The Political Machine

THE ROSTOVTZEFF LECTURES

Institute for the Study of the Ancient World

New York University

The Rostovtzeff lectures are named for Michael I. Rostovtzeff, a Russian ancient historian who came to the United States after the Russian Revolution and taught at the University of Wisconsin and then for many years at Yale University as Sterling Professor of Ancient History. Rostovtzeff's prodigious energies and expansive interests led him to write on an almost unimaginable range of subjects. The Institute for the Study of the Ancient World's Rostovtzeff Lecture Series presents scholarship embodying its aspirations to foster work that crosses disciplinary, geographical, and chronological lines.

David Wengrow, *The Origins of Monsters: Image and Cognition in the First Age of Mechanical Reproduction*

Adam T. Smith, *The Political Machine: Assembling Sovereignty in the Bronze Age Caucasus*

THE POLITICAL MACHINE

ASSEMBLING SOVEREIGNTY IN
THE BRONZE AGE CAUCASUS

ADAM T. SMITH

PRINCETON UNIVERSITY PRESS
PRINCETON AND OXFORD

THIS WORK IS PUBLISHED IN ASSOCIATION WITH THE INSTITUTE FOR
THE STUDY OF THE ANCIENT WORLD AT NEW YORK UNIVERSITY

Copyright © 2015 by Princeton University Press
Published by Princeton University Press, 41 William Street,
Princeton, New Jersey 08540
In the United Kingdom: Princeton University Press, 6 Oxford Street,
Woodstock, Oxfordshire OX20 1TR

press.princeton.edu

Cover photograph: The Karashamb goblet. Courtesy of the Institute of
Archaeology and Ethnography, Republic of Armenia

First paperback printing, 2020
Paperback ISBN 978-0-691-21148-0
Cloth ISBN 978–0-691–16323–9
Library of Congress Control Number: 2014959162

British Library Cataloging-in-Publication Data is available

Publication of this book has been aided by the Institute for the Study of
the Ancient World at New York University

This book has been composed in Sabon Next Pro

For Lori

There are more things in heaven and earth, Horatio,
Than are dreamt of in your philosophy.

—Hamlet, 1.5.166–67

Contents

||||||||||||||||||||||||||||||||||||||||||||||||||||||||||||||||||||||||||||||||||||||||||||||||||||||||||||||||||||||||||||||||||||||||||||||||||||||||||||||||||||

Preface   ix

INTRODUCTION: REVERSE ENGINEERING THE POLITY   1
   The Conditions of Sovereignty   4
   Machine Politics   7
   Bodies and Things   11
   Into the Caucasus   16
   Schematic   20

PART I: The Machinery of Sovereignty

CHAPTER 1. ON ASSEMBLAGES AND MACHINES   27
   Things and Objects   29
   The Exile of Things   33
   Nature Morte   40
   The Assemblage Assembled   43
   The Efficacy of Machines   48
   Sense, Sensibility, and Sentiment   54

CHAPTER 2. ON THE MATTER OF SOVEREIGNTY   59
   Sovereignty Disassembled   61
   Prehistory and the Political   64
   Archaeologies of Sovereignty   67
   Assembly and Assemblage   72
   Origin Myths   73
   Wayward Things and the Dual Sovereign   78
   Exit Objects 1: Liberal Theory and Things   81
   Exit Objects 2: Marx and Matter   83
   Sovereign Matter, Governmental Machines   86
   The Sovereign Conditions   91

PART II: Assembling Sovereignty

CHAPTER 3. THE CIVILIZATION MACHINE IN THE EARLY
   BRONZE AGE   97
   The Kura-Araxes   102

Sensibility   105
Sense   110
Sentiment   122
An Early Bronze Age Public   125

CHAPTER 4. THE WAR MACHINE IN THE MIDDLE BRONZE
AGE   127
The Caucasus in Transition   130
Sensibility   138
Sense   144
Sentiment   148
Territorialization and Contradiction   151

CHAPTER 5. THE POLITICAL MACHINE IN THE LATE BRONZE
AGE   154
The Caucasus at the Beginning of the Late Bronze Age   157
Sensibility   165
Sense   171
Sentiment   178
The Enduring Political Machine   183

CONCLUSION   186
Erebuni-Yerevan   188
Brother Axe   194

References Cited   197

Index   233

Preface

||||||||||||||||||||||||||||||||||||||||||||||||||||||||||||||||||||||||||||||||||||||||||||||||||||||||||||||||||||||||||||||||||||||||||||||||||||||||||||||

This book is an effort to interrogate the role of things in the reproduction of sovereignty, that dense array of practices that simultaneously authorize the polity as a legitimate association and defend its order through various disciplinary institutions—political, juridical, bureaucratic, and so on. My concern is to examine not how a particular regime was initially formed—moments of emergence have already received a significant amount of attention from historians and archaeologists alike—but rather how the ordering framework of sovereign authority came to be sustained across generations, over centuries. The central contention of the book is that this work of sociopolitical reproduction is accomplished in large measure by the operation of material assemblages, what I will call machines, whose efficacy lies in their capacity to sustain communities, orders, and institutions in excess of human intention, and hence enable and constrain human agency, present actions, and possible futures. The political machine, as a historically specific apparatus, arises in the sedimented workings of a dense network of things that have historically established the parameters of sovereignty and that continue to define the possibilities and principles of political association today. This book is thus at once an intervention in contemporary political theory—a field that has long sought to exile objects from an idealized community of (political) subjects—and a contribution to the ongoing material turn in the human sciences, which has often struggled to conceptualize the authority of things. By centering my analysis on the Bronze Age Caucasus, I aim to use an archaeological perspective on the workings of material assemblages to reverse engineer the polity, to take apart the machinery that mediates political association and thereby understand how complex political forms are reproduced.

The lectures that compose the core of this volume were initially presented at the Institute for the Study of the Ancient World in the spring of 2013 under the aegis of the Rostovtzeff Lectures. Although Mikhail Ivanovich Rostovtzeff is best known as a historian of the classical world, his work was also one of the first efforts to draw the oft-neglected archaeology of the prehistoric Caucasus into a wider discussion of the origins of "civilization" (e.g., Rostovtzeff 1922). Rostovtzeff's contributions to our understanding of ancient social and economic history have been much discussed, but for archaeologists his most enduring contribution has been his insistence on the independent epistemological status of material objects in the analysis of the human past. In a radical departure from prevailing early twentieth-century orthodoxy, Rostovtzeff argued that archaeological assemblages are not mere illustrations of the textual record—the proverbial handmaiden to history—but instead provide a fully "independent" account of past human social life (Rostovtzeff 1922: viii; cf. Bowersock 1974: 20; Dow 1960: 546). Today, the autonomy of archaeological datasets and the distinctiveness of archaeological reasoning are both well-established epistemological principles, thanks in part to Rostovtzeff's intervention. My interest in both the original lectures and this book is to honor Rostovtzeff's intellectual legacy by drawing together these two strands of his work—the epistemological independence of the object and the unique prehistory of the Caucasus—in order to explore not only the analytic autonomy of things but also their social efficacy in directing, shaping, and constraining historical transformations in the region over the two and a half millennia of the Bronze Age.

This volume is in many respects a companion to my previous book, *The Political Landscape: Constellations of Authority in Early Complex Polities* (Smith 2003a). In that study, I examined the role that landscapes play in the constitution of political authority, outlining a relational approach to the simultaneous, but often dissonant, workings of spatial experience, perception, and imagination. By working comparatively across early complex polities from Mesopotamia to the Caucasus to the Maya Lowland, I argued that landscapes were, and indeed remain, instrumental to the promulgation of political authority. I suggested that "to leave the political unmoored from the landscape, to allow it to float across society and culture as a conceptual ghost ship, simultaneously anywhere and nowhere, is to obscure the practical relations of authority that constitute the civil sphere" (Smith 2003a: 16). Hence the work aspired to illuminate past constellations of authority and to retheorize the polity from a distinctly archaeological point of view.

As I completed *The Political Landscape*, I was keenly aware of two key missing elements in my theorization of the polity. The first was a sustained account of political reproduction over the *longue durée* (cf. Smith 2003a: 109–11). Archaeology has been so insistently focused on the emergence of complex polities that we have overlooked the real challenge of politics: the preservation of associations through the reproduction of the existing relationship between rulers and ruled. The cross-cultural comparative method that I adopted for a study of landscapes in early polities did not lend itself to the kind of sustained deep history that an inquiry into political reproduction would require. So it was already clear that a study focused on a single region over a considerable swath of time would be critical if I were to address this lacuna. As my collaborative field project in Armenia (known as Project ArAGATS) expanded in both its geographic and temporal scope, it was also evident that a companion volume to *The Political Landscape* would have to center an examination of the deep historicity of political formation in the South Caucasian Bronze Age. This was a matter both of necessity and practicality. Necessity, because our research on the Tsaghkahovit Plain of central Armenia had produced a flood of original data on the village communities of the Early Bronze Age and the fortress-based polities of the Late that demanded synthetic treatment; practicality, because an effort to envelop comparanda from other regions over similar temporal spans, such as Mesopotamia or the Classic Maya, would have produced a book whose weight would have made for a truly burdensome object.

The second element missing from *The Political Landscape* was an account of the political instrumentality of the wider field of material things that lay outside the domain of landscape, place, and built environment. If the political landscape describes the spaces that *we* move through, how are we to conceptualize all the stuff that orbits around us? Although the recent material turn across the human sciences—a logical extension of the earlier spatial turn—has done much to focus attention on the capacities of things to intrude consequentially in social life, it has largely refrained from articulating an object theory of the political. At the same time, the lasting commitment of political thought to a purely ethical account of civil association in large part precludes attention to our attachments to the things of sovereign power, attachments that are often far more profound and durable than our links to a purely human community of fellow citizens.

Taken together, *The Political Machine* and *The Political Landscape* seek to provide an archaeology of the political that works both comparatively and historically to attend to the object matter of civil association. The central question that this book poses is this: What role do material assemblages play in binding political associations, in reproducing the attachments of subjects and sovereigns? In placing my analytical gaze directly on the workings of things, I do not mean in any way to impugn human capacities for political action. I merely seek to set those aside for a moment to consider a set of neglected participants in the polity. But theorizing things into our political lives certainly entails rethinking our role in shaping the constellations of authority within which we live, a matter to which I return in the conclusion to this book.

Like any assemblage, the type and pages assembled in this book are not the result of a singular act of creation but have been formulated, edited, rewritten, thrown out, reinserted, and reworked over many years. In that time, numerous colleagues and friends, along with a number of complete strangers, have provided thought-provoking feedback and rich material for reflection. I must first thank the Institute for the Study of the Ancient World (ISAW) at New York University for the kind invitation to present the 2013 Rostovtzeff Lecture Series. This proved to be an excellent forum for road testing an initial, abridged draft of the present book. The faculty and staff of ISAW were not only thoughtful interlocutors but also generous hosts. I want to thank Roger Bagnall, Lorenzo d'Alfonso, Rod Campbell, Alexander Jones, Ann Macy Roth, and Sören Stark for their thoughtful comments and kind welcome. Thanks also to Kate Lawson for her indefatigable assistance and to Shelby White for her hospitality. I particularly want to extend my gratitude to Karen Rubinson, a dear friend and longtime comrade in the archaeology of the Caucasus, for her encouragement, commentary, and tireless help in tracking down even the most obscure materials from our shared highland home away from home.

The Political Machine was first outlined during a leave year at the University of Chicago's Franke Institute for the Humanities, where James Chandler and my fellow Fellows served as excellent sounding boards for ideas in the early stages of development. My colleagues in the Department of Anthropology at the University of Chicago, including Jean Comaroff, John Comaroff, Shannon Dawdy, Michael Dietler, Alan Kolata, and François Richard, were singularly influential in shaping the basic contours of the project in its earliest phase of development. I was obliged to set the project aside for a time in order to complete the first volume of the reports on my collaborative ongoing fieldwork in Armenia (Smith et al. 2009). But I returned to it during a sabbatical from the University of Chicago that I spent as a John Simon Guggenheim Memorial Foundation Fellow and Fellow at the Cornell Society for the Humanities. I must thank both institutions for their support during a critical year in the development of my thinking on sovereignty and assemblages. I want to extend particular gratitude to my fellow Society Fellows who provided critical feedback on an initial version of what has become here chapter 4, including Jennifer Bajorek, Bruno Bosteels, Joshua Clover, Tracey Heatherington, and James McHugh. Let me extend my special thanks to Tim Murray for making my time in the Society of Fellows so productive and thought-provoking.

The manuscript for *The Political Machine* began to come together in the succeeding year when I left Chicago to join the faculty of Cornell University. I am grateful to my colleagues in both the Department of Anthropology and the Cornell Institute of Archaeology and Material Studies (CIAMS) for suggestions both formal and informal on various portions of the text. Faculty reading groups in both Anthropology and CIAMS have proven to be stimulating forums for rehearsing arguments about materials and materiality. I was also fortunate to participate in a Brett de Bary Interdisciplinary Mellon Writing Group on Material Culture in 2011–2012. I want to thank my co-conspirators in that endeavor—Elizabeth Anker, Elisha Cohn, Renate Ferro, Noor Hashem, Lori Khatchadourian, Stacey Langwick, and Saiba Varma—not only for their comments on an early draft of chapter 1, but also for their consistent intellectual engagement with issues of materials and materiality throughout our nine-month-long discussion. My colleagues in Anthropology provided feedback on various portions of the text. Particular thanks go to Chris Garces, Saida Hodžić, Hirokazu Miyazaki, Paul Nadasdy, Lucinda Ramberg, and Marina Welker for their thoughtful feedback on the penultimate version of chapter 2.

Throughout the development of this book, my students at Chicago and Cornell have had a lasting and durable impact on my conceptions of both assemblages and sovereignty. The participants in my courses on Material Cultures, The Political Lives of Things, Assemblages and Objects, and Political Anthropology have forced me to constantly clarify and revisit key points of argumentation. Among this vibrant community of students, special thanks should go to Charis Boke, Aimee Douglass, Catherine Kearns, Jeffrey Leon, Eilis Monahan, and Kathryn Weber.

Team members from my collaborative field project in Armenia—Project ArAGATS—have been constant inspirations to me in terms of both my thinking on objects and my effort to understand the archaeology of the Caucasus. My project co-founder and friend, Ruben Badalyan, has spent more than two decades teaching me the archaeology of Armenia, and I continue to learn from his vast erudition. The results of our investigations that I discuss here were made possible by the indefatigable work of numerous colleagues from the Academy of Sciences of the Republic of Armenia, including members of the Institute of Archaeology and Ethnography—Armine Harutyunyan, Armine Hayrapetyan, Roman Hovsepyan, Susannah Melkonyan, Hasmik Sarkisyan, and Lilit Ter-Minasyan—and a dedicated team of collaborating scholars from the Institute of Geology led by Arkady Karakhanian. The work would have been truly impossible absent the strong and enduring support that Project ArAGATS has received from two inspiring directors of the Institute of Archaeology and Ethnography: the late Aram Kalantaryan and Pavel Avetisyan. Pavel, a co-director of Project

ArAGATS during our initial seasons, continues to provide not only his administrative support but also his deep scholarly understanding of Bronze Age material culture. Over the last decade and a half, Project ArAGATS has grown from a research project into a supportive community of mutually engaged scholars. Project members Hannah Chazin, Elizabeth Fagan, Kathryn Franklin, Alan Greene, Ian Lindsay, Belinda Monahan, Maureen Marshall, and Kathryn Weber went above and beyond the call of duty, offering cogent commentary and corrections on the draft manuscripts for all of the lectures.

Funding for Project ArAGATS's research in the Tsaghkahovit Plain has been provided by numerous institutions. Without their financial support for sustained archaeological field research, this book would not have been possible. I particularly want to thank the National Science Foundation, the National Endowment for the Humanities, the Wenner-Gren Foundation, the National Geographic Society, the Dolores Zohrab Liebman Fund, the Institute of Archaeology and Ethnography of the Republic of Armenia, the Lichtstern Fund of the Department of Anthropology at the University of Chicago, and the Einaudi Center and Institute for Social Science at Cornell University.

Prior to appearing in the Rostovtzeff lectures, I presented parts of the introduction and chapter 4 at several institutions. I want to extend my thanks to Sue Alcock, John Cherry, and Stephen Houston at Brown University, Ruth Van Dyke and Randall McGuire at SUNY Binghamton, and Robert Preucel and Lauren Ristvet at the University of Pennsylvania. I also want to thank friends and colleagues who took the time to read and comment on one or more chapters, including Geoff Emberling, Bruce Grant, and Ruth Van Dyke. David Wengrow and an anonymous reviewer read the entire series of lectures, offering incisive commentary on both matters of detail and the wider trajectory of the argument that helped greatly in revising the work for this book. I have been deeply impressed by how smoothly the process of moving from lecture to manuscript went, thanks to the skill, professionalism, and patience of Rob Tempio, Kathleen Cioffi, and the staff at Princeton University Press, and of copyeditor Scott Barker.

The last and most emphatic thank-you of all must go to my wife, collaborator, and colleague, Lori Khatchadourian, to our son, Avedis, and our daughter, Ani. Much of the thinking behind this book began during my parental leave after Avedis was born. Few things are more instructive in the workings of the material world than watching an infant gain dexterity with the assemblages that surround him or her. This book strives to stimulate the same kind of curiosity about the workings of things as I saw in Avedis during those early months. In the years since, he has remained a constant source of inspiration. This book was completed just as our second child, Ani, was born. So as much as the work initially emerged from my experiences with Avedis as a new dad, I see it today as a kind of road map for attending to Ani's growth amidst a swirl of things. But the profoundest influence on the work has been my wife, Lori. Lori has been at once my most critical reader, most supportive advocate, and most trenchant interlocutor. Many of the ideas explored in this book were inspired by her deep understanding of the materiality of power, emerging out of years of conversation, argument, discussion, and joint exploration. For her encouragement, care, direction, and unstinting support, this book is dedicated to her.

The Political Machine

Introduction |||||||||||||||||||||||||||||||||||||||||||||||||||||||||||||||||||||||||||||||||||||||||||||||||||||||||||||||||||||||||||||

Reverse Engineering the Polity

Every modern election season seems to bring with it at least one episode where the pressing concerns of the public sphere collide with the absurdity of politics on the hustings. The 2008 U.S. presidential campaign was no exception, thanks in large measure to an extended national conversation on the relation between a single small object and the political community. The topic was introduced early in the primary campaign when a reporter for KCRG-TV in Cedar Rapids, Iowa, asked Barack Obama why he was not wearing a flag pin on his lapel. The reporter noted that these pins had become standard issue for politicians of all stripes since the attacks of 9/11 and so its absence was conspicuous. Obama answered:

> Shortly after 9/11 ... [a flag pin] became a substitute for, I think, true patriotism, which is speaking out on issues that are of importance to our national security.... I decided I won't wear that pin on my chest.... Instead I'm gonna' try to tell the American people what I believe will make this country great and hopefully that will be a testimony to my patriotism. (*New York Times*, 10/4/2007)

The episode was quickly picked up by a wide array of news outlets, and Obama's "refusal" to wear a flag pin became a matter of widespread speculation.

For pundits in the mainstream press, the absent flag pin served as a shorthand for concerns over Obama's shaky relationship with segments of the American public. Charles Gibson suggested in one democratic primary debate that Obama's absent flag pin represented "a major vulnerability" in his campaign for the White House insofar as it bore upon the "general theme of patriotism" and the candidate's commitment to a shared American political culture.[1] For right-wing media outlets, the flag pin was a stalking

---

[1] *New York Times* online transcript of Democratic debate in Philadelphia. http://www.nytimes.com/2008/04/16/us/politics/16text-debate.html?pagewanted=print.

horse for the far more libelous rumors that were circulating about Obama's personal history, which cast him as everything from a smug elitist to an agent of a foreign power.[2] For Obama supporters, the debate was simply witless: cheap trinkets, they retorted, are not indices of the deep sentiments at the heart of the public sphere.[3]

Obama initially held his ground in the media maelstrom, explaining, "I'm less concerned with what you're wearing on your lapel than what's in your heart" (quoted in *Time*, 5/14/2008). Such an argument for the salience of substantive sentiments over simple sensation would appear to have a great deal of intellectual force behind it, a mature retort to the Polonius-inspired superficiality of vesting political community in a "mere" trinket. But the assertion that there was no relationship between material culture and our attachment to the body politic failed to quell the controversy. On April 16, 2008, Obama appeared at a town hall meeting in Pennsylvania and rather dramatically, if a bit awkwardly, donned a flag pin given to him by a veteran in the audience. The charismatic candidate, his promises and policies, were eclipsed by a small $1.35 pin on a black lapel. Indeed, the flag pin became an outsize presence in an election-year debate over patriotism, including a solo appearance on the cover of *Time* (July 7, 2008) above the headline "The Real Meaning of Patriotism."

Though widely lampooned as one of the strangest threads of the 2008 election cycle, the flag pin fuss nonetheless exposed a critical lacuna in both political theory and practice: we remain entirely uncertain as to how political communities are bound to—and bound by—the complex world of things. And yet, the intuition that an account of the ordering of political community must entail an understanding of the order of things lies at the very roots of Western political thought. Indeed, Obama's struggle with the flag pin reads rather astonishingly like a modern retelling—now as farce—of Plato's Allegory of the Cave.

At the opening of book 7 of the *Republic*, Socrates describes for Glaucon how the subjects of a political community are like prisoners in a cave with legs and necks chained so that they are able to see only the wall before them. Behind them, puppeteers carry "all sorts of vessels, and statues and figures of animals made of wood and stone and various materials" (Plat. *Rep.* 514b–c; this and other such translations by Jowett), which pass in front of a large fire and cast shadows on the wall. These shadows are but representations of the real—indeed, they are first- and second-order representations

---

[2] Right-wing pundit Sean Hannity weighed in on the matter, declaring, "Why do we wear flag pins? Because our country is under attack"; see also Brooks 2008; Limbaugh 2008.

[3] Harshaw 2008; Linkins 2008; Mapes 2008.

because they are shadows cast by models and effigies—and yet the prisoners take them as authentic forms since they know no other phenomena.

In order to rule these subjects, one prisoner is freed from his bonds and compelled to see the fire and the marionettes and thus understand the shadows on the wall for what they truly are—simulacra. The prisoner is forced to journey out of the cave, an "ascent of the soul" to the "intellectual world" that imbues him with the knowledge that the objects known to us through sensation are merely shadows of the authentic world of universal Forms. Things are thus revealed to be epiphenomenal to ideas, sensation subservient to understanding. Material things, Socrates concludes, are thus not proper objects of examination in themselves but only as they provide a route to understanding the higher Forms. Obama initially seemed to concur, suggesting that flag pins were mere simulacra whose relation to the deep sentiments of patriotism was a matter of deep skepticism.[4]

When Plato's former prisoner, now in a state of wakefulness, returns to the cave, it is no longer as subject but as ruler, made sovereign by his understanding of the capital G Good (the Form that makes all things intelligible) and by his suspicion of mere lowercase g goods. By ultimately donning the flag pin, Obama seemed less convinced of the efficacy of the flag pin in revealing sentiment than simply cognizant of the ghastly fate that Plato suggested awaits philosopher kings who try to free prisoners from mistaking simulacra for the real—death by mob violence (*Rep.* 517a). And yet the flag pin was remarkably efficacious. Once donned, it effectively ended the debate over the candidate's patriotism. Throughout his two terms in office, the pin has been ever-present, a talisman able to ward off attacks on his affective commitment to the American public sphere.

The media furor over Obama's flag pin was dominated by debates over sentiments of political attachment, but the real dissonance of the episode lay in the striking contrast between the exaggerated sense of the flag pin as public emblem and the underwhelming sensible qualities of the die-cast object itself. Although it would be analytically tempting to cleave the "mere" matter of the object from its representational capacity, such a move would obscure the wider assemblage that allowed the flag pin not only to passively mean but to operate within the field of U.S. electoral politics. That is, the flag pin was enmeshed in a complex assemblage that, in one dimension, extended across the sociotechnical systems of large-scale die-cast metal manufacturing, in another implicated a field of personal adornment deeply

---

[4] Indeed, Obama seemed to echo Henry David Thoreau's (1882: 27) thoroughly transcendentalist (indeed, material-world defying) admonition to "beware of all enterprises that require new clothes, and not rather a new wearer of clothes."

indebted to European traditions of military dress and decoration, and in still another reached into a historically deep field of national heraldry and representation. Each of these assemblages is embedded in the matter of the pin, inseparably binding the material and the representational.[5] Obama's flag pin was thus merely a singular instantiation of a spatially and historically complex material assemblage.

Unfortunately, modern political philosophy offers us distressingly few tools for understanding the object matter of political life, and hence the episode of the flag pin seems at first glance to be merely an electoral grotesquerie. The traditional modern understanding of political association, from Thomas Hobbes to Jean-Jacques Rousseau to John Rawls, has centered resolutely, perhaps obsessively, on the person of the citizen, whose interactions with other members of the body politic establish and reproduce the possibilities and limits of sovereignty. However, the flag pin debate underlined the fact that rarely do we interact with one another directly as citizens. Rather, a vast assemblage of things incessantly intrudes upon our civic practices, from ballots and bullets to licenses, currency, furnishings, robes, and regalia. What does an archaeology of the physical matter of sovereignty reveal about political life and the historical formation of the polity? Moreover, the inverse question is at present no less pressing: What do the relations of authority reveal about the operations of objects? As we shall see in chapter 1, although the emerging wave of materiality theory has keenly focused our attention on things, it has provided less direction in how we should theorize their capacity to shape the relations between sovereigns and subjects that lie at the heart of the political. This book is an effort to address these two overlapping lacunae in our understanding of material assemblages and political association by attending to the machinery that works to reproduce conditions fundamental to sovereignty.

THE CONDITIONS OF SOVEREIGNTY

Our constant and enduring interaction with things poses challenging questions for the human relationships that we traditionally position at the center of our wider social and political worlds. Modern democracies are typically presumed to cohere thanks to the shared interactions of members with one another, defined by the rights and obligations of citizenship en-

---

[5] A point that Webb Keane (2005) makes quite elegantly, working outward from the semiotic tradition.

shrined in constitutions and customary law. However, rarely do citizens encounter one another in forums not mediated by a panoply of things. When we participate in elections—the *sine qua non* of participatory democracy—we enter a booth that explicitly shields us from one another so that we may have an intimate, private encounter with a voting machine. When citizens of modern mass democratic polities attend public rallies, their encounters with those who govern are mediated by televisions, radios, microphones, public address systems, TelePrompTers, newspapers, stretch limos, flags, red, white, and blue bunting, bumper stickers, lawn signs, and a prodigious array of things that enable and constrain relations to one another and to political leaders. What is the impact of all this stuff on political life? Is it possible to define the polity as "we the people" to the exclusion of the things that form, bind, and order? Furthermore, if we include the object world in our understanding of political association, how does this alter traditional understandings of the relationship between subjects and sovereigns?

I should be clear at the outset that to speak of the sovereign is to address not simply a titular figurehead of government but the apparatus of supreme authority *in toto*; not just king, chancellor, or president, but the entire institutional order upon which they rely. The body of the sovereign ruler is often a matter of deep concern as a metonym of the wider political order. To declare in the classical phrasing that "the king is dead, long live the king" is to confirm the uninterrupted reproduction of the polity as a whole (Kantorowicz 1957: 412). The bodies of heads of state are only one element in a wider assemblage, one that embraces not only other official bodies but, central to this discussion, a myriad of things.

In its Hobbesian (Hobbes 1991) sense, sovereignty describes an ultimate authority, an apparatus of supremacy within a delimited territory that insinuates itself into all other domains of association—the home, the workplace, and elsewhere. Michel Foucault (2003: 35–36) consigned Hobbes's account of sovereignty to the premodern era, a form of political power staked on a homology between the body of the monarch and the body politic, in contrast to modern forms of biopolitics that inscribe authority directly on the "docile bodies" of subjects. However, as Giorgio Agamben (1998: 6) has pointed out, modern techniques of authorization and technologies of subjection that draw "bare life" into the political sphere do not represent historical ruptures in a new age of "governmentality." To the contrary, the twinning of life and politics is "the original activity of sovereign power" (ibid.). Thus, the study of sovereignty is not an investigation of a historically restricted formal type of political order, as Foucault suggested, but rather an inquiry into a "tentative and always emergent form of authority grounded in violence that is performed and designed to generate loyalty, fear, and legitimacy from the neighborhood to the summit of the state" (Hansen and Stepputat 2006: 297).

Agamben (1998: 39) locates sovereignty in the articulation of "constituting power" (i.e., the principles that authorize the polity as an association) and "constituted power" (i.e., the practices of governance). Both powers ultimately rest upon forms of violence: an originary revolutionary violence of political foundation and an ordering violence of enforcement and political reproduction (a distinction derived from Benjamin's [1978: 287] distinction between law-making and law-preserving violence). Sovereignty thus resides simultaneously both within and outside of a constituted order, a dual positioning rendered most apparent in the capacity to decide upon exceptions to the enforcement of other claims, whether traditional, juridical, or bureaucratic (Schmitt 1985). Sovereignty, in sum, is not a substantive quality to be possessed but rather a *condition* of political interactions, embedded in the "actualities of relations" (Humphrey 2004: 420) that define both the interiors and exteriors of associations. Specifically, in the chapters that follow, I argue that sovereignty requires the continual reproduction of (at least) three conditions:

1. Establishment of a coherent public defined by relations of inclusion and exclusion that are materially marked and regulated

2. Definition of a sovereign figure (whether individual or corporate), cut away from the community by instruments of social and martial violence

3. Manufacture of an apparatus capable of formalizing governance by transforming the polity itself into an object of desire, of care, and of devotion

The archaeological studies of the three phases of the Bronze Age in the South Caucasus presented in chapters 3, 4, and 5 are organized as investigations into the role of certain highly efficacious assemblages in reproducing these three conditions.

There are two key corollaries to this definition of sovereignty that I want to highlight. First, each condition depends upon the reproduction of specific material assemblages that do critical political work. Second, sovereignty emerges in the historical coalescence of interdigitated assemblages. Sovereignty in this sense is a quintessentially archaeological category, reproduced in the domain of things over the *longue durée*.

An archaeological account of sovereignty necessarily demands an analytical framework that allows us to conceptualize objects at work within a social field defined by power, where objects do not simply mean but operate to enable and constrain social possibilities and historical trajectories. The intuition that civic affairs might be shaped as profoundly by goods as by the Good has been most succinctly captured by the familiar trope of the "political machine."

MACHINE POLITICS

The phrase "political machine" today is largely reserved to describe the urban patronage systems that supported enduring municipal regimes in U.S. cities from the late nineteenth to mid-twentieth centuries. This use of the term to describe a disciplined, hierarchical organization that mobilizes voting blocks in support of autocratic rule is most familiar from Boss Tweed's Tammany Hall in New York City or Richard J. Daley's Cook County Democratic Party. But the trope reaches back to at least the late eighteenth century, when the philosopher John Millar (1796: 87) wrote a letter to the *Scots Chronicle* with this lament:

> No minister can now hope to remain in office, or to be permitted to execute even the most beneficial measures, unless, as it has been emphatically expressed, he greases the wheels of the political machine. For this purpose, pensions are bestowed, sinecure places are instituted.

In this pejorative sense, a political machine is an apparatus for manufacturing authority through a clientelist system run by a boss who secures authority through potentially corrupt *quid pro quo* exchanges of money or other material goods. The term denotes a practical, highly experiential relationship between things and political authority as the former provide the "grease" that ensures the reproduction of the latter. However, the term has a far deeper history, and more richly varied denotation, than current usage typically allows.

The use of mechanical metaphors for political activity has an obscure origin in the rhetorical recruitment of the Latin *machina*—a device of war or siege craft—into political oratory.[6] For Virgil, the Trojan Horse was a particularly sinister *machina*, and for Tacitus, siege engines and war machines were critical to countless Roman victories. It is thus not surprising that such formidable things would percolate into the political lexicon. Cicero drew the military sense of a "machine" into the political arena in his second speech against proposed changes to the agrarian laws, warning, "I

[6] E.g., Tacitus *Historiae* 2.34; Livy 1.43.3, 44.9.2.

perceive that nearly the whole of this law is made ready, as if it were a machine [*machinam*], for the object of overthrowing [Pompey's] power" (Cicero *Agr.* 2.18). Here, the political sense of the mechanical trope is intended quite narrowly to highlight the ability of law to serve as an instrument of legislative combat.

Only at the end of the Middle Ages was the trope of the machine pulled into more substantive terrain, thanks in large measure to its adoption by an emerging scientific literature to describe the physical operation of the earth and solar system. The thirteenth-century astronomer John of Sacrobosco described the earth as a *machina mundi*, an observation that would later reverberate among Enlightenment deists, such as Gottfried Leibniz, who sought to imagine the world as a "great Machine going on without the Interposition of God, as a Clock continues to go without the assistance of a Clockmaker."[7] Ironically, it was the mendicant Augustinus Triumphus who, anxious to defend the powers of the papacy, drew Sacrobosco's divinity-less machinic metaphor into affairs of state less than a century after it was first articulated, arguing that because the "machine of the world is but one realm ... there should therefore be but one ruler" (quoted in Ockham 1992: 18).

But if the machine of the world can run smoothly, it can also break down, an observation made most powerfully by Montaigne. Reflecting on the fragility of political community during France's wars of religion of the sixteenth century, Montaigne (1965: 101) fretted with palpable anxiety: "Who is it that, seeing the havoc of these civil wars of ours, does not cry out, that the machine of the world is near dissolution." Early usages of the mechanical metaphor thus centered on the interdependence of moving parts within a global, as opposed to expressly political, system, so the thrust of the analogy was purely formal—like the ancient *machina*, the world too relies on the smooth integration of component parts, but if those parts are disrupted, catastrophe and misery result.

Rousseau adopted the machine analogy to describe the mechanical interdependence of subjects and authorities that legitimates political authority within the social contract:

The social pact is of a particular and unique nature, in that the people contracts only with itself—that is to say, the people as sovereign body contracts

---

[7] Clarke's first reply to Leibniz (1989: 677). The metaphor of the machine of the world occupied a critical point of disagreement between Leibniz and Newtonian natural philosophy. Leibniz criticized the Newtonians for assuming that God, like a good clockmaker, might need to intervene in the world to ensure its proper running. For Leibniz, the workings of nature were so well engineered that they did not require maintenance.

with the individuals as subjects. This condition constitutes the whole artifice of the political machine and sets it in motion. It alone renders legitimate, reasonable, and free from danger commitments that would otherwise be absurd, tyrannical, and subject to the most enormous abuses. (Rousseau 1979: 461)

Once set into a political frame, tropes of mechanical harmony and disintegration became powerful imaginaries of governmental sustenance and subversion. Hegel, committed to the State as the setting for the realization of freedom, described a critical moment in the formation of the early polity when individual interests were lashed to the collective: "But in a State many institutions must be adopted, much political machinery invented, accompanied by appropriate political arrangements ... involving, moreover, contentions with private interest and passions, and a tedious discipline of these latter, in order to bring about the desired harmony" (Hegel 2011: 23). In contrast, Herbert Spencer, a nineteenth-century proto-libertarian and critic of the state, argued:

When we devise a machine we take care that its parts are as few as possible; that they are adapted to their respective ends; that they are properly joined with one another; and that they work smoothly to their common purpose. Our political machine, however, is constructed upon directly opposite principles. Its parts are extremely numerous: multiplied, indeed, beyond all reason. They are not severally chosen as specially qualified for particular functions. No care is taken that they shall fit well together: on the contrary, our arrangements are such that they are certain not to fit. And that, as a consequence, they do not and cannot act in harmony. (Spencer 1981: 333)

Both Hegel and Spencer set the political machine within the traditional tropic field of the mechanical analogy, defined narrowly by harmonious operation or catastrophic failure. Its power is thus largely descriptive.

A more analytic deployment of the machinic trope attends not only to the integration of parts but also the automotility of the resulting automaton. Most notably, Adam Smith called attention to the political consequences of the aesthetics of machines in motion and the ability to thus implicate human subjects in tending to their operation:

The same principle, the same love of system, the same regard to the beauty of order, of art and contrivance, frequently serves to recommend those institutions which tend to promote the public welfare.... The contemplation of them pleases us, and we are interested in whatever can tend to advance them. They make part of the great system of government, and the wheels of the *political machine* seem to move with more harmony and ease by means of them.

We take pleasure in beholding the perfection of so beautiful and grand a system, and we are uneasy till we remove any obstruction that can in the least disturb or encumber the regularity of its motions. (Smith 1976: 185)

Smith's political machine is thus not simply a descriptive analogy but a powerful analytic that locates an account of political reproduction in our aesthetic commitments to an apparatus of rule.[8]

But although Smith understood the political machine as an engine for inculcating civic virtues, by the nineteenth century the grim aesthetics of industrial technology had wrapped an analytic sense of the term less in pleasure than in terror. As a result, the operation of political machines came to be centered not on producing virtue but on manufacturing subjection. This understanding of the political machine is most acutely described in the work of Marx[9] and, still more perceptively, in that of Engels: "The central link in civilized society is the state, which in all typical periods is without exception the state of the ruling class, and in all cases continues to be essentially a machine for holding down the oppressed, exploited class" (Engels 1990: 274–75). Engels's tyrannical machine is the antithesis of Smith's object of beauty, a terrifying monstrosity that uses technology as a weapon of domination. Most significantly, however, a Marxian conception of the machine is not metaphorical because it points directly to the things—the real machinery (MacKenzie 1984)—that stand in tension with the humans who invent, tend, repair, and utilize them. Acts of spoliation targeting new technologies, such as the riots that greeted the ribbon loom and the wool-shearing machine during the seventeenth and eighteenth centuries or the Luddite movement of the early nineteenth century, were, according to Marx, acts of resistance to the displacement of labor encouraged by mechanization (Marx 1906: 468–69). As a result, Marx presumed that attacks on the machinery of industry were sadly misdirected.

As the analytic of the machine entered into twentieth-century critical theory, however, there was a wider sense that material things possessed not only motility but also autonomy and thus the potential for mastery. Georges Bataille's (1988: 136) argument that capitalist modernity presumes an "unreserved surrender to things," a new politics of human servitude to the independent logics of a world of objects, draws the machine not only into an

---

[8] Smith makes a similar argument in *Theory of Moral Sentiments* (Smith 1982: 316), namely, that our associations to one another are bound most strongly not by naked interest but by the aesthetic pleasure of the "beautiful and noble machine" of human society, whose smooth operation pleases and disrupted workings vex.

[9] See especially the discussion of "Machinery and Modern Industry" in volume 1 of *Capital*.

analytical field but also into a critical one. Thereafter, the image of the tyrannical machine shambles through the modern imaginary, exposing the roots of a deep ambivalence over the political work that things do. On the one hand, Bataille's vision thrives in a scholarly and popular imaginary of things at work to subdue humanity, ranging from the demonic Maschinenmensch of Fritz Lang's (1927) *Metropolis* to the digital enslavement of *The Matrix* (1999), from Oswald Spengler's (1932) dire warnings of impending doom in *Man and Technics* to Herbert Marcuse's (1964) anticonsumerism in *One-Dimensional Man*. On the other hand, Smith's sense of a machine capable of cultivating civic virtue—updated and grounded in specific technologies by Lewis Mumford (1934) in *Technics and Civilization*—reverberates in the contemporary desire to understand information technologies (from Twitter and Facebook to WikiLeaks and Wikipedia) as inherently democratizing technologies, able to dismantle tyranny and empower democracy through the power of a smartphone (Faris 2012; Gerbaudo 2012; O'Connor 2012). What is intriguing about the intellectual history of the political machine is how it highlights both our awareness of the object matter of the polity and our consistent failure to take seriously the political work that things *actually* do, as opposed to the work that we fear, or hope, they do. In chapter 1, I work to develop an analytic of the political machine that does just that.

To forward an analytic of the political machine requires inverting the form of (mis)recognition that Marx described as "fetishism." Where commodity fetishism emerges from laborers mistaking their own action for the action of things, "which rule the producers instead of being ruled by them" (Marx 1906: 86), attending to the political machine means locating sociohistorical forces in the logics of material assemblages *in addition to* (not as a substitution for) the agency of humans. This move entails not only a recuperative project attentive to the motility of objects, but also an effort to theorize the points of articulation that join the organic human body to the inorganic thing. How can we define such heterogeneous points of encounter that stretch from the physical engagement of hands and tools to the imagined vitality of the traditional fetish?

BODIES AND THINGS

On May 15, 1591, the church bell in the Russian town of Uglich sounded the death knell (fig. 1). The young Tsarevitch Dmitri, exiled epileptic third son of Ivan the Terrible, was dead, found stabbed in a courtyard, lying in a

Fig. 1. Detail of Tsarevitch Dmitry Icon showing the sainted prince and the church of the Uglich (eighteenth century, in the collections of the State Museum of the History of Religion, Saint Petersburg). (Source: Wikimedia Commons.)

pool of blood. As the bell tolled, rumors flew through the town that Boris Gudonov, the ambitious regent for Tsar Fyodor, had killed Dmitri in order to remove a potential rival to the throne. Riots followed, leading to the lynching of several local Gudonov agents. In the aftermath, a special commission concluded that the tsarevitch had stabbed himself when he suffered a seizure during a game. Gudonov exiled the leaders of the riots, but a special punishment was reserved for the instigator of the riots: the bell of Uglich. Its tongue (clapper) was cut out, its ear torn off, and it was publicly flogged. The bell was then exiled to Tobolsk, Siberia, where on arrival it was registered as the town's first "inanimate exile" (Batuman 2009: 24). In exile, the bell was treated with reverence as an amulet for the protection of children. The people of Tobolsk refitted it with a clapper and hung it in the church belfry in defiance of Gudonov's orders. Subsequently, it came to be widely believed that water poured over the bell's clapper—the first tongue to mourn the dead tsarevitch—was a powerful elixir for curing sick children.

As an episode of sovereignty both challenged and reproduced by the workings of things, the incitements of the Uglich assemblage—from the tsarevitch's knife to the bell to the ropes that lynched Gudonov's agents to the Tobolsk elixir—provide a succinct schematic of the points of encounter between material things and human bodies. The dramatic tangibility of the plunging dagger and clanging bell demands attention most immediately to the domain of the sensible—the point of articulation between the somatic capacities of human bodies and the physical affordances of material forms. The sensible here refers neither to bodily perception nor to the inherent properties of materials but to the point of experiential encounter between them as they shape and reshape one another. Yet clearly the encounter between the Uglich community and its assemblage cannot be contained by the boundaries of the sensible.

Perhaps most critical to the episode was the sensual quality of the peal of the bell, which Orthodox tradition had long described as the voice of God on earth. To hear Uglich's bell was not simply an aural experience, but a moment of sense perception situated within regimes of sociocultural value. Gudonov's punishment of the bell was a mercilessly physical one—an intervention in sensible technology that rendered it mute—and yet its full violence is most palpable in the domain of sense as an act of iconoclasm, a desecration of the resistive values circulating within an assemblage of resistive things.

Lastly, the episode as a whole, and particularly the Tobolsk epilogue, suggests a field of sentiment that articulated imaginations of the efficacy of things with everyday healing practices that challenged the commands of the sovereign. The prevailing sentiment that a bell might defend a child accords matter a unique capacity to intervene in human affairs. That the bell's actions were understood as defense of legitimate political authority against usurpation suggests that the material world was enveloped within the project of political reproduction.

The riotous assemblage of Uglich thus articulated with the town's denizens across a series of analytically distinct (although experientially simultaneous) human–object confrontations that implicated one another at every turn. The first, *sensibility*, refers most immediately to the physicality of things as they flow amidst relations of power and to their transubstantiation from one state to another as they move: ores become ingots, clays becomes pots, stones becomes sickles. *Sense*, in contrast, is a domain of semiosis, of signs and signification where the encounter of humans and material assemblages possesses not only functional capacities, but evocative potencies. If sensibility is the domain of fact, sense is the domain of value. Whereas the sensible embraces the alteration of material states and distributions, the sensual describes metamorphoses in values—debris become relics, discard becomes art, crafts become commodities. Furthermore, sense also encompasses the transfigurations worked upon our human bodies as our things reposition us within shifting aesthetic terrain. Alfred Gell (1992) described this phenomenon as the "technology of enchantment," the capacity of objects to secure our bodily acquiescence to their demands. Furthermore, Gell grounded the technology of enchantment in what he reciprocally called the "enchantment of technology," the construal of material techniques of production as not simply technical skill, but magical prowess. The magical "halo" that surrounds certain things establishes a social field of *sentiment* that embeds the capacities of things within the objects themselves rather than within our senses. Thus, where sense and sensibility are linked to the direct human encounter with objects, sentiment describes the imagined capacities of things.

The regimes of sentiment within which things are situated are potentially quite expansive, ranging from tropes of maintenance and care that Hodder (2012) describes as "entrapment" to themes of contagion, perhaps best known ethnographically from proscriptions that circulate around the activities of smiths and potters (Gosselain 1999). These represent imaginations of the needs and capacities of things, their potential not just to function, but to take part in social life. To describe these as sentiments is not to argue that they are not also profoundly physical relationships. Sentiments of care clearly entail obligations to constantly attend to the sensible qualities of things. However, maintenance requirements that bind humans to things can be located within a wide array of affective registers, ranging from loving devotion (e.g., the carefully tended model train of the hobbyist, the meticulously cleaned firearm of the gun enthusiast) to tyrannical oppression (e.g., the same firearm to those antithetical to "gun culture"). In the studies of the Bronze Age Caucasus that preoccupy this book, I am most interested in sentiments of captivation that subjugate human action to the operation of objects. Fetishes, talismans, charms, and amulets are all objects of captivation that rely upon the attribution of an inherent power to things. But as we shall see, captivation is more consequentially the power of things to constrain our imagination of alternative lives and sociopolitical orders.

In sum, three key points of intersection between human bodies and material objects provide a basic conceptual platform for an inquiry into their articulation:

- Sensibility: the physical, experiential elements of object form and assemblage distribution that establish the facts of material order;

- Sense: the perceptual, ideological qualities of things that articulate objects with social, political, and cultural values;

- Sentiment: the imaginative domain of affect in which representations place objects within affective regimes.

These three concepts structure the analyses of the Bronze Age Caucasus that I undertake in chapters 3, 4, and 5.

There are clear similarities between this tripartite rubric and the triad of experience/perception/imagination that I explored in *The Political Landscape*, based on conceptual schemas defined by Henri Lefebvre (1991) and David Harvey (1989). Both of these triads proceed from the immediate physicality of encounter (sensibility and experience), to the apprehension of an exteriority (sense and perception), to representations of the order of things (sentiment and imagination) that embed the material world within dense layers of meaning and action. Both triads are heuristic devices that necessarily partition our mutually penetrating points of contact with the material world in order to muster the distinct epistemologies and analytical tools that each component of the triad demands. A study of commodity desire necessarily utilizes different tools than, say, an account of the techniques of craft production. But both are clearly integral to a holistic relational ontology of the material world.

I conceptually distinguish our encounters with things and landscapes for one fundamental reason, namely, that our bodies move across and within landscapes, but things circulate around us. This real and potential motility suggests the possibility of substantial divergences in our relation to such very different elements of our material world, even though the line between landscape and object is by no means stark. A hillock of tuff can be cut into portable building blocks that move long distances before settling into the walls of a building, which when it falls into ruins is itself quarried, setting the stones in motion once again. Hence, although things and landscapes may be analytically distinct vis-à-vis human sociality, they are clearly mutually implicated elements of the expansive material world.

INTO THE CAUCASUS

There are few places more mythologically well suited for an inquiry into the object matter of sovereignty than the Caucasus (fig. 2), the land of Prometheus. Having stolen fire from Olympus and bequeathed it to humanity, the fate of Prometheus (which I discuss at greater length in chapter 1) was to be shackled and nailed to the bare slopes of the windswept Caucasus for eternity; humanity's fate was thereafter to be lashed inextricably to the devices and contrivances that followed from their newly acquired skills in the pyrotechnic arts. The Great Caucasus range traverses over 1,100 kilometers along the northern end of the isthmus that divides the Eurasian steppes from southwest Asia. The slopes and foothills north of the Great Caucasus ridge are generally referred to as the North Caucasus, a region that incorporates the southern provinces of the Russian Federation. The South Caucasus, the primary focus of the archaeological studies in this book, comprises the territory south of the Great Caucasus ridge to the Araks River, including the three independent states of Georgia, Azerbaijan, and Armenia, along with the disputed regions of Abkhazia, South Ossetia, and Nagorno-Karabakh. Although today defined by modern political boundaries, in topographic terms the South Caucasus flows uninterrupted into the Armenian Highland, the highest of the uplands that make up the northern sectors of the Near East.

Two major river systems drain the South Caucasus: the Kura, which cuts through the Lesser Caucasus before dropping into the Shirvan Steppe, and the Araks, which rolls through the Ararat Plain before joining the Kura for a short sprint to the Caspian Sea. The South Caucasus can be divided into four basic geographic provinces based on climate and land cover. The highlands of northern Caucasia are defined by the middle Kura River and its associated drainages, including the Pambak/Debed system and the Agstef (Akstafa) River. The province is characterized climatically by hot, dry summers and mild, dry winters, and the vegetation consists primarily of temperate grasslands. Western Caucasia consists of the Colchian Plain, drained by the westward-flowing Rioni and Inguri rivers. The climate tends toward mild summers and damp winters, supporting mixed deciduous and conif-

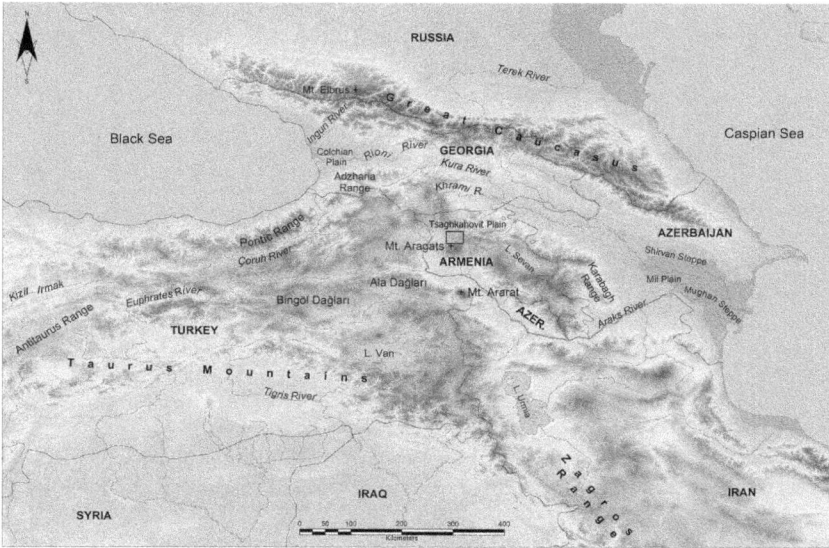

Fig. 2. Map of the North and South Caucasus, including major river drainages and geographic provinces; box identifies the Tsaghkahovit Plain. (Map Credit: Adam T. Smith.)

erous forests. Annual rainfall averages approximately 2,500 millimeters, making it the wettest province of the South Caucasus. Eastern Caucasia (the steppes of Azerbaijan, crossed by the lower Araks and Kura) is a similarly low-lying area characterized by broad open steppe terrain with riverine vegetation. Summers tend to be mild and winters humid, though little rain falls throughout the year (in general, less than 200 mm) in this, the driest of Caucasia's provinces (Cole and German 1961; Dewdney 1979; Plashchev and Chekmarev 1978).

Southern Caucasia includes the highland middle Araks River and its drainages. Average elevation is between 1,200 and 1,800 meters above sea level, dipping below 1,000 meters only in the Ararat Plain. Summers are hot, dry, and short, but winters tend to be long and harsh, with moderate accumulations of snow (Hewsen 1997, 2001). The vegetation tends to steppe/prairie but varies significantly with elevation from the salt marshes of the Ararat Plain to the deciduous forests of Syunik, to the alpine regimes of the upper mountain slopes. Cultivation is difficult in the region without irrigation because rainfall is generally light (between 150 and 300 mm annual precipitation in the Ararat Plain) and concentrated in the spring (Tardzhumanian 1984). Irrigation historically has concentrated as much on

Fig. 3. Photo of the Tsaghkahovit Plain and the north slope of Mt. Aragats. (Photo Credit: Adam T. Smith.)

the capture and storing of snowmelt as the exploitation of river systems, since the latter tend to rest at the bottoms of deep gorges.

Resting atop the watershed between the Kura and Araks drainages sits a region known today as the Tsaghkahovit Plain (fig. 3), bounded by the north slope of Mt. Aragats, Mt. Kolgat, and the southwestern flanks of the Pambak range. I call attention to this small intermontane plateau because its prehistory will play an outsize role in the discussions in chapters 3, 4, and 5. Since 1998, I have co-directed a collaborative archaeological program in the region known as Project ArAGATS or, more expansively, the Joint American-Armenian Project for the Archaeology and Geography of Ancient Transcaucasian Societies. Our continuing program of field research has provided a view of this single region of unprecedented detail (Avetisyan et al. 2000; Badalyan et al. 2003, 2008, in press; Khatchadourian 2008a, 2014; Lindsay 2006, Lindsay et al. 2007, 2010, 2014; Smith et al. 2004, 2005, 2009; Smith and Leon 2014). Throughout this book, I contextualize regional developments in the South Caucasus in reference to changes in the Tsaghkahovit Plain. In addition, for the sake of simplicity, I utilize the Project ArAGATS chronology for the Bronze Age (fig. 4) and refer the reader elsewhere for a wider discussion of chronological issues in the region and its neighbors (Badalyan and Avetisyan 2007; Badalyan 1996; Smith et al. 2009).

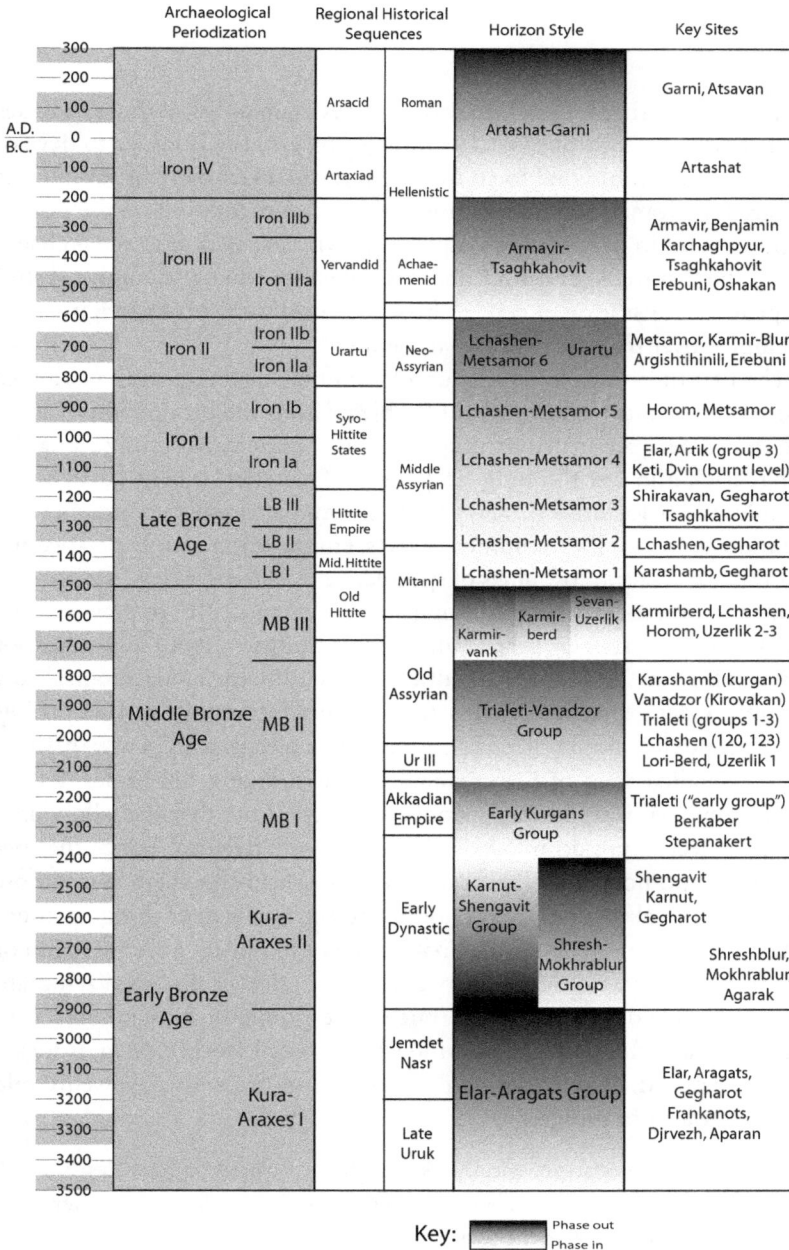

Fig. 4. The Project ArAGATS chronology for the Bronze and Iron Ages in the South Caucasus. (Figure Credit: Adam T. Smith.)

SCHEMATIC

In the chapters that follow, I draw on sources from political thought to aesthetic theory to anthropological studies of materiality in order to develop the conceptual tools vital to an inquiry into the machinery of sovereignty. In part 1, I advance two intersecting lines of argumentation on the politics of things, and in part 2, I flesh out the analytic in relation to the archaeology of the Bronze Age South Caucasus. Taken together, the empirical studies provide a historical survey of how the conditions of sovereignty were assembled over the course of two millennia.

The first theoretical intervention of the book, taken up in chapter 1, examines modernity's effort to banish objects from the production of social life alongside a series of counterprojects that have consistently smuggled things back into our thinking. The current "material" (Hicks 2010) or "archaeological" (Boelhower 2005) turn in the human sciences represents only the most recent of these counterprojects, embracing multiple perspectives from the abstract philosophies of speculative materialism (e.g., Meillassoux 2008) and object-oriented philosophy (e.g., Harman 2010) to grassroots social movements, such as permaculture (e.g., Mollison 1990) and transition towns (Hopkins 2008).[10] My intention in situating the archaeological turn within a wider genealogy of our struggle to understand the world of things is not to provide an intellectual history of materialism (cf. Frow 2010) or even a detailed map of the current state of thinking (cf. Miller 2005b). Rather, my goal is to develop a conceptual repertoire that will allow us to accord objects a presumption of difference—an analytical stance that neither anthropomorphizes their operation nor dismisses them as unknowable. It is critical that we attend not just to the qualities of things in themselves (what Ingold [2007] calls "materials") or to our interior reflection on the "thingly" character of things (what Latour [2007] calls "idealized materialism"; cf. Heidegger 2001: 26) but to the points of human–object encounter where the political, and indeed the social world *in toto*, is forged and reproduced. Three orienting theses emerge from this avowedly relational ontology of things:[11]

1. Objects are not sociologically meaningful as isolated singularities, but only relationally, set within heterogeneous assemblages whose encounters with human bodies define the social field.

[10] My thanks to Charis Boke for calling my attention to these movements.
[11] On relational ontology, see Smith 2003: 69.

2. Assemblages are not agentive, but they do have what I will call, following Jane Bennett (2010), "efficacy." This efficacy lends synchronic assemblages a diachronic motility, a capacity to define the logics of transformation that constitute "machines."

3. These machines operate simultaneously along multiple points of encounter with human bodies that I describe as sensibility, sense, and sentiment. This heuristic rubric seeks not to partition the human–object encounter, but to allow a multimodal epistemology that can grapple as sensitively with materials as with "materiality" (Crossland 2010; Meskell 2005b).

The second theoretical intervention of the book, presented in chapter 2, examines the sources and consequences of traditional political theory's exile of objects. The reduction of things to inert property, an innovation of Enlightenment liberal thought, provided a critical foundation for a modern politics that staked governance on resolving problems attendant to material distributions (e.g., distributions of capital, of tax revenues, of the means of production). The governance of human communities was thus closely elided with the regulation of a sensible world of things bereft of sensuality or sentiment. This account of the distributive state relied upon an ethical narrative of the origins of political association grounded in either the consent of the governed or the coercion of recalcitrant subjects. However, this severely limited understanding of the origins of political community gave rise to a fundamental paradox, what has traditionally been referred to as the "*aporia* of the one and the many" (Quillet 1988: 528). This *aporia* worries the puzzling solidarity of political communities despite the fragmentation and social fissures at the heart of their operation, the peculiar unity of the "world-machine" (Mueller 1944: 47) that rests upon the simultaneous integrity and sublimation of individual parts. In chapter 2, I argue that the relation of the one to the many is only aporetic if we ignore the operation of our human-built machines in the reproduction of the polity, discrete assemblages that work continuously to reproduce both the one and the many and mediate their relations.

In part 2, I examine the operation of three intricately related machines of sociopolitical reproduction that were forged during the Bronze Age in the mountainous South Caucasus, attending to their efficacy in securing the reproduction of sovereignty. Chapters 3, 4, and 5 pull apart the apparatus of sovereignty by distending the emergence of its conditions across two and a half millennia. In doing so, I do not intend to suggest that any kind of teleology inheres in the manufacture of the political machine. Quite the contrary, I hope to demonstrate through this distinctly archaeological analytic how the machinery of sovereign conditions works not only to enable but also stall, frustrate, and undermine the reproduction of the polity.

The first of these machines, what I call the civilization machine, encompasses an assemblage of objects that manufactures distinction and polices boundaries between those who are members and those who are not. Although Ernst Cassirer was certainly correct that the state's first aim is to "create the sort of subjects to whom it can address its call" (Cassirer and Gay 1954: 62–63), it does not begin with a blank slate. Rather, aspiring sovereigns must work with communities whose collective formation is already in process in both the short term and *longue durée*. In particular, subjects must first recognize one another as real or potential associates. What is particularly intriguing about the civilization machine is how it establishes a mode of reckoning based on the qualities of materials—the distinctive shape of a house, the unique decoration of a cooking pot—and their imbrication in social practices. However, the civilization machine does not simply sort members of different communities through an array of material cues. It also polices social boundaries, elevating formal and aesthetic differences into moral and political privileges. In chapter 3, I investigate the making of a civilization machine in the Early Bronze Age Caucasus, when the region became part of a material culture horizon known as the Kura-Araxes, a distinctive assemblage that at its height united communities across an extensive territory, from southern Russia in the north to the Levant in the south, from central Anatolia in the west to the central Zagros Mountains in the east.

In chapter 4, I examine the breakdown and redevelopment of the civilization machine during the Middle Bronze Age alongside a fearsome new assemblage that (following Deleuze and Guattari 1986) is best described as a "war machine." The operation of the war machine entailed not only the reproduction of political violence but also the dissection of social orders, severing a sovereign body from the bodies of subjects—those who command from those who obey. Through the conspicuous consumption of Middle Bonze Age mortuary ritual, the war machine reproduced the terms on which social order was predicated—charisma, violence, and distinction. However, built into the conjoined operations of the civilization and war machines was a contradiction. As the one (the erstwhile sovereign) pulled away from the many (the constituted public), demands upon material resources exceeded capacities. Moreover, territorial fragmentation and military stalemate—consequences of the war machine's proliferation—threatened to undermine the workings of the civilization machine, dissecting a previously expansive public into smaller and smaller segments. As a result, the central principle of charismatic authority was put at risk insofar as political power flowed from the provision of needs through conflicts successfully waged.

Trapped in a paradoxical state of contradiction, as the operation of the war machine eroded the integrity of the public assembled by the civilization machine, polities in the South Caucasus during the Late Bronze Age developed a new assemblage directed toward transforming charismatic authority into formal sovereignty. In chapter 5, I examine the assembling of this political machine, which drew the civilization and war machines into an extensive apparatus of rule, one that resolved the paradox at the heart of the joint operation of both. This novel political machine did not supersede the war and civilization machines—those continued to operate and indeed remain critical to political reproduction today. Rather, the political machine cloaked their contradictions, allowing the relation of the one to the many to persist as a "mystery" of sovereignty. The political machine not only provided the instruments of judicial ordering and bureaucratic regulation—instruments vital to containing state violence and regularizing the demands of a political economy—but it also transformed the polity itself into an object of devotion, securing not simply the surrender of subjects but their active commitment to the reproduction of sovereignty.

The final chapter of the book returns to the overarching question that opened this introduction—how do objects shape our political lives?—by drawing insights gained from the Bronze Age Caucasus into a wider reflection on the political work of things in contemporary moments of revolution and reproduction. However, before confronting the political, it is critical that we come to an understanding of what exactly objects are and how we can conceptualize them at work. It is to this problem that I turn in the next chapter.

PART I

The Machinery of Sovereignty

On Assemblages and Machines

The animated figures stand
Adorning every public street
And seem to breathe in stone, or
Move their marble feet.

(Pindar O. 7: 95–97)

The series of mythic tales surrounding the titan Prometheus has become a wellspring for theoretical reflection on the articulation of things and humans, an Iron Age urtext for today's material turn (e.g., Bredekamp 1995; Kaufman-Osborn 1997; Sennett 2008). Aeschylus's version of the story, based on the account in Hesiod's *Theogony*, centers on the punishment of humanity's savior. Zeus, unimpressed by "witless" mortals, had resolved to destroy humanity (Aesch. *PB*: ln. 444; trans. Smyth). In order to save them, wily Prometheus instructed humans in the workings of the object world, teaching them how to use wood and brick to build homes, how to yoke animals to bear burdens and plow fields, how to harness horses and build boats to travel great distances, how to devise medicines to heal the sick, how to read the sun and stars to understand the seasons, how to discern portents in the flights of birds and other auguries, how to represent the world in numbers, and how to preserve the memory of these arts in letters (Aesch. *PB*: ln. 450–70). But it was the defiant titan's theft of fire from Olympus that doomed Prometheus. Zeus ordered that he be bound to the bare mountain rock of the distant Caucasus for his transgression. Humanity was saved, but we too were bound, chained ever after to labor and its instruments, an object world without which the species that Hannah Arendt (1958) described as "*animal laborans*" (cf. Sennett 2008: 6) would surely perish.

In *Works and Days*, Hesiod attended less to Prometheus's woes than to the consequences of humanity's transgression against Zeus. In retaliation for Prometheus's intervention, Zeus commanded Hephaestus to fashion

Pandora "[to] mix earth with water and to put in it the voice and strength of human kind, and fashion a sweet, lovely maiden-shape, like to the immortal goddesses in face ... And he charged Hermes the guide, the Slayer of Argus, to put in her a shameless mind and a deceitful nature" (Hes. *WD*: ln. 60–70; trans. Evelyn-White). Zeus bequeathed this unfortunate golem—a product of craft (Sennett 2008: 11)—on Epimetheus, Prometheus's brother, along with a jar containing all the ills, plagues, and miseries of the earth. Epimetheus was captivated by this gift of Olympus, misrecognizing Pandora's anthropomorphism for humanity, her "endowments" for gifts. Driven by curiosity, Pandora opened the jar and let out the evils therein, allowing "countless plagues" to "wander amongst men" (Hes. *WD*: ln. 100).

As the philosopher Bernard Stiegler (1998: 186ff) has persuasively argued, the story of Prometheus alone makes little sense without the doubled figure of Epimetheus, who links the survival of humanity to its fall into the world of *animal laborans*. However, the mediating role in the story that ties together its key components—Prometheus's theft and Epimetheus's scourge—is played not by humans but by material things. In the first half of the story, objects serve as instructors to humankind, elevating the species from its rude state by teaching us crafts that are simultaneously material (e.g., how to build) and social (e.g., how to dwell). In the second half of the story, anthropomorphized material—a sentient compound of earth and water in human form—brings evil into the world. The caution in the Promethean cycle is not against the terrors of things acting per se but rather against things conscripted to act like, and appear like, humans, á la Pandora. This Promethean recognition is an archaeological insight, an acute awareness of the workings of things in human society (for Aeschylus, Prometheus's legacy) and a caution against conflating the operation of objects with the actions of humans (the mistake of Epimetheus when he welcomed Pandora).

Posthumanist philosophy has waged a powerful assault on the traditional hierarchy of things, arguing for a project of ontological leveling by pointing out how things from electrical grids (Bennett 2010) to Amazonian worms (Latour 1999) act agentively "like" humans. "A touch of anthropomorphism," Jane Bennett argues, "can catalyze a sensibility that finds a world filled not with ontologically distinct categories of beings (subjects and objects) but with variously composed materialities that form confederations" (Bennett 2010: 99). I am in sympathy with the political agenda that animates Bennett's intervention, an effort to check the "earth-destroying fantasies of conquest and consumption" (Bennett 2010: ix) that have been fed by representations of a passive material world, ready for exploitation. But anthropomorphism inevitably leads directly back to anthropocentrism, reinscribing the categories of human action as the only conceivable form of action in the world. As the Promethean cycle makes clear, objects interact with us, but they act like us only at our peril. Instead of forcing things to behave like we do, our focus should instead be on understanding their forms of action. But if objects do not act like us, how do they operate?

THINGS AND OBJECTS

It is difficult to define the operation of the things that surround us when we have only a vague sense of what they are. Despite our aesthetic captivation by commodity forms from the ridiculous (e.g., the catalog of things advertised on late-night American television) to the sublime (e.g., the inventory of Gary Hustwit's 2009 documentary *Objectified*), despite the dependence of the global economy on colossal migrations of raw materials and finished products, and despite our dedication to negotiating social distinction through material diacritics, we lack even a basic census of the world of things. A recent study conducted in Seoul found that the average South Korean household contained more than 10,000 individual objects (Nojima 2005). To roughly generalize from these data would suggest that there are between 8 and 17 trillion objects in households around the world, to say nothing of the factories, government offices, military bases, museums, archaeological sites, and, of course, landfills, where generations of past things now pile up in a purgatory between disposal and decay (Rathje and Murphy 1992; Reno 2008). And this population of things continues to grow ineluctably. It is difficult to imagine a theorization of the material world that does not also chart what for lack of a better term we might call not demography or biography, but *resography*, an account of material composition and distribution, formation and decay, topology and technology.

More concerning than the absence of even basic resographies is the lack of detailed studies that examine the mechanisms through which the sea of material culture shapes our lives. There is no shortage of studies that celebrate, deplore, or simply note the power of things in the contemporary moment (e.g., Findlen 2013; Glenn and Hayes 2007; Henare et al. 2007), but there are surprisingly few that provide an encompassing account of how we should theorize the human–object encounter. Archaeology has been steadfast in documenting humanity's phylogenetic encounter with things, which began more than 2 million years ago with the production of the first stone tools. However, the discipline has also tended to undervalue its unique intellectual mandate to define the forceful forms of historical and social determination embedded in our relationship to things, instead sublimating the object world into the ethnographic concepts of culture (e.g., Kidder 1924; Taylor 1948), system (e.g., Flannery 1968; Plog 1975), or text (e.g., Hodder 1986: 122; Tilley 1991: 16–17) and the historical epistemologies of events (e.g., Schliemann 1875), personages (e.g., Carter and Mace 1977), and thick description (cf. Snodgrass 1985).

Our ontogenetic ties to objects, which begin at birth if not before, are largely unexplored and yet do point to the profundity of our mutual engagement. A provocative recent study conducted in Japan sought to quantify infant interactions with objects versus interactions with their own and their parents' bodies (Shingaki and Nojima 2006). At four months of age, roughly half of child interactions were with things and half with other organic bodies—parents, siblings, other caregivers, and so on. By ten months, that ratio had soared as three-quarters of all child interactions were with objects. Similarly, a developmental pediatrician at Johns Hopkins recently estimated that as many as 25 percent of young American women go to college accompanied by a childhood transitional object, such as a teddy bear or blanket (Klass 2013). Parents might reasonably ask who, or rather, what, is raising our kids?

The suspicion that things are actively shaping our lives is by no means new. It is the anxiety that lies behind asceticism (both religious and secular) and the desire that drives commodity consumption. In a 2013 op-ed in the *New York Times*, Internet entrepreneur Graham Hill wrote: "I had a giant house crammed with stuff... Somehow this stuff ended up running my life ... the things I consumed ended up consuming me" (Hill 2013). Tellingly, in order to free himself from things, Hill designed a 420-square- foot New York apartment that used folding tables, hideaway furniture, and moveable walls to allow a single space to serve as bedroom, living room, and dining room. Liberation from our things, it seems, requires the help of a great many other things.

Recent studies of human "materiality," a critical conceptual force within the wider material turn, have argued persuasively for the co-constituted nature of things and social practices, ranging from colonialism (Thomas 1991) to Christianity (Bynum 2011) to capitalism (Maurer 2005). The materiality movement has succeeded admirably in resuscitating the object world as an analytical concern beyond the disciplinary confines of archaeology (e.g., Bennett and Joyce 2010; Braun and Whatmore 2010a; Brown 2001; Coole and Frost 2010; Daston 2004; Miller 1987, 2005a; Myers 2001). And within archaeology, materiality studies (e.g., Boivin 2008; Knappett 2005; Meskell 2004; Olsen 2010; Tilley 2004) have worked to extend an earlier concern with the social power of landscape to embrace a wider sense of material instrumentality (e.g., Alcock 1993, 2002; Harmanşah 2007; Johnson 2007; Khatchadourian 2008b; McGuire 1991; Smith 2003). Yet they have not produced a conceptual apparatus for detailing the operation of things sufficiently robust to match the rich lexicon for detailing the actions of human individuals, collectivities, and institutions. As a result, the things themselves rather quickly disappear from view (Hodder 2012: 1), overwhelmed by the myriad forces of psychological, cultural, and institutional determination grounded in the singularly powerful figure of the modern human subject.

One response to our anemic conceptual repertoire for detailing the operation of things has been to destabilize the distinction between human subject and material object, thus appropriating the traditional terms of human activity to do new work in the world of things. Things are then open to description in distinctly anthropomorphic terms as having lives (Appadurai 1986) and thus biographies (Gosden and Marshall 1999; Kopytoff 1986); they are vibrant (Bennett 2010) and unruly (Hodder 2012: 85–87). Although highly productive as both a "methodological philistinism" (Gell 1992: 42) and a critical stance, the extension of human qualities to things is, in ontological terms, a violation of the Promethean recognition, an imposition of our logics upon theirs. Ironically, dismantling the traditional divide between knowing subject and known object, rather than empowering things, entails a real danger of anthropomorphizing everything, leaving the human figure as the sole point of reference for imagining causation, agency, or determination.

If we seek to understand the object world in terms that more closely approximate its own, then we must heed the Promethean recognition and accord things an epistemological presumption of difference. The object world must be given the opportunity to operate differently than humans do, much as archaeologists and ethnographers must presume that distinct epochs and communities operate in ways native to their own histories and understandings (Meskell 2004: 3). An anthropology of the object world necessarily entails a rejection of what Meillassoux (2008: 5) calls "correlationism," the post-Kantian conceit that we can never gain knowledge of a thing outside us "in itself" but only as an appearance to an observing subject. As Meillassoux (10) keenly observes, correlationism excludes the possibility of understanding a world outside of—or "ancestral" to—human subjectivity. And yet the co-constitution of objects and subjects necessarily entails a world forged by relations established among objects, a *"great out-doors"* (7; italics in original) exterior to, and partially autonomous from, human consciousness. As Meillassoux's analysis clearly implies, the episte-mological task that faces contemporary material thought is not how we can collapse humans and objects into equivalent social forces but rather how their distinctive capacities articulate with one another to forge, reproduce, and undermine specific sociopolitical formations.

The central preoccupation of much philosophical reflection on the ma-terial world has traditionally been the object. However, the object is merely a conceptual abstraction. There is no empirically demonstrable thing that is not first and foremost something else before it is an object. Phones, com-puters, mugs, and paper, for example, are only objects insofar as we seek to impose homogeneity and singularity upon a field defined by heterogeneity and multiplicity. That is, there is no such thing as an object, there are only a myriad of distinct material forms. This is not to say that objects are de-fined solely by particularity but rather to argue that what holds material forms together is not their status as objects but their mutual participation in *assemblages* (see below). The particular assemblage of computer, coffee mug, pen, and paper now on my desk is fundamental to the writing of this book, but it is inseparable from an array of other things—manufacturing equipment, global transport technologies, digital networks, pulp mills, cof-fee plantations—that it implicates. To focus on the object would be to ig-nore not only the particularity of material forms but also the extensive ties that link forms into assemblages.

Assemblages, as I will use the term here, are arrays of material forms that, to use Nicholas Thomas's (1991) evocative term, "entangle." Assem-blages make our practices social, by mediating links between humans and material forms that are at once spatial—generating relationships of posi-tion and movement—and historical—demanding continual investment and attention. I will use the terms "object" and "thing" interchangeably throughout this book to refer to the heterogeneous components of assem-blages. This is not to suggest that elsewhere distinctions between the terms might not be of consequence—a prominent thread in contemporary the-ory worries exactly this conceptual difference to productive ends (Bennett 2010: 5; Brown 2001: 4)—only that these arguments are not at stake here. What is at the center of concern instead is the assemblage.

Assemblages can embrace the organic and inorganic, the durable and ephemeral, and may envelop human bodies in forms such as mortal re-mains, chattel slaves, and transplanted organs. The assemblage thus flows into the assembly—the community of persons—across blurred rather than sharply drawn borders. The Promethean recognition requires carving out theoretical terrain where things can operate in ways that are uniquely their own, irreducible to anthropomorphic metaphors, but the edges of this conceptual space must necessarily be porous, allowing for the kinds of movement back and forth that generate complex relations. Assemblages are not simply congeries of materials but rather are constituted by material forms linked by distinctly social relationships with assemblies of humans that are likewise defined by the engagement. A person not defined by the assemblages that surround—both their presence and their absence—is, to borrow a phrase from Aristotle (*Pol.* 1253a1), either too bad or too good, either an exile from the real or a decorporealized divinity.

Three questions loom large in working toward an archaeology of our engagement with assemblages. First, how can we define the assemblage as a synchronic unit of analysis? Is the assemblage a set of four wheels, the engine and mechanics that drive the wheels forward, the car interior in which drivers and passengers sit, or the systems of manufacturing and representation that have placed the automobile at the heart of global transport economies, settlement dynamics, and the poetic imagination of freedom (Kerouac 1957; Kunstler 1993; Safdie and Kohn 1997)? Second, how can we describe assemblages in action and the particular quality that lends them the capacity to participate in the historical production and reproduction of social life? If things are not agentive in the same way that people are, how can we describe their social operation? Last, how can we define the parameters of our human articulation with assemblages? To observe the determinative potential of things is to presume points where their logics impinge upon human bodies. How precisely can we conceptualize these points of encounter? In order to address these issues, it is critical that we historicize them within both traditions of philosophical reflection and the current material turn (cf. Parika in Dieter 2013: 24).

THE EXILE OF THINGS

The implications of the Promethean recognition have in large measure been overlooked by a Western philosophical tradition built not on Aeschylean dramaturgy and Hesiodic poetry but on Platonic ontology. Aristotle's response to Plato's theory of the Forms (see this book's introduction) was to argue against the separate existence of universal qualities apart from the objects in which they inhere. For example, on this page the text is black and the page is white, particular qualities of an object, the book. Whereas for

Plato, blackness and whiteness existed apart from all individual appearances as higher order Forms that distinguished sensing from knowing, for Aristotle (1966: 26–29), these universal qualities were intrinsic to objects. That is, for Aristotle, even though we identify the text on this page thanks to our knowledge of blackness and whiteness, we will never find these qualities in the world apart from particular things (Fine 1993).

As taken up by medieval Christian realism, the debate between an Aristotelian account of universals and a Platonic theory of the Forms was yoked to a distinctly theological outlook, allowing all things to be understood as instantiations of the divine idea (Tillich 1967: 6). Thomas Aquinas struggled to resolve contradictions between Platonic and Aristotelian ontologies by positing that universals live first as ideas in the mind of God (a theological extension of the Forms) and secondarily in things themselves (as objects of sensory encounter). To help clarify, Aquinas (1964: 69) distinguished between the relation of objects to God and humans by drawing an analogy to a house. A house comes into existence because of the conception of a dwelling in the mind of the architect. In contrast, passersby come to understand the house because of their direct experience of it. Deviations of experience from the idea of the house are errors of the builder who carried out the architect's instructions; similarly, if passersby were to mistake a house for a church, factory, or school, then their understanding has failed to apprehend the idea. In other words, our intellect conforms itself to the idea intrinsic to the object, even as objects conform themselves to the universal idea in the mind of God.

One implication of Aquinas's ontological realism[1] was to articulate all things, animate and inanimate, with the deity. Aquinas defended the veneration of relics, including things associated with the life of Christ and the saints, arguing that they both represented the holy person and had physical contact with the venerated (Aquinas 1965: 197–99). Things were thus endowed with a spirit derived from God that parallels the infusion of a soul in every individual human body. An understanding of the holy as residing in material objects created distinct theological tensions because of the second commandment's prohibition on the worship of graven images (Exodus 20: 4–5). Medieval realism was predicated upon a living world in which the sacred could burst forth from any given thing through the animating intervention of the creator: "The basic way of describing matter—the default

---

[1] I use the term realism throughout this book in the medieval sense of the term, roughly equivalent to what Kant (1872: 307) termed transcendental idealism, to denote various strands of thought that insisted upon the independence of the properties of things from perception and mind.

language, so to speak, into which theorists tended to slip—was to see it as organic, fertile, and in some sense alive" (Bynum 2011: 30).

The Middle Ages were rife with active things that revealed the mind of both the deity and the devil. Medieval Europe boasted a robust market in the things of saints and the life of Christ, including body parts and contact relics, such as clothing, water, bones, and hair. These objects contained within them powers to heal, protect, and incite the faithful (Bynum 2011: 20). Relics of the *Arma Christi*, or instruments of the Crucifixion, circulated through Europe both as physical objects of pilgrimage and devotion and imagined representations of God's intercession in the world—media par excellence. By the late Middle Ages, holy matter had become increasingly lively—witnesses report that statues moved, relics bled, hosts cured—in what Caroline Bynum (2011: 128) calls "miracles of metamorphosis." Sculptures became flesh and blood that winked and wept. As things became more animated, so too did human reactions to the workings of objects; relics were bowed to, prayed to, kissed, dressed, and adored. Moreover, they initiated new patterns of human mobility as pilgrimage routes developed around relics and reliquary, forging complex exchange economies. Holy relics themselves became objects of intense competition and exchange as institutions vied for pilgrim revenues. But even as prizes, objects were not passive; as a case in point, a cross relic owned by Jane Mary of Maillé reportedly bled when divided in two for distribution to a second reliquary (Bynum 2011: 139).

If during the late Middle Ages "to materialize was to animate" (Bynum 2011: 125), what navigates the distance between then and our current conditions of late modernity when reification entails fixity, immobility, and inanimacy? I suggest that three key transpositions were critical to the exile of things from the *via moderna*: the austere division of the animate from the inanimate world, the compression of things into a singular "object," and the shackling of material forms into a subservient utility. Let me begin with the issue of animacy, because the rigorous division of the world into the animate and inanimate set the ontological conditions for the other intellectual transformations.

Animacy

The exile of the object in philosophical contemplation traces its roots most directly to the various forms of antirealism forwarded by William of Ockham—often distinguished as nominalism and conceptualism—which ushered in a significant new effort to discipline the object world. Ockham's nominalism denied the reality of metaphysical universals. Such universals were, he argued, simply created in the act of thinking about several objects simultaneously:

> I say that there is no such a thing as a universal, intrinsically present in the things to which it is common. No universal ... is a thing existing in any way outside of the soul, but everything which can be predicated of many things is by its nature in the mind either psychologically ("subjective") or logically ("objective") and nothing of that sort is of the essence or quiddity of any substance. (Ockham 1974: 291–92)[2]

Qualities of objects, for example redness or sphericity, exist not as separate ideas (or Forms) but only in our reflection upon a group of things that share these qualities: a red ball, the planet Mars, a balloon, a meatball, a gumball. Universals, Ockham argued, were thus not things (*res*) but names (*nomina*); knowledge of the world, he concluded, is predicated on the direct experience of objects; understanding is thus built upon sense perception.

Ockham's nominalism dismantled the medieval accord between Christian revelation and Platonic realism that had been brokered, most powerfully, by Aquinas. His insistence on the immediacy of the world of things opened the *via moderna* and established the foundations for empiricism (Oberman 1987). As a result, Ockham is often regarded as the father of epistemology (Tornay 1936: 245). Yet what most interests me here is the ontological transformation in the nature of things that his thought advanced. Ockham's nominalism created a distinctly human-centered ontology. Far from being potential media for God's intercession in the world, or possessed of their own spirit, be it beatific or satanic, things were only what humans made of them. As a result, objects were cast out of the world of movement, action, and causation and redefined *a priori* as inanimate, immobile, and inert. As Foucault (1989: 54–55) noted, the foundations of the modern episteme rest upon the strict ordering of this divide between animate and inanimate worlds, between a human sphere of sense, value, and thought and an external object world of passivity, fact, and mechanics. It is this metaphysical work of the Enlightenment that Bruno Latour (1993: 11) has aptly described as "purification," a radical simplification of the world that makes possible the certainty of the Cartesian subject, the universalization of "objectivity," and, consequently, the exile of things from social life to "the balmy elsewhere beyond theory" (Brown 2001: 1).

---

[2] Ockham engages with the problem of universals and the Forms in two key passages: *Ordinatio* I d.2 qq.4–8 and *Summa Logicae* 1.xv–xvii.

Compression

The project of purification that defined the *via moderna* was a profound departure from the *via antiqua*. The Heraclitan roots of classical epistemology set forth a world in constant flux: "All things move and nothing remains still" (Plat. *Crat.* 401d; trans. Fowler). Classical philosophy in general was highly attentive to object variation and dynamism and curious as to the origins of such heterogeneity. For the Roman poet and philosopher Lucretius, things possessed a shared vitality derived from their emergence from primal bodies possessed of their own unique power. Lucretius mocked the reduction of the panoply of things into a singular category suggestive of a singular origin:

> For if things came out of nothing, all kinds of things
> Could be produced from all things. Nothing would need a seed.
> Men could arise from the sea, and scaly fish
> From earth, and birds hatch in the sky.
>
> (Lucretius 1997: 1.160–63)

Instead, he argued, each thing arose from, and ultimately dissolved back into, its own unique "seed" possessed of "a distinctive power" (1.172) of its own:

> And why do roses flourish in the spring
> And corn in summer's heat, and grapes in autumn,
> Unless because each thing that is created
> Displays itself when at their own due time
> Fixed seeds of things have flowed together, and the seasons
> Attend, and safe and sound the quickened earth
> Brings tender growth up to the shores of light?
> [...]
> All things grow slowly, as is natural
> From a fixed seed, and growing keep their character.
>
> (Lucretius 1997: 1.173–79, 189–90)

Lucretius's world of variation, ebb, and flow clearly remained broadly Heraclitan in its attentiveness to heterogeneity and flux. What is most immediately striking about Lucretius's account is the luxuriant, highly poetic, representation of a dense material world from plants and animals to stones, weapons, furniture, and tools, all at various stages of becoming or receding.

The complex sensible world of antiquity stands in remarkable contrast to the abstract, unrecognizably compressed object world of Enlightenment thought. Although Ockham initiated the exile of objects from historical determination, it was not until several centuries later that the Lucretian world of things was effectively stripped of its variation. This process of compression was well under way by the mid-seventeenth century when Thomas Hobbes (1991: 13) defined the "object" generically as any "accident of a body without us." The external world was collapsed into a single undifferentiated, homogenous category defined primarily by a negation: "not us." The opening created by a radical distillation of the world of things into the singular category of "object" was a Cartesian division that sundered not simply body from mind, but physics from metaphysics, allocating the former to the scientific gaze and the latter to philosophical reflection. Both forms of knowledge are defined by a fierce impatience with the world of things, moving brusquely past sensory apprehension to locate allegedly deeper wells of determination and solidity.

Graham Harman (2010: 95) has recently railed against philosophy's long-standing reduction of the object world, wondering whether the discipline can truly "remain satisfied with not addressing any . . . objects by name, so as to confine itself to a 'more general' discussion of the condition of the condition of the condition of possibility of ever referring to them?" Harman continues: "Will philosophy continue to lump together monkeys, tornadoes, diamonds, and oil under the single heading of that-which-lies-outside?" For Harman, as for Meillassoux (2008; see above), knowing the world entails coming to terms with the panoply of things and their relationships to one another.

Subservience

Hegel noted the predicament that faced the object world when reduced to being only a category for abstract thought or material for practical use. On the one hand, as matter for theoretical reflection, objects reside as lonely exiles in a prison of objectivity, walled off from each other and from human contact by the presumption of their independence and the "subjugation of subjectivity" (Hegel 1988: 112). On the other hand, as material for practical labor, objects are systematically annihilated as work demands "altering them, molding them, forming them, canceling their qualities, or making them work upon one another, e.g., water on fire, fire on iron, iron on wood, and so on." Hegel concludes, "Thus now it is things which are deprived of their independence since the subject brings them into his service and treats and handles them as *useful* .... The objects have become unfree, the subjects free" (Hegel 1988: 113; italics in original). Trapped in a state of pure utility, only the beautiful object manages to escape the double bind into which the combined forces of modern philosophy and craft production have thrust the object: "[The contemplation of beauty] leaves objects alone as being inherently free and infinite; there is no wish to possess or take advantage of them.... So the object, as beautiful, appears neither as forced or compelled by us, nor fought and overcome by other external things" (Hegel 1988: 114). Hegel thus leaves us stranded between an idiosyncratic object of contemplation, dense in particularity and defined by an aesthetic encounter, and a mass of undifferentiated things reduced to subservient utility.

It is ironic that Ockham's "hard-headed" nominalism and the various forms of "clear-eyed" empiricism that followed from it have left us not soberly mindful of things, but deeply naïve as to their capacities and efficacy. How can we "maintain that hitting a nail with and without a hammer, boiling water with and without a kettle, fetching provisions with or without a basket, walking in the street with or without clothes, zapping a TV with or without a remote ... are exactly the same activities" (Latour 2005: 71). One version of these activities is prosaic, the other parodic. The difference lies in the work accomplished by the assemblages involved. To reduce the object world to mere subservience is to ignore all of the activity that our assemblages not only make possible but even imaginable. It is not only the captivation of the work of art that entangles us, obligates us, makes demands of us. We are constantly serving our things: maintaining homes, repairing automobiles, nurturing plants and animals, shepherding goods from factory to market to landfill. Most of us spend our day tending to the needs of things that, presumably, reciprocally tend to ours, relations that Ian Hodder (2012) defines as dependency and dependence. Material assemblages can only be understood as subservient to human will if we can imagine performing consequential activities without them.

Proponents of new forms of materialism (e.g., Harmann, Meillassoux, and Latour) are currently engaged in directly confronting the legacy of Ockham's assault on realism, but the ongoing "material turn" is by no means the first effort to resist the exile of things from our understanding of social life. A similar effort to preserve the heterogeneity of assemblages and illuminate the consequential force of things has motivated a number of historical counterprojects. Let me turn now to highlight just two of these practical engagements with material forms that illuminate the conceptual terrain critical to defining the operation of things.

NATURE MORTE

Although the philosophical exile of objects from the *via moderna* heralded the passing of the object world from an ontological state of lively "vitality" to one of cold inertia, it by no means augured a radical historical rupture. As Bynum (2011: 22) points out, objects became more animated in the later Middle Ages—after Ockham—rather than less. And, indeed, even today unruly things occasionally erupt in the public sphere in distinctly medieval ways; witness the piece of cheese toast said to possess an image of the Virgin Mary that sold on eBay in 2004 for $28,000. Yet such transgressions across the heavily policed line between the animate human world and the inanimate sphere of things are no longer set within an epistemological framework that might allow such moments to serve as episodes for contemplation and investigation. Instead, they are derided as preposterous archaisms, the "residue of a primitive, childlike way of thinking" (Lurie 2007: 19).

The transition from an "infantile" presumption of things as participants in the world to the "mature" modern mind inured to the efficacy of objects was made across a wide array of the arts and sciences of Europe's seventeenth century. But nowhere was it as succinctly formulated as in André Félibien's (1668) hierarchy of artistic genres, a pictorial adaptation of Aristotle's great chain of being. Félibien formalized Enlightenment anthropocentrism by elevating representations of the human figure while derogating the genre of still life. Images of the human form provided material for contemplation and moral instruction, pedagogical qualities absent from the lowly still life:

> Thus the one who paints perfect landscapes stands above the one who represents only fruits, flowers, or shells. The one who paints live animals is worthier than the one who represents only things dead and without motion. And as the figure of man is the most perfect work of God on Earth, it is certain that the one who makes himself an imitator of God by painting human figures is much more excellent than all the others. (Félibien, quoted in Skira 1989: 38)

Capable of simple reportage but bereft of moral force or artistic imagination, the still life's studious contemplation of material assemblages focused attention on the everyday and thus, for Félibien, they were allegedly incapable of providing instruction in the virtues of great men or the lessons of history. Joshua Reynolds (1975[1769]) reinscribed the still life's lowly position, arguing that overindulgence in such prosaic "exercises" would preclude artists from gaining proficiency in the higher genres. Yet no genre was entirely without merit:

> Even the painter of still life, whose highest ambition is to give a minute representation of every part of those low objects, which he sets before him, deserves praise in proportion to his attainment; because no part of this excellent art, so much the ornament of polished life, is destitute of value and use. (Reynolds 1975: 52)

Faint praise.

As Norman Bryson (1990: 8) notes, the genre's "inevitability and indispensability have not helped it generate much corresponding light (or heat) in critical discussion." But still lifes have long been one of the most popular genres of painting and can boast a long list of influential practitioners in Caravaggio and Chardin, Picasso and Cezanne (to name only a few). They are as ubiquitous as landscapes and can be as mannered as history paintings. Long "the neglected stepchild of high art" (Sims and Rewald 1996: 11), the rise of industrial consumer society, particularly in the United States, has prompted some critical reevaluation:

> American concern for objects has always been thought to be both a specific and somewhat native one. There is a love of the way things in this country look, and yet at the same time a resentment that these objects fill and obliterate the landscape. (Cathcart 1983: 28)

Although critical studies of landscape painting have witnessed a resurgence in recent decades, marked by a considered effort to articulate these representational spaces with the sociopolitical forces driving transformations in lived spaces (e.g., Bermingham 1986; Mitchell 1994), still lifes have generally not provided the same invitation to retheorize the object world.

Yet, early modern still lifes are works of deep moral and existential anxiety that appear to worry both the coming of capitalism and the dispiriting enervation of things at the heart of the *via moderna* (cf. de Vries 1999; Honig 1998). So-called *vanitas* paintings, like medieval *momento mori* and Roman *mors omnia aequat* images, use skulls alongside the tools of science, industry, and the arts to grapple with the paradox posed by the ultimate perishability of human endeavor and the immortality of the material object (Bryson 1990; Ebert-Schifferer 1999). Humans pass even as things endure—an eminently archaeological insight to be sure. More subtle in their perception of the object world are the Haarlem *banketje* and Amsterdam *toebakje* paintings that shifted the artistic gaze away from tightly composed scenes of highly formalized object groups to scenes of assemblages in disarray. What

Fig. 5. Willem Claesz Heda, *Banquet Piece with Mince Pie* (1635). (Source: Courtesy National Gallery of Art, Washington, D.C.)

is most engaging about paintings like Willem Claesz Heda's *Banquet with Mince Pie* (fig. 5) is the way they freeze the motility of things—upended goblets, dirtied plates, smoldering pipes—in contexts devoid of humans. Indeed, human action in such scenes is entirely implicit, highlighting the very impossibility of the social worlds that coalesce around the dining table absent a heterogeneous collection of things.

The still life provides rich terrain for an exploration of the articulation of human and object worlds. Although preoccupied with material objects, the still life is not exhausted by them. The boundaries of the genre are remarkably elastic—allowing animals, scenery, and at times people into the frame—but the focal point of representation dwells on social engagement of things. In this sense, they reverse the epistemic virtues at work in the domain of scientific illustration, which developed in parallel. Daston and Galison (2007: 42) argue that scientific illustration in the eighteenth century was governed by a code of "truth-to-nature," which produced idealized representations that relieved objects of their idiosyncrasies by perfecting "nature's imperfect specimens." Still lifes, in contrast, revel in idiosyncrasy. More than just simple studies of static material form, still lifes are proto-archaeological encounters that explore the possibility of the very same "great outdoors" that Meillassoux (2008; see above) longs to bring to philosophical reflection. They thus constitute a critical dissenting opinion in the construction of the *via moderna*, even as Félibien's derogation of the genre aided in the wider project of relegating things to the world of inertia and immobility. Whereas philosophy has been intent on exiling things, still lifes provide a haven for representing the operation of assemblages. They thus constitute a vernacular form of resistance to the exile of things from philosophical reflection. However, what the genre could never provide was a conceptual framework for understanding how objects cohere not as random encounters, but as systematically articulated with one another within a social field. For that, we must turn to another counterproject running against the tide of modernity: archaeology.

THE ASSEMBLAGE ASSEMBLED

Like the still life, archaeology traces its origins to an abiding intuition that the world of objects is complexly interwoven with our social lives and their historical transformation. Even as Enlightenment philosophy exiled things to the inert world of inanimacy, seventeenth-century antiquarians were avidly smuggling them back in as material for contemplation as part of a historically grounded inquiry that sought to, in John Aubrey's words, "make the stones give evidence for themselves" (Aubrey, quoted in Schnapp 1997: 193). The European cabinets of curiosity that began as jumbles of ephemera, bric-a-brac, and oddments—secularizations of ornate relic altars—had, by the eighteenth century, developed into an increasingly systematic approach to apprehending the object world. This incipient archaeology attended less to singular artifacts than to the relations between objects, places, and contexts, ultimately giving rise to one of the discipline's central analytical concepts: the assemblage.

The Reverend James Graves—so aptly named for both his ecclesiastical profession and antiquarian avocation—was among the first to use the term "assemblage" to describe a discrete collection of material objects drawn together by a shared set of relations. Reporting on J. Richardson Smith's "diggings" in a "pagan" cemetery at Ballon Hill in Carlow County, Ireland, Graves (1853: 301) described the recovered ceramic vessels as a "matchless assemblage of examples of the fictile [plastic] art of the primitive inhabitants of Ireland." This sense of an assemblage highlighted the articulation of objects sharing the same raw material (e.g., ceramic), and hence broadly similar production processes (e.g., molding, pyrotechnics, etc.), both within and between sites. But the term was not broadly adopted by archaeologists of the nineteenth century. Although the assemblage was already in general use by naturalists, geologists, and paleontologists to describe congeries of physical properties (Mohs 1825: 20) and collections of fossils (Cuvier 1818: 362), seminal archaeological texts of the late nineteenth century (e.g., Layard 1853; Pitt-Rivers 1887; Schliemann 1875; Squier and Davis 1848) avoided the term even as principles of stratigraphy imported from geology were focusing new attention on associations among material forms (e.g., Worsaae 1849). Where the term assemblage did appear, it often carried a sense not of close material association but of simple co-occurrence: "For not the least remarkable feature observed in reference to the altars of the mounds is, that their deposits do not exhibit a miscellaneous assemblage of relics, like the contents of an Indian ossuary or grave-mound" (Wilson 1862: 375). It was John Lubbock's groundbreaking *Pre-Historic Times* (1865, but esp. the 1872 third edition) that assertively forwarded the concept of assemblage to define collections of materials that co-occurred in one location, "particularly when his purpose was to compare a collection from one location with that from another" (Joyce and Pollard 2010: 295). What is striking in these early uses of the term is a consistent understanding of the assemblage as defined not primarily by relations of objects to humans (as producers or consumers) but by independent spatiotemporal relations among themselves.

It was not until the second quarter of the twentieth century that the assemblage began its migration to the center of the discipline, as archaeologists began to look at assemblages as remains across an array of media that co-occurred within the same depositional context. As American archaeology, in particular, came to be increasingly dedicated to culture-history and material taxonomy, "it became commonplace to associate all artifacts and features in a stratum and to refer to the conglomerate as an assemblage" (Lyman et al. 2003: 158). This conventional sense of the term as defining a single unit of archaeological recovery tended to presume that their co-occurrence was the result of direct discard rather than a product of postdepositional site-formation processes (Schiffer 1987), and hence the nature of their association was historical and not coincidental. This sense of meaningful co-occurrence was often expanded beyond the stratum to provide a material summary of an entire epoch. It was this sense of the assemblage that V. Gordon Childe (Childe 1950a: 2) codified when he defined an archaeological culture as "an assemblage of artifacts that recur repeatedly associated together in dwellings of the same kind and with burials of the same rite. The arbitrary peculiarities of implements, weapons, ornaments, houses, burial rites and ritual objects are assumed to be the concrete expressions of the common social traditions that bind together a people." Hence, Robert Braidwood and colleagues (1952: 6) deployed the term simultaneously to describe an "upper phase assemblage," a "Matarrah assemblage," a "Hassunan assemblage," and a "Near Eastern village assemblage," clearly demonstrating the scalar plasticity of the term to draw together materials from discrete deposits, a single site, a regional spatio-temporal horizon, and a broadly defined sociocultural phenomenon. David Clarke (1968: 22) later formalized the place of the assemblage within a scalar classificatory nomenclature that described the "fundamental entities" of analysis as extending from "the attribute, the artefact, the artefact-type," to the more embracing categories of "the assemblage, the culture and the culture group."

However, alongside this capacious sense of spatial co-occurrence emerged a more complex understanding of assemblages as toolkits unified by practical function. Childe also repeatedly used the term to refer to a collection of objects that define specific economic practices. The co-occurrence of food animal remains and instruments related to their preparation at the Neolithic site of Skara Brae in the Orkneys constituted a "typical kitchen-midden assemblage" (Childe 1931: 198); the predominance of domesticated animal remains, sickles, and sickle blades in late Chalcolithic settlements of the central Eurasian steppe defined "an assemblage indicative of settled farming" (Childe 1942: 134).[3] This definition of an assemblage as a closely cohering toolkit established a new understanding of things as united by their distinctly social activity. It is this sense of the assemblage that Gordon Willey and Philip Phillips (1958) embraced as they sought to sever it from its purely taxonomic usage and thus to understand it as the "imperishable" materials used by a defined group of people within a defined location at a defined point in time. This sense of the assemblage was thus itself scalable and plastic, capable of describing both the personal toolkit of a single individual in the past or the complete inventory of a single

[3] In a similar use of the term, Emil Haury's (1950: 73, 193) report on excavations at Ventana Cave described assemblages of both faunal remains and tools.

period of a site or a durable set of materials made and used by a people across board regions. What is critical is that assemblages were defined not by formal or stylistic qualities but by activities.

It was the New Archaeology of the 1960s that elevated the assemblage to the central object of archaeological study, displacing earlier rivals, such as the site, the monument, and the artifact. In setting the agenda for archaeology's high modernist processual movement, Lewis Binford (1964: 433) dedicated the discipline to the assemblage by arguing that "the aim of archaeological investigation is the definition of the structure of an archaeological assemblage in addition to its content." For Binford, the structure of an assemblage—its patterns of heterogeneity and homogeneity distributed across space and time—was critical to any effort to examine social and cultural processes as systemic instead of purely idiosyncratic. That is, to understand patterns of social change entailed delineating variation and continuity within the associations that defined what David Clarke (1973: 15) would refer to as "mutual assemblage affinities." Although Binford does not directly implicate assemblages in historical transformations—his sense of culture remained largely idealist, and the mediations of material culture were largely limited to adaptation (Binford 1962, 1965)—his understanding of the assemblage as materials set within a field of independent associations was critical to both the intellectual mission of archaeology and the current material turn. The processual sense of the concept that Binford ushered into the discipline largely assumed that the assemblage was a residue of purposeful human actions, mitigated by the social and environmental forces that shape the archaeological record (Schiffer 1983).

Even as the New Archaeology came under a withering critique from the various forms of postmodernism that defined the so-called postprocessual movement (Hodder 1986; Preucel 1995; Shanks and Tilley 1987), the assemblage was retained largely intact—an indispensable conceptual apparatus that allowed for the articulation of disparate materials across media to define contexts of practice, embodiment, and interpretation (e.g., Hodder 1999: 182; Shanks 1995: 222). However, the postprocessual turn focused new attention on the forces assembling the assemblage. Studies of ritual deposits (e.g., Garber 1983; Walker 1995) and public performances (e.g., Inomata 2006; Kus and Raharijaona 2006) highlighted the scripted nature of some depositional contexts, challenging the traditional processual sense of autonomous, intentional human action as the source of assemblages (Walker 2002). As a result, assemblages were redefined as not simply a residuum of human behavior but constitutive of the mutual engagement of objects and people, opening the possibility that historical determination might lie as powerfully in what Ian McEwan (1987: 7) has called the "conspiracy of objects" as in the traditional agentive capacities ascribed to persons.

The product of archaeology's century and a half of reflection upon assembling and assemblages is a sense of the concept grounded in two key foundations. First, assemblages are heterogeneous in that they extend across media, form, type, and style. Second, they are emergent in that the principles of association are constantly in flux and thus any assemblage is inherently synchronic—a slice across an even more complex web of "entanglements" (Hodder 2012). As a consequence, assemblages are drawn together by social engagement within the community of people and things and not by features inherent to the material (e.g., affordances) or ideational (e.g., the traditional culture concept) alone. The linkages that define the assemblage are established by, to use Manuel DeLanda's (2006: 18) terminology, relations of exteriority. Where relations of interiority—such as part to whole—constitute the identity of the component parts (e.g., an engine is part of a car and that role defines it), relations of exteriority are highly contingent, multiple, overlapping, and simultaneous. Elements in an assemblage are thus coherent in themselves and hence self-subsistent; they can be easily detached from one and attached to another.

This distinctly archaeological notion of the assemblage stands as the vital antithesis to the modernist philosophical "any accident of a body without," heterogeneous and polysemous instead of singular, flat, and monotonous. The assemblage is fundamentally an affirmation of the sociality of the things that surround us, composed not only of component objects, but also of the relations that articulate them, including relations to human practices and bodies. I should note that the assemblage is not the same thing as Latour's (1999: 182) association of actants, which describes how action arises in symmetrical relations between humans and nonhumans (e.g., the human who transforms the gun into a weapon and the gun that transforms the human into a killer). The assemblage attends specifically to relations among objects themselves.[4] However, because assemblages are synchronic, articulations of material forms at a single moment in time, it remains unclear how we can conceptualize their operation diachronically and thus their capacity to set sociopolitical production and reproduction in motion.

---

[4] Among these objects, as noted above, we may find human bodies and body parts, but the assemblage is not a concept meant in the first instance to envelop the totality of the human and nonhuman worlds.

THE EFFICACY OF MACHINES

As Gilles Deleuze notes, the relations constitutive of any assemblage are external to their components (Deleuze and Parnet 2002: 55). "The glass is on the table" is a relationship exterior to either the glass or the table and subject to a wide array of decompositions and reformations—either can move, either can break, the wooden table will decompose but the glass will not, the glass can be stolen more easily than the bulky table, more glasses and tableware can join the glass on the table, new furniture can join the table, liquid can fill the glass and condensation can mar the table. Among the first to recognize the assemblage as fertile ground for a critical project, Deleuze and Guattari reversed the traditional philosophical compression of the material world into the singular "object" by detailing the envelopment of the human body in the complex "machinic systems" of the assemblage:

> For the moment, we will note that assemblages have elements (or multiplicities) of several kinds: human, social, and technical machines, organized molar machines. . . . We can no longer even speak of distinct machines, only of types of interpenetrating multiplicities that at any given moment form a single machinic assemblage, the faceless figure of the libido. Each of us is caught up in an assemblage of this kind, and we reproduce its statements. (Deleuze and Guattari 1987: 36)

Assemblages are not infinitely mutable because of the material properties that inhere in substances, like the hardness of rock or the suppleness of clay, but because of the social properties that arise in our interactions with things—their flows across territorial domains, their perduring anachronism derived from a distinctively nonhuman temporality, their metamorphoses from one sociomaterial state into another, their transformation of value and transfiguration of human bodies. These operations of the material lie at the heart of the machinic assemblage, or what I will simply call "machines." What separates a synchronic assemblage from a diachronic machine is the capacity to operate in the world, to make a difference in social life over time. Assemblages are everywhere, constantly embracing us in our co-constitution of the social. But to understand their historical workings—their role in both the production of new social forms and the reproduction of existing orders—we must define the elements within the wider assemblage that do not just articulate, but operate.

Agency and Efficacy

A central theme in the contemporary material turn has been an effort to theorize the workings of things, their capacity to intrude into a field of historical determination that has long been occupied by an exclusively human figure. Yet, as the Prometheus cycle makes clear, things put in motion historical forces that can and do overwhelm any possibility of human agency. Jane Bennett (2010: 23) pushes Deleuze and Guattari's account of assemblages in exactly this direction, describing them as "ad hoc groupings of diverse elements, of vibrant materials of all sorts." These collectives are made manifest most conspicuously when the "vital force" of each thing within the assemblage works in concert to create an effect in the world, such as a hurricane, or a blackout, that is irreducible to human intention or will. At times, Bennett's account of the assemblage appears largely synonymous with the broad domain of unintended consequences, thus recentering analysis not on determinative things but on the limited knowledge of human actors (cf. Giddens 1984: 293–97). However, her account opens critical analytical ground insofar as her assemblages emerge out of the interactions of their component parts.

Latour (2005: 72) has waged a strong assault on the traditional view that objects can "'express' power relations, 'symbolize' social hierarchies, or 'reinforce' social inequalities, and yet "cannot be at the origin of social activity." Latour protests that, in traditional sociology, things "live at the margins of the social doing most of the work but [are] never allowed to be represented as such" (Latour 2005: 73). Objects, he thus argues, are "full-blown" (72) actors in the social field, capable of not just passively symbolizing relations, but explaining them. Latour's assemblage, like DeLanda's, is thus dynamic and motile—a radical redefinition of the traditional philosophical object.

Yet there are clear hazards in describing things as "actors." Although epistemologically provocative, such a move represents a contravention of the Promethean recognition, of the dangers that inhere in failing to recognize the autonomous condition of the world of things. A number of scholars have noted the consequences for our understanding of human agency that would follow from broadening the concept to embrace all kinds of movement in the world (e.g., Jones 1996), but equally concerning are the implications for our reflection upon the workings of objects. To collapse the workings of things into agency, and the heterogeneous object world into the category of actor, defers theorizing the unique kinds of intervention in the world that arise from the articulation of things within assemblages and their operation as machines of social (re)production. Although both Latour (2005) and Bennett (2010) work assiduously to strip the concept of agency of its underlying humanity, collapsing human and object actions into a single agent provides little space for Meillassoux's (2008) "great outdoors" where things work in ways that are not reducible to models defined by human language and cognition. As a result, the compression of human and object agency threatens to leave the object world trapped in an analytic incapable of understanding not simply the unique mechanics of things (e.g., how a dam holds water), but also their efficacy (e.g., how holding water creates political authority in one sociohistorical moment and not in another). And, indeed, it is precisely this form of efficacy that both Bennett and Latour have so eloquently placed on the agenda of social thought.

The term efficacy thus warrants some elaboration. Bennett (2010: 31) describes efficacy as "a capacity to make something new appear or occur"; it is one element in a swarm of affiliates, including trajectory and causality, that compose agency. Most importantly, efficacy is that aspect of activity most clearly centered on material assemblages within Bennett's wider effort to define a confederate sense of agency. Bennett's account of efficacy provides a good starting point for defining the work of things in the world. My only amendment would be to delete the word "new." So much of the work of things is not in making new things happen, but in making the things we take for granted happen again and again. The efficacy of things is not simply a feature of a traditional theory of transformational agency. It is also, perhaps more formidably, critical to the routines of social reproduction. Bennett notes how breakdowns, system failures, blackouts, shortages, and so on bring the efficacy of things to our attention (as does Hodder 2012: 68). But the consequences of these moments of machinic malfunction merely underline their everyday efficacy in reproducing an existing state of affairs. We may notice their work in the world more when it gives rise to novel effects, but that in no way diminishes the everyday efficacy of things in ensuring reproduction. To reinvoke the cases discussed in this book's opening, Obama's flag pin did not make something new appear, but it was remarkably efficacious in reproducing the standard figure of a political candidate; the bell of Uglich did not produce revolution but rather a reconsecration of Tsarist succession. Things in this sense participate differentially—just as people do—within an expansive apparatus of reproduction that constantly recreates the existing conditions of social and political life.

Reproduction and Transformation

It is important to note that to observe the efficacy of machines in securing social reproduction is not to limit their operation to mere recalcitrance (cf. Latour 2004a: 81),[5] or what Ankersmit (1996: 9) calls "sheer inertia, an immense and immovable weight that even the collective can never succeed in overcoming." Current approaches to materiality that highlight human dependency on things regularly struggle with how to theorize them into, as opposed to outside of, historical change. When human–object relationships are theorized as webs of mutual dependency, it is not surprising that entanglement appears to be a highly synchronic condition rather than a diachronic tension: things are normally assumed to be in place (Olsen 2010: 158). The resemblance of so-called tanglegrams (e.g., Hodder 2012: 181)—graphic representations of webs of object entanglement—to traditional systems theory flow charts is not coincidental. It arises from a shared sense of social life as fundamentally homeostatic. Things, Bjørnar Olsen argues, "enable and *stabilize* society" (Olsen 2010: 139; italics in the original). Or as Michel Serres (1995: 87) puts it: the object "makes our history slow." When efficacy is limited to obstinacy, objects are reduced to historical anchors, weights that work forcefully to fix the contemporary in place (Hodder 2012: 98–101).

Sometimes things do stabilize society but sometimes they do not, exposing institutions, communities, and polities to tremendous forces of transformation. One need look no further than the automobile and the combined geopolitical pressures of oil dependency and global warming to see things working to undermine social reproduction. So how then can we theorize social change without losing sight of human–material entanglements? If we are ill-advised to use terms for causation derived from human sociology, like actor, to describe the workings of things, how can we define the operation of things? Deleuze and Guattari's (1987) invocation of a machine metaphor to describe the operation of material assemblages highlights the autonomous motility of things—their capacity not simply to mediate but to transform human thought and action. But as William Connolly (2013: 81–83) points out, self-organizing processes (an intrinsic quality of any machine) are inherently fragile, susceptible not simply to breakdown but to paradox wherein their operation over time creates the conditions for their own obsolescence.

---

[5] Latour's sense of recalcitrance embraces both object and human actors.

It is important that we not overestimate the impact or the extent of the machinery critical to sociopolitical reproduction lest we mistake attention to the efficacy of things for a totalizing form of technological determinism. Machines are efficacious not in isolation but in their encounters with us, in relation to our own forms of action. But how can we theorize the encounter of machines with human bodies that reserves some autonomy for both their, and our, unique ways of working in the world?

Bodies and Machines

To attend to the machinery of social reproduction is not to eclipse the corporeal, but rather to reinscribe it in relation to the assemblages that surround it, push it, and, in both the political and aesthetic sense, grab hold of it. Eric Santner (2011) has described the "affective grip that a social formation is able to call forth" in its members. But where Santner examines the libidinal work of fantasy—"spectral 'things'" (2011: 72)—in this grip, I am more concerned with the object matter of excitation: the assemblages that *captivate*. However, doing so entails destabilizing our traditional understanding of the relation between what Diana Coole (2010: 92) has critically described as "the inertia of matter and the generativity of flesh": passive things set in motion by agentive humans. Certainly the efforts discussed above to attend to the "vitality" of things have done much to undermine this understanding, but so too have recent studies of the "thinginess" of bodies. It is this turn to the historicity of embodiment that opens critical analytic terrain for examining how assemblages come to grip bodies, to hold them, remake them, and redefine them.

Much as Western thought had compressed the diversity of the material world into the abstract category of "object," so too had the body been generally conceptualized as a singular biological entity set apart by a putatively unique form of consciousness encapsulated by the Cartesian *cogito*. This understanding was called into question by early feminist theorists, such as Simone de Beauvoir, who argued in a pointed rejoinder to Merleau-Ponty that "to be present in the world implies strictly that there exists a body which is at once a material thing in the world and a point of view towards the world; but nothing requires that this body have this or that particular structure" (de Beauvoir 1953: 7). This body, de Beauvoir noted, lives in the world quite differently for women than for men, marking a critical opening for probing the social construction of experience that has since been explored through the lenses of psychoanalysis (Irigaray 1985), philosophy (Butler 1990), anthropology (Martin 1989; Strathern 1988), and other disciplines beyond the purview of the present discussion. The critical distinction that de Beauvoir drew between a material body and a social body—often reread as a biological body defined by sex and a social body defined by gender—established a fulcrum point that continues to shape contemporary thinking on the body between first the discursive and now the material turns. Judith Butler (1993: ix), for example, has noted this common response to her studies on the social construction of the body in discursive performances: "What about the materiality of the body?" Or as Elizabeth Grosz has phrased the issue: there is "an elision of the question of nature and of matter in Butler's work. Mattering becomes more important than matter! Being 'important,' having significance, having a place, mattering, is more important than matter, substance or materiality" (Grosz, in Ausch et al. 2000). Grosz's (2008: 24) work emphasizes relocating the body within, rather than in distinction to, a material world, highlighting "the virtualities, the potentialities, within biological existence that enable cultural, social, and historical forces to work with and transform that existence." As such, Grosz offers a view on bodily "affordances" situated within worlds of things that overlaps considerably with recent archaeological thinking on the body.

In archaeology, an initial emphasis on the "social skin" (after Turner 1980)—the cultural operation of surficial materials like dress and adornment—has given way to a broader turn toward understanding embodiment—the material practices that call "bodies" into being, shaping and transforming them over the course of a lifetime and over generations (Crossland 2010: 388; Joyce 2005). As Olsen (2003) has noted, however, the distributed sense of personhood that the dissolution of the universal body entails has not fundamentally dislodged the primacy of human agency in social thought. To do so necessitates a move away from embodiment and toward an object-aware approach to human corporeality. Joanna Sofaer's (2006: 77) "theoretical osteoarchaeology" offers an analytically powerful account of the body as "the site of articulation between the material and the social." She argues compellingly that skeletal remains are the product of "the development of specific kinds of bodies in terms of a temporal process that takes place through a network of heterogeneous materials" (140). The body is thus itself a kind of material culture, shaped and reshaped by a lifetime of encounters with things.

Sofaer's sense of the body inserted in a field of heterogeneous materials draws consequentially on Latour's sense of networks. Indeed, Latour argues for a critical recalibration of corporeality, suggesting a focus upon the intersection of humans and the world:

The body is thus not a provisional residence of something superior—an immortal soul, the universal or thought—but what leaves a dynamic trajectory by which we learn to register and become sensitive to what the world is made of. Such is the great virtue of this definition: there is no sense in defining the body directly, but only in rendering the body sensitive to what these other elements are. (Latour 2004b: 206)

This understanding of a sensitive body necessarily directs attention to the points of encounter between bodies and assemblages, the linkages where bodies reach out to the world and things reach in to "grip" flesh. It remains unclear; however, how are we to conceptualize these points of articulation that are ultimately generative of that human–thing collaboration we typically call "the social"? Where, in other words, does the material assemblage meet the human assembly?

SENSE, SENSIBILITY, AND SENTIMENT

The articulation of material assemblages and human assemblies has been, within traditional post-Enlightenment philosophy, strictly delimited. The *via moderna* entailed a severe constriction in the points of encounter between things and bodies, torn between a rationalism wary of the sensible (that is, the physical sensory encounter with things) and an empiricism staked on it. In his *Meditations*, Descartes framed rationalist suspicion of sensibility as a necessary hedge against the fickle mutability of things:

Let us take, for instance, this piece of wax. It has been taken quite recently from the honeycomb; it has not yet lost all the honey flavor. It retains some of the scent of the flowers from which it was collected. Its color, shape and size are manifest. It is hard and it is easy to touch. If you rap on it with your knuckle it will emit a sound. In short, everything is present in it that appears needed to enable a body to be known as distinctly as possible. (Descartes 2006: 16)

However, when the wax is placed near a flame:

The remaining traces of honey flavor are disappearing; the scent is vanishing; the color is changing; the original shape is disappearing. Its size is increasing; it is coming liquid and hot; you can hardly touch it. And now when you rap on it, it no longer emits any sound. Does the same wax still remain? (Descartes 2006: 16)

Even though the material state of the wax has changed—its appearance, texture, smell, taste, and even sound—we still recognize the object as wax. For Descartes, this could only mean that objects outside ourselves are not understood through sensibility but rather through the sense of "the mind alone" (Descartes 2006: 17).

For Locke, Descartes' argument merely demonstrated the sovereignty of sensibility, since an understanding of wax can emerge only from those material qualities that are perceptible through experience:

> I think it is not possible for any man to imagine any other qualities in bodies, howsoever constituted, whereby they can be taken notice of, besides sounds, tastes, smells, visible and tangible qualities. And had mankind been made but with four senses, the qualities then which are the objects of the fifth sense had been as far from our notice, imagination, and conception, as now any belonging to a sixth, seventh, or eighth sense can possibly be. (Locke 1959: 2.3)

Understanding, for Locke, was thus organized by sensibility, a faculty of feeling immersed in experiences of the world; we apprehend even imagined things in relation to qualities we know by direct encounters through taste, touch, smell, sound, and appearance. Thus, for Locke, our engagements with things proceed inductively, through the amassing of experience upon minds that begin in infancy as *tabulae rasae*.

The impasse between sensibility and sense that lies at the root of the debate between Lockean empiricism and Cartesian rationalism can be drawn out into a series of "ancient dichotomies" (Keane 2005: 182)—subject–object, form–substance, symbol–material—that have come under sustained attack. In contemporary studies of material culture, the tension between sensibility and sense is most clearly visible in an ontological schism that Tim Ingold (2007) has insightfully framed as "materials against materiality." Although the extremes of Ingold's argument may well be inhabited by straw men, the contrast effectively illustrates the bind that post-Enlightenment philosophy has created for any effort to define the points of articulation between material assemblages and human assemblies. For Ingold (2007: 9), where "materiality" studies are preoccupied by the general quality of things ("what makes things 'thingly'" to us), examinations of "material" emphasize the unique physical properties of objects that are independent of human cognition yet fundamental to our practical engagement with them; qualities of things as opposed to qualities of perception.

There is an argument to be made that attention to materiality forwards a Cartesian privileging of sense, such that by centering our account of human engagements with things solely in the observing, thinking subject, the things themselves largely disappear, overwhelmed by a relentless interior monologue that may be about "thing-ness" but is rarely about the social, cultural, or political work that they do. This is a critique that Keane (2005: 184) presents in his seminal effort to return the material to the semiotic: "We remain heirs of a tradition that treats signs as if they were merely the garb of meaning.... As this tradition dematerializes signs, it privileges meaning over actions, consequences, and possibilities." Moreover, limiting the field of human–object encounter to sense leaves us with few tools for historicizing either subjects or objects, as both are excluded from the dynamic social world of transformation. As a result, the past comes to be a pale reflection of the present, ceded little autonomy, much less distinction.

Conversely, the kind of material study that Ingold advocates does not, unfortunately, fare much better. Ingold (2007: 14) is concerned with understanding how things live in the world through their own material properties: "To describe the properties of materials," he argues "is to tell the stories of what happens to them as they flow, mix and mutate." Where materiality privileges sense, Ingold valorizes sensibility and the apprehension of things that follows from practical engagement with the physical characteristics of substances. Yet Ingold's program suffers from many of the same limitations that bedevil materiality approaches. In centering analysis on the properties of materials, it is unclear where one might locate historical change and variability. Moreover, by focusing on the physical properties of things and their impact on human craft, a materials-centered approach works so strenuously to recuperate production that it tends to neglect consumption and exchange, dramatically narrowing the social contexts of human–object encounters.

The conceptual poles represented by materiality and material both fall short in providing an encompassing account of the social co-constitution of humans and things, not because either sense or sensibility are unimportant, but simply because each is insufficient. Indeed, Ingold (2007: 15) concludes on just this point, highlighting the "total surroundings" that engage objects "in the currents of the lifeworld." But what is traditionally left unexplored in both materials and materiality approaches to this lifeworld is the imaginative domain of sentiment—a point of encounter between bodies and things that has historically been richly shaped by representational genres as disparate as *xenia*, still lifes, and of course, archaeology itself.

Sensibility, sense, and sentiment describe three points of articulation between the human body and material assemblage. Let me clarify exactly what these terms mean here.

Sensibility refers most immediately to the physicality of things, including their flow across distinct sociospatial locations and their transubstantiation from one state to another, as wool is spun into thread, marble is hewn into sculpture, bones are cut into tools, toys, and flutes. Transubstantiation and material flows clearly draw us into a consideration of the nature of substances presented by Ingold—the distribution of physical resources and their inherent characteristics. But to attend to the sensible, and not just the material, is to locate the physicality of things not in their universal properties but in the efficacy of things within, rather than outside of, human sociality.

Sense, in contrast, is a domain of evocation, of signification, where assemblages work to (re)define value. The sensual thus describes the metamorphoses that transform detritus into artifact, craft into relic, and art into commodity (Benjamin 1968; Clifford 1988: 224). Furthermore, sense also encompasses the transfiguration of human bodies that are made possible as things reposition us within shifting affective terrain. The anointed body, the draped body, the bejeweled body are all forms of transfiguration accomplished by the work of complex machines.

Whereas sense and sensibility are linked to the human encounter with form, sentiment describes the imagined capacities of things, the sympathetic magic that allows them to project their qualities onto human bodies. Here, emblems work within a field of representations to captivate, that is, to subjugate the human capacity for action to the operation of assemblages. An array of "magical" things, from icons and relics to fetishes and amulets, all operate through various highly visible forms of captivation as they rely upon the attribution of an inherent power to objects. Sentiment thus hinges upon our imagination of the efficacy of things—the power we accord to them to intervene in, and transform, social life.

I recognize that the terms sense, sensibility, and sentiment might appear to fit more comfortably in a discussion of the nineteenth-century novel than the archaeology of political life, so let me briefly defend their utility and clarify exactly what these terms mean for this discussion. For Jane Austen (1922), sense and sensibility represented conflicting approaches to sociality. Her *Sense and Sensibility* opens with the contrast between Elinor, who possessed "strength of understanding and coolness of judgment" and her sister, Marianne, who was "eager in everything" and hence "her sorrows, her joys could have no moderation" (Austen 1922: 4). Whereas sensibility described the emotional immediacy of subjective feeling, sense described prudence and the strategic capacities of objective reason. Sentiment, in Austen's novel, refers to the worldviews that emerge from the twinned workings of sense and sensibility, the "propensities of mind," "inclinations," and "tastes" that root judgment in a particular imagination of the proper ordering of the world (15). As Terry Eagleton (1990: 13) has pointed out (and indeed Austen concludes by the end of her novel), sense and sensibility are not opposed dispositions but dependent elements of the aesthetic encounter—the confrontation of thinking humans and a material world that "strikes the body on its sensory surfaces … takes root in the gaze and the guts and all that arises from our most banal, biological insertion in the world." This aesthetic, as Jacques Rancière (2006) has persuasively argued, is fundamentally political in that it orders the articulation of fact, value, and judgment that governs the "distribution of the sensible," the relation of part to whole, the one to the many, the subject to the polity. Hence sense and sensibility define not simply personalities but relations to the material world that should not be corseted within the narrow domain of literary reflection.

Although sense, sensibility, and sentiment provide us with a framework for understanding the points of articulation between the human and object worlds, nevertheless what remains uncertain is how to theorize these encounters as socially grounded and politically generative. How, in other words, do things work across the domains of sense, sensibility, and sentiment to participate in shaping publics and political orders? It is to the role of things in the production of sovereignty that we turn in the next chapter.

On the Matter of Sovereignty

We do not ride upon the railroad; it rides upon us.

(Thoreau 1882: 146)

Arguably the most consequential—and controversial—figure in contemporary global politics is neither statesman nor diplomat but a highly efficacious machine: an assemblage of unmanned aerial vehicles (UAVs) and their support and control technologies represented most emblematically by the MQ-1 Predator drone. Equipped with variable aperture TV and infrared cameras, the Predator was originally developed in the 1990s by the Central Intelligence Agency as a medium-altitude reconnaissance aircraft. The drone has a range of more than 675 nautical miles and can loiter above areas of interest for more than forty hours, and it is connected via satellite to control systems located on bases in the United States.[1] UAVs initially gained prominence in the Pentagon's military planning in response to the public's perceived unwillingness to wage wars that risked the lives of U.S. soldiers (Singer 2009: 136). The 1999 NATO air campaign in Kosovo was considered the paragon for a newly automated approach to waging war; the ill-fated 1993 intervention of U.S. Marines in Somalia was, inversely, the anathema. The Predator's genealogy thus originates in the solution to a specifically political problem—a reluctant public—rather than a military one.

The Predator's mission changed substantially with deployment to Afghanistan in 2001 where it was fitted with Hellfire anti-armor missiles and tasked with engaging Taliban insurgents and al-Qaeda operatives. That same year, section 220 of the National Defense Authorization Act endorsed the strategic automation of the U.S. military, mandating a rapid escalation

---

[1] According to the 1995 report of the Defense Airborne Reconnaissance Office, archived by the Federation of American Scientists. http://www.fas.org/irp/agency/daro/uav95/endurance.html.

in the Pentagon's unmanned air and land combat capabilities.[2] By late 2013, estimates suggested that more than 400 drone strikes had been conducted by U.S. operations in Pakistan, Yemen, and Somalia, killing at least 3,000 people.[3] Predator strikes in northwest Pakistan, an erstwhile U.S. ally in the Afghanistan war, have been particularly controversial for their unsanctioned intrusion on Pakistani territory, their high potential for civilian casualties, and their corrosive effect on civil society (Williams 2010).[4] Indeed, the Predator has come to be a "terrifying presence" in Pakistan (Rohde and Mulvihill 2010: 238), the perceptible buzzing of its engines engendering fear and paranoia among armed fighters and civilians alike. In the United States, however, reaction to Predator's military mission has been muted. As Scott Shane noted in the *New York Times* in 2009:

> The [bipartisan] political consensus in support of the drone program, its antiseptic, high-tech appeal and its secrecy have [*sic*] obscured just how radical it is. For the first time in history, a civilian intelligence agency is using robots to carry out a military mission, selecting people for killing in a country where the United States is not officially at war.[5]

The Predator represents not simply a new technology for waging a different kind of geopolitical combat, but one whose operation remains largely invisible to all but a few protestors in the countries that deploy them (in contrast to their locations of deployment),[6] raising the far larger question as to what other things might be at work shaping the conditions of sovereignty.

In this chapter, I work to define an object-aware account of sovereignty, one attentive to the articulations of human bodies and assemblages (and

---

[2] Section 220 of the National Defense Authorization Act for Fiscal Year 2001, entitled "Unmanned Advanced Capability Combat Aircraft and Ground Combat Vehicles," stipulated that "it shall be a goal of the Armed Forces to achieve the fielding of unmanned, remotely controlled technology such that—(1) by 2010, one-third of the aircraft in the operational deep strike force aircraft fleet are unmanned; and (2) by 2015, one-third of the operational ground combat vehicles are unmanned."

[3] Strike and casualty estimates based on research by the Bureau of Investigative Journalism's Drone warfare project. http://www.thebureauinvestigates.com/category/projects/drones/.

[4] Reporting by thelongwarjournal.com suggests the drone war in Pakistan has resulted in a total of 2,716 casualties, 5.6% of those civilian. http://www.longwarjournal.org/pakistan-strikes.php.

[5] *New York Times*, 12/3/2009. http://www.nytimes.com/2009/12/04/world/asia/04drones.html?pagewanted=all&_r=0.

[6] See remarks made by Cornell West on drone warfare and protest movements: http://www.c-span.org/video/?316282–1/activists-examine-drones-around-globe. On protests against drones in Pakistan, see the 11/23/13 report in the *New York Times* by Mahsood and Mehsud: http://www.nytimes.com/2013/11/24/world/asia/in-pakistan-rally-protests-drone-strikes.html?_r=0.

their distinct ways of working) rather than "oriented" explicitly to the object (Harman 2010). My goal is not to provide a review of contemporary theories of sovereignty (for those, see Agamben 1998; Bartelson 1995; Hansen and Stepputat 2006; Humphrey 2004; and Santner 2011, among others). Rather, my aim in the first portion of the chapter is to examine what happened to the political in archaeology and to detail its recent resurgence within a range of studies that attend to the matter of sovereignty. The second portion of the chapter then examines the reciprocal problem—how political theory lost sight of things—and outlines the intellectual foundations for regrounding the polity in the machinery of sovereign reproduction. Thus the chapter moves from a broad focus on the political—that borderless mass of relations defined by the operation of a power that aspires to map the contours of an ordered community—toward a more focused attention on sovereignty as a *condition* of political interactions, embedded in the relations of authority. In this project, the Predator provides a useful point of entry precisely because it is widely seen as reshaping not simply our sense of the political writ large, but the foundational conditions of sovereignty.

SOVEREIGNTY DISASSEMBLED

As the icon for a new generation of unmanned robotic weapons systems, the Predator has sparked a broad conversation on the legal, moral, and political repercussions of machines at war. Much of the concern has focused on the adequacy of current legal frameworks for dealing with things that appear to blur the traditionally stark line between the organic person on the one hand—a rights-bearing subject and the irreducible locus of culpability—and the inorganic object on the other—mere chattel. Predators are emphatically not cyborgs, in the sense Donna Haraway (1991) used the term more than two decades ago. They are not hybrids (Latour 1993) of organic flesh and inorganic matter but rather complex machines (see chapter 1) that supersede the physical and political limitations of the human by pushing controllers to the very margins of action. In his study of robots at war, P. W. Singer (2009: 64) reports that the human body in many defense technologies is considered to be the "weakest link" in the system, limited by biological constraints on atmospheric pressure, oxygen, g-forces, and so on. Robotic systems can withstand conditions that human bodies cannot while operating at digital speed. Moreover, their decision-making apparatus is programmable, in a way humans are not, and impervious to second-guessing and reticence. This capacity for decision making has created considerable anxiety in scientific and legal circles about the impending moment when the last slender thread connecting controller and weapon, person and instrument will be severed entirely (Asaro 2006; Lin et al. 2012). If robotic weapons gain practical autonomy, observers worry, what happens when their decisions transgress the rules of engagement or treaty obligations, such as the Geneva convention (Arkin 2009; Strawser 2013)? Who, for example, is prosecuted for a war crime committed by a robotic weapon system that assessed a target incorrectly before launching its missiles? Currently, war crimes prosecutions require not just a demonstration of a fact of violation—for example, the death of civilians in a war zone—but also evidence of intent to target noncombatants as a tactic of war. Can a robot, even an apparently autonomous one, have criminal intent?

Although legal scholars and engineers wrestle with the implications of machines that boast animacy and autonomy—distinctly anthropomorphic renderings of technological operations—the moral debate over sending robots to war has centered primarily on machinery's absent humanity. As Singer (2009) points out, by removing human operators from the military apparatus of violence, drones fight on a battlefield bereft of moral sentiments, such as empathy and restraint. In this sense, it is not just the autonomy of machines that is of concern, but their lack of certain affective dispositions and their inability to make complex decisions in the context of feelings of fear, grief, loss, guilt, hope, and remorse. A 2010 report by the United Nations special representative on extrajudicial executions was particularly concerned by the moral hazard that semiautonomous machines pose for their distant human controllers. The report found that placing soldiers on a battlefield drained of affect, experienced solely through the aesthetic field of the machine, engendered a "PlayStation mentality" toward killing on the part of remote pilots and their commanding officers. In other words, rather than our moral conscience safeguarding the actions of machines, complex human affects appear to be diminished by mechanical dispassion and calculation.

But the most far-reaching of the Predator's effects to date has been political. The United Nations special representative on extrajudicial executions identified several risks to the global community posed by the increasing deployment of UAVs. The report suggested that drones, like the Predator, threaten to undermine existing global constraints on the use of military force. By reducing the human cost of waging war, unmanned weapons systems make military solutions to geopolitical crises more appealing to decision makers than if such choices risked the lives of citizens. Violence without human cost was, of course, the very reason for the militarization of the Predator in the first place. It is paradoxical that technologies designed to reduce the hazards of warfare may increase the likelihood of war.

Even more concerning are the implications of the Predator's operation within the territorial space of allied governments. The intrusion of UAVs into allied airspace effectively overturns the global regime of sovereign nation-states that took root in Europe after the Peace of Westphalia in 1648 and subsequently spread as a world order following decolonization and World War II. Even as the traditional nation-state has found itself under pressure from a range of local and global forces—resurgent claims of indigenous communities, the demands of large-scale humanitarian relief, obligations of international economic coordination, and legal institutions that claim a global reach (e.g., the International Criminal Court)—only the Predator has succeeded in fully breaching the traditional Westphalian presumption of territorial primacy. The result is not simply an infringement on "traditional" understandings of the political (Glanville 2013) or the resurrection of a political tradition where "force 'trumps' law" (Schmitt 1985; cf. Derrida 2009: xi) but rather a fundamental reconceptualization of sovereignty.

To many observers (e.g., Boyle 2013; Krasner 2005; Marcus et al. 2012; Williams 2010), the Predator seems to herald the coming of a new age of animate, autonomous things that has replaced conventional Westphalian geopolitics with a new form of conditional sovereignty (see below). But although the robotic technology of the UAV and its broader assemblage is clearly cutting-edge, the operation of a complex machine to define, reproduce, and reconfigure the principles of sovereignty is not new. Things have long been at work in human communities, reshaping our social orders, political institutions, and moral intuitions. Warning bells now sound decrying the advent of an era of robotic technologies that compromise human values and alter our politics, but in fact the premises of political association have been reproduced by machinic assemblages for millennia. And today it is still those less conspicuous assemblages whose logics continue to define the conditions of sovereign power and its reproduction. The Predator is thus less an opening in an entirely new political moment than an invitation to undertake an archaeology of sovereignty, an inquiry into the world of things that has largely eluded theorization into the political. Let me turn first to archaeology's own struggle with theorizing the political and a new movement toward understanding the matter of sovereignty before turning to the fate of things in political thought.

PREHISTORY AND THE POLITICAL

A concern with the political is relatively new to archaeology.[7] Over the last century, the field has scrutinized royal iconography (e.g., Bahrani 1995; Schele and Miller 1986), surveyed the Urban Revolution (e.g., Adams 1966; Childe 1950b; M. Smith 2003), tracked the rise and fall of civilizations (e.g., Flannery 1972; Trigger 2003), and detailed the evolution of formal sociopolitical types, such as the chiefdom and the state (Carneiro 1970; Earle 1997; Kirch 2010; Wright 1977). However, none of these conceptual foci attends directly to political association, to the creation and maintenance of sovereignty in practical negotiations between formalized authorities and a community of subjects. This is not to argue that archaeologists have ignored themes critical to politics, such as bureaucracy and kingship, tribute and taxation, hierarchy and order (see Johansen and Bauer 2011). But the discipline has consistently sublimated the dynamics of sovereignty into other relationships constitutive of economic exchanges, ecological systems, bureaucratic flows, cultural ties, or social rankings. As a result, politics traditionally has been framed as a competition over exotic trade goods, subsistence resources, raw materials, information, or status. Only rarely has archaeology understood politics as politics: as a negotiation over the logics of authorization and subjection that stitch together the polity and differentiate the terrain of personal will from that of sovereign privilege (Richardson 2012). Yet it is precisely this dynamic of sovereignty that has defined the political at least since Aristotle (and likely long before) and preoccupied post-Enlightenment political theory.

Why has archaeology traditionally been so reluctant to attend to politics *qua* politics in favor of proxy concepts, such as cities, civilizations, chiefdoms, and states? In part, archaeology's reticence arises from hoary restrictions placed on the historical reach of politically organized societies. Victorian cultural anthropology posited just two known forms of association: "The first and most ancient was a social organization founded upon gentes, phratries, and tribes. The second and latest in time was a political organization, founded upon territory and property" (Morgan 1877: 62). For archaeologists working beyond the geographic and chronological limits of early "civilizations," there was thus no domain of the political to be found in "traditional" societies. Childe (1950b: 16) effectively codified this division,

[7] Portions of the discussion in this section and the next are drawn from Smith 2011.

suggesting that the State arose only with the substitution of political ties of co-residency for kinship ties of consanguinity.

Although this rigid separation of genealogical versus political societies remains extant in contemporary archaeology (e.g., Kirch 2010: 3; Trigger 2003: 152–53), it has recently begun to erode. Anne Porter (2010: 74) has forwarded the most detailed archaeological attack to date on the division of genealogical from political societies. She observes that kin-based systems for social reckoning, rather than replacing the political in fact operate alongside it: "Kinship, despite long academic traditions of assumption otherwise, implies nothing about political operation." Porter's critique complements that of Pierre Clastres (1989), who argued from an ethnographic perspective that egalitarian communities cannot be understood in terms of the absence of the political but rather represent a highly developed understanding of both sovereignty and its infringements. Thus not only must we consider the role of kinship within complex polities, but we must also reconceptualize the political within communities dominated by genealogical systems for reckoning status.

Within late nineteenth- and early twentieth-century investigations of early "civilizations," the institution of kingship largely exhausted the political.[8] A presumed isomorphism between the kingly body and the body politic allowed monumental building programs and visual art to be read as expressions of broadly shared dispositions rather than as instruments of power vital to the production of authority (Smith 2003: 195). Childe (1957) did much to implicate a wider sociological terrain in the operation of political authority, including bureaucracies, temples, and exchange economies; however, he sharply curtailed the historical relevance of political institutions, arguing that they had little autonomy from the economic relations of production. Political institutions served merely to concentrate an economic surplus coerced from the peasant masses into ready capital available for redeployment by the ruling class (Childe 1957: 3, 6–7). The operation of political institutions was thus dissolved into the workings of "totalitarian economies" (8), auguring a turn toward economic determinism that was further etched into archaeology's theoretical orthodoxy by the ecological turn (e.g., Steward 1955: 37), by mid-century functionalism (e.g.,

---

[8] A similar opinion prevailed among ancient historians (e.g., Rostovtzeff 1922) well into the twentieth century, who presumed that the ancient world possessed only the most anemic sense of sovereignty, grounded primarily in the legitimacy conferred by might, preserved through the tools of war and repression, and theorized as a natural order of domination by the strong over the weak (cf. Thuc. 1.76).

Clark 1954), and by the materialist eco-utilitarianism of late processualism (Gould and Watson 1982: 376). By the 1980s, the political had completed its migration to the margins of archaeological interpretation in tandem with a significant recalibration of political anthropology that accompanied a turn away from political structures and toward everyday forms of power (Spencer 2007: 1; Vincent 1996: 428).

There are (at least) two reasons why the processual archaeology of the 1960s and 1970s held the political in particularly low regard. First, politics was understood to be a domain of radical contingency and thus beyond the scope of a discipline focused on homeostatic systems. This was a Thucydidean understanding of politics rather than an Aristotelian one, attentive to histories of idiosyncratic governments, the fickle *demos*, and the unpredictable fortunes of war rather than to formal theories of the principles and dynamics of political life. Politics, for many archaeologists, has thus traditionally been epistemologically suspect, impossible to systematize or submit to analytical rigor, and dismissed as archaeologically invisible. In 1983, Fred Plog and Steadman Upham (1983: 200) declared: "We suggest that it is currently close to impossible to effectively utilize in a prehistoric context . . . concepts such as social control, sanction, reinforcement, power, authority, custom, and law." The discipline's ingrained suspicion of the political is satirically voiced by the character of "Dr. Science," in Timothy Pauketat's (2007: 29) parable of chiefdoms in North American archaeology, who declares to a student, "'you wouldn't want to exaggerate the importance of hierarchy and politics.' Any mention of hierarchy and politics, to Dr. Science, usually seems an exaggeration." Efforts to reassess the salience of the political during archaeology's theoretical reformation of the 1980s came initially from studies of political interaction (e.g., Renfrew 1986), structure (e.g., de Montmollin 1989), and centralization (e.g., Gledhill et al. 1988), investigations that defended the analytical autonomy of a political sphere and refused to reduce the relationship between authorities and subjects to an economic model of resource domination.

A second force behind processual archaeology's suspicion of the political was its own commitment to a politics grounded in either liberal utilitarianism or, more rarely, Western Marxism. Both traditions are highly skeptical of the political sphere (Kehoe 1998; Smith 2004). For the latter, political authority is simply parasitic on privileges created by relations of production that drive historical change and shape daily life. For the former, politics is always secondary to the more robust institutions of the private sphere—kinship, corporate group, and market. Hence, an archaeology of the political would necessarily overlook the "real" forces of historical determination that presumptively lie elsewhere.

As the Foucauldian turn in the human sciences transformed archaeology's understanding of power, politics began to move back toward the center of archaeological research, dramatically expanding the social terrain shaped by negotiations over the terms of authority and relocating rule as powerfully in ideological and cosmological practices as in economic calculations (e.g., Demarest and Conrad 1992; Joyce and Winter 1996; Schele and Freidel 1990). Undoubtedly the most dramatic consequence of "postmodern" thought for archaeology has been the dismantling of social evolutionism and the concomitant opening of new possibilities for conceptualizing the historicity of the political. The attack on social evolutionism and the desublimation of the political were largely ground-clearing projects—efforts to sweep away vestiges of traditions that had left the archaeology of political association moribund by the early 1990s (Chapman 2003, 2007; McGuire 1983; Pauketat 2007; Smith 2003; Yoffee 1993). A new archaeology of sovereignty has emerged in their wake, forming at the intersection of a reinvigorated archaeology of practice and a wider archaeological turn in the social sciences that has brought things, places, representations, and the political work that they do to the center of debate.

ARCHAEOLOGIES OF SOVEREIGNTY

In 1984, George Cowgill presciently bemoaned political anthropology's traditional focus on building generic types, lamenting that categorical accounts of the State had precluded assembling "a picture of how any specific real state may have worked" (Cowgill, in Claessen 1984: 371). A significant number of authors have recently employed strikingly similar phrasing to emphasize the critical need to recenter analysis on what polities do rather than what type they resemble (see Campbell 2009: 823; Cooper 2010: 88; Smith 2003: 102). As Dietler (2001: 65) declares, "we need to think seriously and realistically about political life as it is lived and experienced if we are to fill our analytical categories with meaningful content." The emerging archaeology of sovereignty's distaste for typology thus arises out of a concern to focus instead on practical regimes of authorization and subjection—on the embodied regimens, rituals, habits, and activities that reproduce, and undo, sovereignty in interactions from the spectacular to the everyday.

Recent efforts to understand the spectacle of sovereignty have focused on the aesthetics of performance and the role of affect in practices of subjection and authorization. The most expansive archaeological reflection on the role of performance and spectacle in political life to date is a collected volume edited by Takeshi Inomata and Lawrence Coben (2006). In their overture, the editors posit that

> the development of large, centralized polities would have been impossible in any historical context without frequent public events in which agents of political power presented themselves in front of a large number of spectators and the participants shared experiences through their bodily copresence. (Inomata and Coben 2006: 11)

The aesthetics of awe that accompany grand performances ground the theatricality of large-scale events in an affective regime, locating practices of subjection within a world order (Houston 2006). As a result, spectacle simultaneously binds community through participation even as it cuts lines of difference through the close regulation of sensory and bodily engagement and exclusion (Baines 2006; Coben 2006; Houston and Taube 2000; Inomata 2006).

As John Baines and Norman Yoffee (1998) note, the spectacular describes a range of highly aestheticized practices, ranging from festivals to funerary rituals, that position political elites between novel techniques of power and embedded traditions of social order. In ancient Mesopotamia and Pharaonic Egypt, this negotiation was worked out through a range of material practices, including writing and visual media that established a shared political culture and generated the centripetal forces that bound subjects and authorities. Furthermore, as Michael Shanks (1999: 72) points out in his sketch of archaic Korinth, political culture is not solely located in a fixed series of ritual events, but rather establishes the terms of sovereignty through incessant negotiations over key aspects of publicity, including religious dedications, martial violence (both civil and foreign), and tropes of iconographic representation.

The spectacle of sovereignty embraces not only the singularity of event but also practices of publicity. Several recent studies of memorialization practices have emphasized the role that public media play in "fixing history" (Rowlands and Tilley 2006: 500), in reinforcing the values of the spectacular in the everyday, allowing for the perduration of the aesthetics of political performance (Bradley 1998; Hutson 2002). Shackel (2001) provides a particularly intriguing study of publicity and memory, arguing that post–Civil War landscapes, monuments, and public ceremonies worked to simultaneously occlude some parts of the past while lionizing others, creating a nostalgic sense of political belonging that reinforced contemporary orders of racial domination. Similarly, in an examination of Urartian images of spectacle, I suggested that the reproduction of sovereign authority relied upon deities who could mediate between the demands of royal authority and the acquiescence of subjects. As a result, demand and subjugation "are more than simply stratagems of power; they are right, good, beautiful, desirable, and sublime in their accordance of the particular individual with the course of the universe" (Smith 2006: 125).

Central to the political work of the spectacular is the representation of the violence at the heart of sovereignty (Bahrani 2008; Brumfiel 1998; Inomata and Triadan 2009; Porter and Schwartz 2012). Inomata (2006: 199), for example, details evidence that Classic Maya temple staircases served as stages for the presentation and torture of captives to throngs of subjects gathered in open-air plazas. Such events are the very substance of sovereignty in that they allow for the bodily enactment of subjection (onlookers), exclusion (captives), and the reproduction of authority through the reduction of the human body to bare life.

Perhaps the most extensive discussion of political performance has taken place under the rubric of feasting practices and commensal politics (see Bray 2003; Dietler and Hayden 2001; Mills 2004). Feasts, in Dietler's (2001: 67) definition, are "public ritual activities centered around the communal consumption of food and drink." Mills (2007: 211) points out that, as public rituals, feasts are performances: "Each feast has its own dramaturgical order that includes the choice of particular foods; the sequence of food preparation, presentation, and consumption; who partakes; and who watches." The feast, in other words, is a critical site for defining inclusion and exclusion. It thus can be a defining locus for the enactment of sovereignty. In one sense, the political work of the feast hinges upon bringing into the public sphere traditions and practices marked as inherent in the private. Performances thus are legitimized through elision with quotidian routines of the household. Feasts also open up avenues for contestation as forms of participatory politics.

A complete review of the feasting literature is unnecessary here, but three points in particular bear upon any effort to forge an archaeological account of sovereignty. First, as Dietler points out (2001: 77), feasts are politically polysemous in that "they both unite and divide *at the same time.*" Such is the stuff of sovereignty, simultaneously stitching together a community of subjects and cutting this public through forms of violence, both real and symbolic. The feast is thus fundamentally a practice of sovereign reproduction (Fiskesjö 2003), whether as a forum for elite alliance building and competition (e.g., Nelson 2003; Pollock 2003), the production of obligation and privilege (e.g., Cook and Glowacki 2003), or as a context for negotiating the aesthetics of distinction (e.g., Bray 2003; cf. Elias 1994). Second, the feast is a critical medium for the penetration of practices of sovereignty into the material order of the everyday. As Gero (2003: 287) points out, feasting provides a means of bodily training, for the promulgation of rules of etiquette by which subjects come to embody their own subjectivization. Moreover, the economy of commensal politics extends well beyond the immediacy of the table (Bauer 2010; Minnis et al. 2006). The feast thus pushes us to articulate the practices of political spectacle with everyday contexts of lived experience.

What makes these examinations of political performance elements in an emerging archaeology of sovereignty is their concern with two key processes: the (re)production of a public out of a mass of subjects and the (re) production of the sovereign body as cut away from the wider body politic. As a complement to investigations of public spectacle, a parallel movement to locate the political in everyday practices has opened an inquiry into still a third condition of sovereignty: the regular operation of an apparatus of governance that defines the terms of association.

The geopolitics of institutional interaction and territorial integration is the starting point for most definitions of sovereignty. Lisa Cooper's (2010) recent study of the site of Ebla and its hinterland in northwest Syria assesses the archaeological evidence for garrisoning, tribute payments, bureaucratic administration, and the kind of elite emulation critical to regional political interaction. Cooper finds that Ebla's hold on its hinterland during the mid-third millennium was "loose and transitory," contradicting the more strident claims of the textual sources. In trying to make sense of the varying data sources, Cooper, following Alan Kolata (2006; Sahlins 2004), suggests that the situation at Ebla might best be described as "hegemony without sovereignty" in that ad hoc interactions with local polities created informal obligations resulting in a recognition of an Eblaite privilege. Here, hegemony is meant in the sense native to international relations (rather than Gramsci's sense) to denote how Ebla's rulers secured regional authority by creating relations of obligation that inscribed their privilege without imposing the costs of direct administration. Geopolitical hegemony ultimately reinforces sovereignty by defining the subjects of subordinate rulers to be outside the hegemon's superordinate order and yet ultimately still answerable to its claims—a logic not so far removed from that which supports contemporary UAV strikes on allied nations.

Lori Khatchadourian (n.d.) refers to the nested relations of sovereignty as "the satrapal condition," the double bind that draws subjects into the everyday logics of political reproduction as a requirement for the reproduction of their own situated authority. Khatchadourian's (2008a; 2013) study of the social logics of empire in Achaemenid Persia investigates the hegemonic (in the Gramscian sense) operation of sovereignty between the metropole and the Armenian satrapy. In the metropole, Khatchadourian, following Root (1979), notes public media portraying the active participation of the conquered in upholding the empire; the sovereign is literally held up by the conquered, not as vanquished slaves, but as members of a political association. In discussing the satrapy, Khatchadourian illuminates the making of political community in a series of practical contexts, from the columned halls of regional centers that drew on models from Persepolis to everyday life in small communities. On the northern fringe of the empire, in the village of Tsaghkahovit in central Armenia, she details novel techniques of everyday subjection and authorization, including intriguing evidence for the practice of ritualized ceremonies associated with the Persian imperial apparatus. Khatchadourian's study joins a number of related investigations into how communities situated beyond the immediate reach of formal bureaucratic administration were lashed to the project of sovereignty (e.g., Bachand 2006; Pauketat 2000; Routledge 2004; Wesson 2008; Yaeger 2000).

The emerging archaeologies of sovereignty share a common concern to illuminate how assemblages condition the political relationships that are determinative of social life broadly, from economic production and exchange to the aesthetics of representation (Glatz 2009; Halperin and Foias 2010; Richard 2010). Curiously, however, much of the recent turn to understand the "materiality" of things within archaeology has largely evacuated the political from our interactions with things (Meskell 2004; Tilley 2004; cf. Khatchadourian n.d.). Things are often described as "powerful" (Meskell 2005a: 52), but this is a power to signify, not a power to authorize or make subject (cf. Rowlands 2005). Hodder (2012: 213) concludes his seminal study of human–thing entanglements by noting that power is largely implicit in his account of their mutual dependencies. Clearly a certain kind of power—a power to—is fundamental to our dependence on things to make, build, work. But there is nothing inherent in this "power to" that leads inexorably into the logics that produce a "power over"—an ability to establish the rules of civil order, enforce them, and regulate exceptions (a point Hodder gamely concedes [2012: 222]). In part, this is a critical lacuna in contemporary materiality. But it is more conspicuously a failure of contemporary political theory. Only rarely has modern political thought allowed objects to intrude into our conception of authority, the problem to which we now must turn.

ASSEMBLY AND ASSEMBLAGE

If archaeology has worked over the last decade to understand the political force of the materials that it has long placed at the heart of its disciplinary project, political theory has had a far more difficult project in attending to "political matter and the matter of the political" (Braun and Whatmore 2010b: xxii). Within the intellectual traditions of both liberalism and Marxism, things traditionally have been situated most fundamentally in a relationship of possession, of ownership, and hence have been largely dissolved into the passive category of "property" (cf. Engels 1990; Locke 1988). Active things, from Marx's (1906: I.1.i.4) fetishized commodities to Thoreau's (1882; cf. L. Marx 1964) tyrannical machines, have been imagined as illusions or pathologies—wayward objects that must be cast out from the body politic, not theorized into it.

And yet political practice remains deeply in thrall to the objects that make the modern polity possible—locomotives, automotives, and airplanes, telegraphs, televisions, and newspapers, computers, bombs, and ballots, museums, monuments, and antiquities. Even more emphatically, public policy is consistently captivated by the capacities of objects to solve problems from the geopolitical to the procedural: think of the Predator and the extraterritorial projection of force or efforts to reengineer voting machines after the botched 2000 U.S. presidential election, or smart phones and social networking during the Arab Spring. Andrew Barry (2001: 2) has detailed how this contemporary "political preoccupation with the problems technology poses, with the potential benefits it promises, and with the models of social and political order it seems to make available" has reconfigured not only our understanding of the polity but also our image of the capacities of the citizenry. Sovereigns and subjects alike look to the possibilities of things for solutions to political challenges, and only as a last resort do they make demands upon the behaviors of us humans. Things are tasked with a dazzling array of political work: responding to geopolitical security threats through remote monitoring, creating more transparent regimes by harnessing the Internet to open government initiatives, policing streets, cities, and borders with increasingly omnipresent surveillance technologies, and cataloging citizens through an extensive network of analog and digital techniques.

These challenges are pushed onto objects rather than taken up by human denizens of the polity through alterations to our everyday practices—more sophisticated approaches to diplomacy that might defuse geopolitical conflicts, greater forthrightness by political leaders, and reaffirmations of civility and community against criminality. Former New York City mayor Michael Bloomberg's controversial recent effort to restrict the size of the cups used to serve sweetened soft drinks provides a clear case in point. Faced with a growing epidemic of childhood obesity and an array of related health problems, including increased rates of type 2 diabetes, Bloomberg sought a solution in the world of things. Rather than working to alter the behavior of humans directly, Bloomberg's proposal worked to limit the size of the cup to no more than 16 ounces (approx. 0.5 liters).[9]

The vast array of things tasked to intervene in contemporary sociopolitical matters suggests the need for a radical inversion of our traditional thinking on humans and things. Humans appear to be strangely passive, unable on their own to alter ingrained behaviors and understandings. Things, in contrast, do much of the work that we traditionally think of as political. They solve problems, address concerns, and bind the community into a coherent public—all feats humans alone could not possibly accomplish. Political thought and practice thus offer us fundamentally divergent accounts of the object—at once theoretically marginal and inert, but practically at the center of any intervention in public affairs.

ORIGIN MYTHS

The intuition that objects are critical to political order is a strikingly ancient one. Arguably the earliest known theory of political association—of the unity of sovereign, subject, and object—comes not from the oft-cited sources of classical philosophy but from a small inlaid wooden box uncovered in the Royal Cemetery at the city of Ur in southern Mesopotamia (fig. 6).[10] Dated to the mid-third millennium, the side panels and both ends of

---

[9] The proposal limiting soft drink serving sizes was approved by the Board of Health in 2012 but overturned in 2013 by a state appeals court, a decision affirmed in 2014 by the New York Court of Appeals, the state's highest court.

[10] Specifically, chamber D of tomb 779. The box is 21.59 cm high and 49.53 cm long (Woolley 1934: pl. 91–93),

Fig. 6. The Standard of Ur (ca. 2550 BC) from tomb PG 779, chamber D in the Royal Cemetery at Ur: (a) the "Peace" mosaic, (b) the "War" mosaic. (© The Trustees of the British Museum.)

this trapezoidal hollow box were decorated with inlaid figurative and geometric mosaics of white shell, red limestone, and lapis lazuli set in three vertical registers. The function of the box remains uncertain,[11] but the scenes on its two long side panels, typically nicknamed "war" and "peace," depict the assimilation of sovereign and subject, as mediated by a dense array of animals and objects, within the practical regimes of productivity on the one hand and violent destruction on the other.

In the "peace" mosaic, the upper register depicts a banquet presided over by the seated sovereign, rendered as an oversized figure wearing a flounced skirt and holding a cup in his right hand. Before him, on identical chairs, six seated figures hold identical cups in their right hands. Three attendants

---

[11] The excavator, Leonard Woolley (1934: 266–74), suggested that the box, found near the shoulder of one of the interred, may have been carried on a pole as a standard. But as Hansen (1998: 45) notes there is little evidence to support this interpretation.

provide for the seated figures as two musicians (one a lyre player, the other perhaps a singer) serenade the gathering. The two lower registers of the panel depict a parade, from left to right, of the animals, humans, and objects that provide for the feast above. The center register focuses primarily on products of the pastures and the marshes, including fish, bulls, sheep, and the tools of animal husbandry. The lower register attends to the bounty of the field with laborers carrying sacks of produce on their shoulder or in heavy backpacks supported by headbands and leading asses by ropes attached to nose rings.

On the other side, in the "war" mosaic, we find the sovereign, again in the upper register, but this time as an oversized standing figure in the center of the composition holding a staff or short spear and receiving naked and bound captives at the end of a battle. He is flanked on the left by three figures of augmented stature (perhaps some of the same figures from the banquet), each bearing a spear in the left hand and an axe in the right, and a four-wheeled chariot drawn by a team of onagers. In the lower two registers, we find the divisions of military practice. In the bottom register are the chariots and charioteers trampling the vanquished enemy underfoot; in the middle register, the infantry, marked by standardized uniforms and swords in hip scabbards, is shown entering battle from left to right, culminating in scenes of violence in the center that resolve into captives being led away on the far right. Interestingly, the lower two panels portray a quickening of pace, viewed from left to right, as the battle is joined with the most violent tableaux located directly below the figure of the ruler.

The Standard of Ur provides an account of political community that is extraordinarily complex, one that describes both the proper ordering of the polity and the dynamic mediations of things. First, authority quite clearly rests upon the articulation of the sovereign with a well-ordered public, a community of herders, farmers, brewers, musicians, wheelwrights, soldiers, smiths, and charioteers, defined by the assemblage represented in the Standard. In the peace mosaic, not only does the polity embrace an array of goods, but the entire field of political economy is also mustered to the commensal politics of the feast. What flow between the panels from the pastures and fields to the table of the ruler are not people—those are rigidly separated by the frames of the composition—but a panoply of things. In the war mosaic, we again find a rigidly ordered political community divided among the sovereign and his peers at the top, the infantry in the middle register, and the chariotry at the bottom. Here, war is not the inverse of peace, but rather a complementary domain of political practice that serves to distinguish the sovereign from his subjects. But the most potent division in this panel is from left to right as the action of the battle is joined. Again, objects provide critical mediations in each register—the staff of the ruler at top, the weapons of the infantry in the middle register, the trampling war chariots at the bottom. Taken as a whole, the mosaics argue for the reliance of the polity not only on the systematic ordering of human bodies constitutive of differences in status or rank, ally or enemy, but on the efficacy of things in mediating those associations.

The Standard of Ur is typically interpreted as a representation of the twin principles of Sumerian kingship: command of the military and administration of prosperity (Hansen 1998: 47). But it can equally be understood as an account of the conditions of sovereignty centered on a constituted community of subjects, a distinctive body of the sovereign cut away from the masses, and an apparatus of regulation for tying the two together. These relationships are then naturalized by the aesthetics of their representations, literally written in the stones of the mosaic.

Object theories of the polity like that presented on the Standard of Ur percolated through much pre-Aristotelian political thought. In one of the more troubling episodes of the *Republic*, Socrates reluctantly admits that his ideal *polis* must be founded upon an origin myth or, as he calls it, a "needful falsehood" or noble lie (Plat. *Rep.* 414c). The rulers, soldiers, and people of the *polis* were to be told that their youth was a dream. In reality, that time had been spent in the "womb of the earth where they themselves and their arms and appurtenances" were manufactured (Plat. *Rep.* 414d–e). Since the land of the *polis* had been their mother and nurse, they are bound to her as her children. Yet they were not all formed in this terrestrial womb as equals:

> Some of you have the power to command, and in the composition of these [God] has mingled gold ...; others he has made of silver, to be auxiliaries; others again who are to be husbandmen and craftsmen he has composed of brass and iron; and the species will generally be preserved in the children. (Plat. *Rep.* 415a–c)

There are two elements of Plato's noble lie of particular interest here. The first is the suggestion that the human body and the artifacts, the "appurtenances," of political rank and occupation developed together in the womb of the *polis*—the body of the soldier and his bronze shield are cast as elements of a single natural process of ontogeny. The second is its effort to provide an origin myth that naturalizes the affective attachment of subject to polity and the authority of an elite to rule. The noble lie is thus a rare example in political thought of an ontogenic origin myth—one focused on the mutual cultivation of the citizen/object as the origin of political cohesion in the face of both economic inequality and status distinction.

Earlier in book 2 of the *Republic*, Plato provides a quite different, phylogenic origin myth for the polity as an association:

> "The origin of the city [*polis*], then," said I, "in my opinion, is to be found in the fact that we do not severally suffice for our own needs, but each of us lacks many things. [...] As a result of this, then, one man calling in another for one service and another for another, we, being in need of many things, gather many into one place of abode as associates and helpers, and to this dwelling together we give the name city or state, do we not? [...] Come, then, let us create a city from the beginning, in our theory. Its real creator, as it appears, will be our needs. [...] Now the first and chief of our needs is the provision of food for existence and life. [...] The second is housing and the third is raiment and that sort of thing. [...] Tell me, then," said I, "how our city will suffice for the provision of all these things. Will there not be a farmer for one, and a builder, and then again a weaver? And shall we add thereto a cobbler and some other purveyor for the needs of body?" (Plat. *Rep.* 369)

In this account, the polity arises organically from need—an association charged with supplying for the whole community what each individual cannot provide for oneself. From these needs spring not only the basic assemblage of the polity—domestic architecture, subsistence goods, clothing—but also the specialized employments of builder, farmer, shepherd, tailor, and cobbler that go with them. An unexplained insufficiency of this basic assemblage necessitates importation of goods from elsewhere and thus a class of merchants charged with ferrying things from place to place and salesmen to oversee them in the market. Still further demand for goods sparks competitions for more land with neighbors and hence a further need for armor, weapons, and a class of individuals to bear them.

As origin myths of the polity go, this is one of the most popular, repeated by Aristotle (*Pol.* 1252b) a century later and formalized as a first principle of political economy by Adam Smith (1976: 18–20). However, as an account of historical emergence, the phylogenetic account of need, complementarity, and competition is no less an exercise in myth-making than Plato's noble lie. Complex political associations characterized by radical social inequality and centralized institutions of authority arose episodically across the globe beginning only in the late fourth millennium in southern Mesopotamia and the Nile valley. And yet human needs had clearly been met for millennia, since at least the beginning of the Neolithic "revolution," if not far earlier in the human career. The egalitarian villages of this earlier

epoch could just as confidently be described as associations formed to sat-
isfy need, and yet the key features of the polity—occupational specialization, class differentiation, and political inequality—were absent in whole or
in part (cf. Sahlins 1972). Need is thus an insufficient explanation for the
production of the specific relations between humans and objects that define the polity.

However, as an object theory of the machinery of sovereignty, Plato's
phylogenetic origin myth is incisive and compelling. The polity, it is important to point out, is in Plato's rendering a place of objects, an assemblage
cared for by humans rather than things that care for us. What is of most
interest in his phylogenetic theory of the *polis* are the unexamined links
between human requirements of things—that is, "needs"—and the obligations upon humans that things impose. Having fulfilled basic needs with a
largely self-sufficient village, it appears to be less human needs that drive
the expansion of the *polis* than the needs of things—arms need soldiers to
bear them, imports need merchants to carry them. The needs of humans
are displaced onto the needs of a complex machine. But what then can account for the recession of things in modern political thought?

WAYWARD THINGS AND THE DUAL SOVEREIGN

The neat ordering of objects in both the Standard of Ur and the Platonic
origin myths was of course an aspiration. However, this idealized order
clearly suggests that the regulation of things was at least as constitutive of
sovereignty as the governance of human bodies. But how does sovereignty
come to order things and, just as importantly, how does it discipline things
that misbehave? It is not coincidental that rules governing wayward things
provide a key point of articulation between the object-aware polity of the
ancient world and a modern political theory bereft of things. During the
medieval era, the triumph of Ockham's nominalism (see chapter 1) was
shadowed by legal institutions that enshrined the capacity of things
not just to work, but to misbehave, most notably in the English law of
deodands.

The historically shifting suite of legal practices governing deodands (derived from the Latin *deo dandum*, "to be given to God") dates back to at
least the eleventh century and perhaps to the ninth-century legal reforms of
Alfred the Great. Objects that had caused the death of a human—knives
that stabbed, irons that brained, tubs that drowned—were classified as deodands and thus "forfeited to God, that is, to the King, God's lieutenant on

earth, to be distributed in works of charity for the appeasing of God's wrath." The deodand was not enshrined in parliamentary statute or ecclesiastical decree but rather was solely a matter of common law, decided upon by juries and enforced by the office of the coroner. The principle of the deodand was encapsulated by the phrase *omnia quae movent ad mortem sunt deodanda*.[12] A wagon that killed a pedestrian was subject to deodand law, including the horses and goods within, as was a mill whose sails caught hold of a miller during a sudden squall, throwing him over the building to the ground and killing him (Sutton 1997: 48). Bennett (2010: 9) aptly describes the institution of the deodand as a recognition of an object's "particular efficacy." (See chapter 1.) In one sense, the immediate efficacy of the deodand lies in its criminality. Objects subject to seizure as deodands became property of the sovereign, imprisoned for their malfeasance and disposed of at the king's pleasure. Deodand law in this sense brought wayward things into the polity as subjects of law and punishment. But in another sense the more enduring power of the deodand lay in its reproduction of the sovereign as the agent of God, simultaneously within and beyond the political community. The transgressive object was thus an element in reproducing the sovereign as a figure with one foot on earth and the other with the divine, a figuration of sovereignty most emblematically theorized by the Tudor-era lawyers at the center of Ernst Kantorowicz's (1957) account of *The King's Two Bodies*.

This sense of the duality of the sovereign was formalized in political theory by Thomas Hobbes, who transformed the polity itself from an organic community into an assemblage, an automaton manufactured to rule. The famous frontispiece for Hobbes's *Leviathan* (fig. 7) represents one of the most compelling efforts to visually represent the assemblages that ground political association since the Standard of Ur. In the upper register, a hirsute giant rises from a settled landscape of rolling hills below an epigram from the book of Job that reads, *Non est potestas Super Terram quae Comparetur* (Job 41:24).[13] In his right hand, the awe-inspiring sovereign brandishes a sword, in the left a bishop's pastoral staff. The body of this "artificial man"— a kind of "automata"—is composed of the subjects of the sovereign's authority, who together constitute the body politic (Hobbes 1991: 9). It is this upper portion of the image—a representation of the corporal form of Hobbes's sovereign automaton—that has received the lion's share of the attention from modern political theorists (Brandt 1982, 1987; Bredekamp

[12] "What moves to death is deodand (to be given to god)" (Pervukhin 2005: 237–38).

[13] "There is no power on earth to be compared to him." Hobbes thus explicitly links the sovereign to the monstrous Leviathan of biblical lore.

Fig. 7. Frontispiece to *Leviathan* (1651), by Thomas Hobbes. Etching by Abraham Bosse. (© The British Library Board 31.k.14 frontispiece)

1999, 2007; Gamboni 2005; Malcolm 2003; Martel 2006; Schaffer 2005). But despite the awe-inspiring drama of the giant, it is the lower frame of the image that provides a glimpse into the mechanics of sovereignty, the hidden gears and levers that give "life and motion" to the automaton above (Hobbes 1991: 9).[14]

[14] Callon and Latour (1981: 284) have faulted Hobbes for failing to mention the equipment that makes the sovereign formidable, yet it is right there on the bottom of the frontispiece.

The left panel of the lower frame is devoted to the instruments of worldly power; the right panel portrays the objects of ecclesiastical might. Each is divided into frames that correspond to one another in a series of horizontal juxtapositions: the castle and the church, the coronet and the miter, the cannon and the lightning of excommunication, the artifacts of war and the tools of logic, the battlefield and the disputation. This unique assemblage represents neither goods fundamental to political economy nor a mytho-logical origin myth. Instead, Hobbes's assemblage is composed of the ma-chinery of seventeenth-century sovereignty—tools for enforcing the social contract that establish civil society and keep the state of nature at bay. As such, the assemblage nicely illustrates the central argument in the *Levia-than* by emphasizing the polity as a product of artifice, an artificial machine held together by the artifacts of human craft and given life by an artificial soul known as sovereignty. This insight served to radically denaturalize the principles of political association and created an opening for the rearticula-tion of an object theory of the polity. But as the contract came to be taken seriously as a model for the polity, objects were again banished to the mar-gins of political thought, shackled by the conceptual limits of a newly vig-orous, human-centered concept of "property."

EXIT OBJECTS 1: LIBERAL THEORY AND THINGS

Arguably, the critical watershed in the Enlightenment dematerialization of political thought was John Locke's labor theory of property. How is it, Locke wondered, that a world of things bequeathed by God to "mankind in common" has come to be held in "private dominion" (Locke 1988: 286–87), appropriated for personal use? Locke suggested that although God's in-junction placed the earth and "inferior creatures" in common, it reserved to every individual "a property in [their] own person," a private right to their body and, most consequentially, the labor that this body accomplishes. This labor accomplishes a magical transformation in the things that it touches, not only forming products from raw materials but also extending the bodily right of property to the created object itself. As long as numbers were few and resources plentiful, the encroachment of property upon the common produced little cause for injury. Political society emerged, Locke argued, when the preservation of property required laws to deter and pun-ish transgressions against it: "And the commonwealth comes by a power to set down what punishment shall belong to the several transgressions which they think worthy of it committed amongst the members of that society . . .

all this for the preservation of the property of all the members of that society as far as possible" (Locke 1988: 324).

In one sense, the labor theory of property sets the disposition of things at the very heart of the political—"the increase of lands and the right employing of them is the great art of government" (Locke 1988: 297–98). Governance is defined as fundamentally an ordering of the world of things (a world including human bodies as the original property belonging to the self). However, the object world is framed politically solely in relation to two conceptual possibilities—common and property—that is, to a relation of possession that locates determination exclusively in human activity, labor. Things are given no role whatsoever in defining the nature of labor, its capacities or potential; as a result, they are rendered as passive objects to be governed with no capacity to shape the character, direction, or possibilities of governance.

Yet manifestly, the qualities of objects are critical to the very possibilities of labor. The fruitless application of labor to transform, say, raspberries into a house does not lead to a private domicile any more than efforts to make jam from stone result in a nourishing breakfast. In this sense, the material affordances of the object world can frustrate and dissipate any value that labor seeks to add. But the affordances of things are never solely located in only their physical properties. The work of mining copper ore in the Neolithic produces nothing more than a pile of useless rocks absent a pyrotechnic assemblage that can extract the metal. Hence the wider assemblage pushes back on human labor, constraining it, directing it, in ways that Locke failed to recognize. Labor in this sense is not the work of the isolated human but the conjoined exertion of a material assemblage.

The tradition of liberal political thought that follows from Locke has further exaggerated the marginality of the assemblage, reaching an apogee in John Rawls's (1971) theory of justice as fairness. Just principles for civil association can be derived, Rawls argued, through reflection upon an "original position," a hypothetical state for manufacturing public agreement on principles of fairness. However, to achieve this state, Rawls required that members of the civil community be placed behind a "veil of ignorance" so that they do not know how general principles of justice might affect their own particular fate:

> No one knows his place in society, his class position, or social status; nor does he know his fortune in the distribution of natural assets and abilities, his intelligence and strength, and the like. [...] More than this, I assume that the parties do not know the particular circumstances of their own society. That is,

they do not know its economic or political situation, or the level of civilization and culture it has been able to achieve. [...] It is taken for granted, however, that they know the general facts about human society. They understand
political affairs and the principles of economic theory; they know the basis of
social organization and the laws of human psychology. (Rawls 1971: 137)

In other words, in the original position, members of the political community are ignorant of their location amidst the assemblage of things that
constitutes wealth, marks status, crystallizes identity, preserves memories,
enables production, mediates exchanges, and concretizes beauty. The promulgation of shared principles of fairness requires shielding the civil community from the object world, creating a purely discursive encounter shorn
of the dismaying influence of things.

EXIT OBJECTS 2: MARX AND MATTER

The radical disengagement of human activity from the material world of
things entailed in liberal thought encountered its earliest resistance in the
work of the mid-nineteenth-century thinker Ludwig Feuerbach, younger
brother of the archaeologist Joseph Anselm Feuerbach. Best known for his
influence on Marx, Ludwig Feuerbach's *Principles of the Philosophy of the
Future* (1966) called for a radical break with the tradition of Cartesian philosophy, most notably "the abstraction from all that is sensuous and material" (Feuerbach 1966: 13) out of which the conception of a *cogito* separated
from the material world first arose. For reflection upon the world to avoid
becoming "a prisoner of the ego" it must begin not with thought but with
its antithesis, sensation, which is determined by the activity of the object.
The promise of Feuerbach's approach was an analytic that allowed sensuous objects to operate in some measure independently of the tyranny of the
human "conceptual object." However, this promise was largely extinguished
by Marx's *Theses on Feuerbach*: "The chief defect of all previous materialism—that of Feuerbach included—is that things, reality, sensuousness are
conceived only in the form of the object, or of contemplation, but not as
sensuous human activity, practice, not subjectively" (Marx 1998: 572).

Marx's effort to envelop human thought as itself a material process engaged by the physical world had the corollary consequence of once again
establishing the human as the unrivaled source of social change: "It is men
who change circumstances" (Marx 1998: 573). Humans make history having secured the possibility of material life—"eating and drinking, housing,

clothing, and various other things"—acts that in themselves create new needs, and thus drive the expansion of material appropriations and the technologies that define the world of things (a progress outlined conceptually by the various "stages of development" of the division of labor described in *The German Ideology* and more rigorously charted by the evolutionary anthropology of Engels's *Origin of the Family, Private Property, and the State*). It should be noted that Marx possessed an acute understanding of the functional operation of industrial machinery and the economic implications of tools that operated without human action as their motive source (Marx 1906: 406ff). Moreover, technologies clearly create the conditions of possibility for historical epochs by making possible certain relations of production and not others. However, Marx's materialism was never a project to attend to the social operation of things per se but rather to attend to the matter of humanity (cf. Miller 1987 for an extended critique of Marxian materialism). As Marx (1906: 198) argues in volume 1 of *Capital*:

> A spider conducts operations that resemble that of the weaver, and a bee puts to shame many an architect in the construction of her cells. But what distinguishes the worst architect from the best of bees is this, that the architect raises his structure in imagination before he erects it in reality. At the end of every labour process we get a result that already existed in the imagination of the laborer at its commencement.

As other have pointed out, Marx's "productionist metaphysics" (Thomas 2012: 224) implies that the significance of things—including their political operation—is removed from the domain of things, leaving them to languish under the onslaught of human cognition, body, and mind.

Historical transformation—which for Marx entailed both political revolution and a reordering of the relations of production—was driven by contradictions in class relations defined by a singular relationship to the object world: "In order to become an unendurable power, i.e., a power against which men make revolution, [estrangement] must necessarily have rendered the great mass of humanity 'propertyless'" (Marx and Engels 1998: 54). Thus, though Marx maintained a rich sense of the *functional* operation of things, the object world was *socially* inert, limited to a relation of ownership, of possession. A critical exception to this proposition lies in Marx's account of the fetish in which commodities gain a "mystical" quality, appearing "as independent beings endowed with life, and entering into relation both with one another and the human race" (Marx 1906: 83). Commodity fetishism is, however, for Marx, a pathology of capitalist production to be cast out of the social body rather than theorized into our material order (cf. Pietz 1993).

By the latter half of the twentieth century, Western Marxism had ironically worked its way to a sublimation of the object world not far removed from that advocated by Rawls, most notably in the work of Jürgen Habermas (1984), whose thought exhibits a similar impatience with things. For Habermas, only an "ideal speech situation" can provide a legitimate context for political decision making. In this situation, participants know one another solely through the discursive power of argument—all other kinds of understanding are stripped away, including things indicative of particular kinds of personhood. Like Rawls's veil of ignorance, the ideal speech situation is more a regulative ideal for political practice than a model for the interaction of members of a civil community, and as such seems to be at pains to divorce itself from politics in order to ground itself in ethics. Both, however, highlight an abiding suspicion that the object world inhibits the discursive realization of just political communities. Both elevate an Aristotelian *Homo loquens*—speaking man (Herder 1986)—over *Homo faber*—man the creator (Bergson 1911: 139)—insofar as humans are presumed to be political because of the capacity for speech, not because they can produce the machinery of political association depicted with such force on the Standard of Ur, in the Platonic origin myths, and on Hobbes's frontispiece to *Leviathan*.

What the liberal and Marxist traditions share is a drive to atomize the relationship between things and people as direct relations of ownership that promote singular senses of the good, be it advancement in the pursuit of "life, liberty, and estate" (Locke 1988: 323) or the satisfaction of "species being" (Marx 1978: 76–77). But our relations to things are not reducible to the one-to-one dynamic of ownership. Rather, an account of the ties between ourselves and our things only makes analytical sense when examined corporately, as a relationship not between one individual and one object, but rather between civil communities and the machinic assemblages that shape politics in practice. This larger sense of the "thingness" of political association finds its most cogent expression in Max Weber's account of bureaucratic regimes:

> A lifeless machine is congealed spirit. Only as such does it have the power to force people into its service and to determine with such dominance their everyday working life as is actually the case in the factory. Congealed spirit is also that living machine represented by bureaucratic organization with its specialization of trained skilled labour, its demarcation of responsibility, regi-

mentation and hierarchically organized relations of obedience. Combined with the lifeless machine, bureaucracy is at work creating the housing of that future enslavement in which perhaps people will, as with the case of the Fellahin in the Ancient Egyptian state, be forced helplessly into line if a purely technical value—i.e. a rational civil service administration and provision of needs—becomes the ultimate value which is to determine the manner in which their affairs are directed. (Weber, quoted in Scott 1997: 562)

What is at stake in utilizing a mechanical metaphor for Weber is, first, the autonomous operation of a domain of administration and, second, the self-regulation of this machine that, once operational, carries on its work of production independently. Weber's metaphorical deployment of the mechanical nature of political rule reinforces the machinic sense of the efficacy of things developed by the Deleuzian tradition of materiality described in chapter 1. Moreover, Weber's attention to the mechanics of political regulation returns us to the central question of this chapter: How can we reinsert things into the body politic?

SOVEREIGN MATTER, GOVERNMENTAL MACHINES

To suggest that the object world is more intimately involved in the production and reproduction of political association is thus to challenge the central premises of modern Western thought. Even a cursory juxtaposition of liberal and Marxist politics of objects serves to underline the inattention, or even hostility, with which things have come to be regarded within theoretical treatments of the political. What is noteworthy about the culmination of both liberal and Marxian traditions is their shared effort to first promote consensus on the fundamental principles of association and then produce a corresponding redistribution of the material world to correspond—a translation of the ideal into the material. However, political practice has tended to approach the issue oppositely, ordering first our relations to objects and thereby secondarily reordering relations among citizens within human political communities (cf. Barry 2001: 7ff). Take just the example of U.S. civil rights legislation, which sought to reform political subjects steeped in centuries of discrimination. These efforts did not culminate in a reordering of the object world, but they began there, redefining the legal status of relations between people and an array of things—schools, buses, homes, automobiles, water fountains, uniforms, sports equipment—and thereby altering relations of citizens to one another. The practice of sovereign authority has never lost sight of things, even as assemblages retreated from theories of the political that defined the *via moderna*.

This tension is rather neatly described by Foucault (2007: 97) as a product of a sixteenth-century opposition between the Machiavellian concern to protect the relation of the sovereign to territory and the anti-Machiavellian effort to define the "arts of government" wherein "to govern means to govern things." For Foucault, this split augured a rupture from a political regime dominated by structures of sovereignty to one centered on the techniques and technologies of governance, a move made possible by the erosion of the family as a model of political community and the solidification of the population as the object and instrument of biopower. Agamben (1998) has pointedly shown the antiquity of biopower and the enduring envelopment of life within sovereign power. However, the corollary observation is also key, namely, that the ordering of things is fundamental not simply to a recent form of bureaucratic administration but to the reproduction of sovereignty. Hence, to reclaim things for an account of the political entails attending to their inclusion at the very heart of the principles and practices of sovereign power. To adopt a turn of phrase from Agamben (1998: 6), it might even be said that the reproduction of an order of things is an original activity of sovereign power. In contrast to the dematerialized political of modern Western theory, sovereignty has long been a persistently physical principle of the polity, one that is both fundamentally located in space and materially articulated with the corporeal body.

The traditional Western "myth" of sovereignty, reified by the Treaty of Westphalia in 1648, centered on a single spatio-political principle: one ruler in one territory. A geographic space (as opposed to a people or a confession) thus defined the maximal extent of *de facto* sovereignty and a territory's borders defended its *de jure* inviolability. The territorial account of sovereignty is most closely associated with Weber's (1994: 316) definition of the state as a "monopoly of physical violence as a means of rule within a territory," but its genealogy as a formalized principle clearly extends at least back to Machiavelli. As John Agnew (2009) has perceptively argued, the reduction of sovereignty to simple territoriality—and the corollary equivalency of territory with statehood—obscures the complex spatiality of authority (see also Smith 2003), even as it clearly demarcates the sovereign's embeddedness in a material world. Moreover, as Agamben has noted, the territory of a sovereign is heterogeneous, marked both by spaces of inclusion and spaces of exception. This spatial heterogeneity is necessarily (re)produced by an array of historical practices from security regimes to nationalist rhetorics (Howland and White 2009).

Sovereignty as practice necessarily implicates a consequential set of relations between human bodies and assemblages, relations whose points of articulation extend from the sensible apparatuses of security and policing to the sensual pleasures of performance to sentiments of orders both possible and desirable. The originality of Kantorowicz's analysis of "the king's two bodies"—a principle of sovereign dualism articulated by Tudor-era lawyers—has in large measure focused attention on the corporate corporeal entity, the union of a body natural (mortal and tangible) and a body politic (immortal, perfect, in a word, mysterious). However, Kantorowicz also attended to the duality of sovereign things. The crown, most notably, exists as both a "visible, material, exterior gold circle or diadem with which the Prince was vested and adorned at his coronation" and as "an invisible and immaterial Crown—encompassing all the royal rights and privileges indispensable for the government of the body politic—which was perpetual and descended either from God directly or by the dynastic right of inheritance" (Kantorowicz 1957: 337).

> As opposed to the pure *physis* of the king and to the pure *physis* of the territory, the word "Crown" ... indicated the political *metaphysis* in which both *rex* and *regnum* shared, or the body politic (to which both belonged) in its sovereign rights. (Kantorowicz 1957: 341; italics in original)

For Kantorowicz, the immediate value of the crown lay in its sensible qualities—a metallic durability that was superior to both the "physical *rex*" and the "geographical *regnum*" (Kantorowicz 1957: 341).

Yet hardness clearly does not exhaust the political work of regalia, be it crown or flag pin (see introduction). The efficacy of these assemblages clearly also lies in their sensible portability that enables them to shape social relationships across "inter-subjective spacetime" (Munn 1986: 11; cf. Geertz 1977), their sensual aesthetics that allow pomp to bedazzle (e.g., Geertz 1980), and their sentimental representation, always more than their manifest forms.[15] The regalia of sovereignty thus operate not only as a kind of dynastic engine, transporting the weight of majesty across generations that neither the royal body nor the territory can bear, but as a cog in the

---

[15] The best example of the latter in the domain of regalia is the mace, long an emblem of sovereignty from Pharaonic Egypt to the crown jewels of numerous monarchs of modernity. The mace in many respects is the original instrument of sovereign violence, as depicted in the Narmer Palette (O'Connor 2011) and other images of ancient kings engaged in acts of war and repression. But the ceremonial mace deployed in rites of political pomp is useless as a weapon. Its violence has been rendered purely as anachronism, a form of captivation engendered by a weapon fully drained of its capacity for consequential violence.

machinery of sovereign reproduction, charged with reproducing fiscal solvency, aesthetic captivation, and an enduring desire to be ruled all at the same moment. Clifford Geertz (1980: 123ff) understood this as the mutual implication of power and pomp, of reality and representation, in the Balinese "theater state"; Benedict Anderson (1990: 22) attributed the matter of sovereignty to a distinctly Javanese political theory that embraced into the political the vital energy that is manifested "in every aspect of the natural world, in stones, trees, clouds, and fire"; Lori Khatchadourian (n.d.) has uncovered an Achaemenid Persian (sixth to fourth centuries B.C.) theory of political order (Old Persian: *xšaça*) that "categorically refused the separation of power and matter," insisting that substances were not simply raw materials for the realization of power but were themselves part of the divine unity of sovereignty.

That histories (Kantorowicz), ethnographies (Geertz, Anderson), and archaeologies (Khatchadourian) have all noted the object matter of sovereignty suggests that the practices of rule have never lost sight of things, even as assemblages retreated from theories of the political. As Agamben (2011) suggests, sovereignty is founded not in distinction to the "arts of government" described by Foucault (2007), but rather grounded in both *oikonomia* (power as management) and glory (power as ceremonial regality) by the steady operation of a "governmental machine" (Agamben 2011: xi). To clearly locate Agamben's "machine" entails first understanding his account of the production of subject bodies, particularly the body of *Homo sacer*, a peculiar figure in Roman law, who, having committed a certain kind of criminal violation, (e.g., oath breaking) was exiled from the social community and the legal protections of rights. This "sacred man" could be killed by anyone but could not be sacrificed in rituals of worship. Agamben notes that *Homo sacer* is a mirror image of the sovereign in that both are excluded from law but continually "under its spell." The sovereign's exteriority to the polity enables the suspension of law not simply for *Homo sacer* but for the polity as a whole, a state of exception where the protections of law and custom are suspended for all subjects (cf. Schmitt 1985). As such, the work of the sovereign has the capacity to both define and control the bare life (*zoe*) of subjects quite apart from their "being" (*bios*) as political subjects/citizens.

Yet the production of *Homo sacer* involves not simply a legal reclassification of a body, but an explicit repositioning of persons within a vast "apparatus": "a machine that produces subjectifications, and only as such is ... also a machine of governance" (Agamben 2009: 20). For Agamben (2005), the apparatus of subjectification is defined by the "machines" implicated in modern spaces of exception—Auschwitz, the Gulag, Guantanamo Bay, Abu Ghraib (Fiskesjö 2003)—that work to exclude law and reduce being to bare life. This work is, for Agamben (2004: 37), one product of an "anthropological machine":

> If, in the [anthropological] machine of the moderns, the outside is produced through the exclusion of an inside and the inhuman produced by animalizing the human, in [the more ancient anthropological machine] the inside is obtained through the inclusion of an outside, and the non-man is produced by the humanization of an animal: the man-ape, the *enfant sauvage* or *Homo ferus*, but also and above all the slave, the barbarian, and the foreigner, as figures of an animal in human form.

Politics, for Agamben, is the very product of this "anthropological machine" and its efficacy in defending the distinctions between categories that manufacture the figure of "humanity" (see also Ingold 2012: 86). This entails not only creating a distinction between humans and other organic beings (especially animals but also plants) but also the envelopment of the ontological category of the inorganic within the apparatus (cf. Haraway 1985).

Given the analytical attention that has been focused on the material apparatuses at work in states of exception, it is important to keep in mind that the classical understanding of *bios* was also a world of things, raising the critical question of how sovereignty lies not simply in the "governance of things" or even "governance by things" but "governance as thing." Governance as the proper regulation of a material world in order to make possible the good life (*eudaimonia*) lay at the heart of classical philosophy's major strands of thought. If for Aristotle the good life entailed the deployment of the intellect in fulfilling work, a life guided by practical reason (*bios theoretikos*, i.e., contemplation relating to action in the world), for Epicurus *eudaimonia* was realized in the pursuit of pleasure (*bios apolaustikos*). Both the Aristotelian and Epicurean understandings of the good life are embedded in activity conducted within and through a material world of things.

This material world is composed of machines quite like those that populate the world of Agamben's *Homo sacer*; their operation is both regulated by and constitutive of the "governmental machine" (Agamben 2011: xi) that allows the sovereign not only to control the conditions of *zoe*, but also to make *bios*, even *eudaimonia*, possible. Hence the work of sovereignty entails not simply operating on bodies, reclassifying them and marking them, but the constant maintenance of the machinery that makes possible both the conditions of subjection and sovereign power. Sovereignty is thus constituted by its apparatus, the machines that define the human community of real and potential subjects (Agamben's anthropological machine) and enact its dictates in the world of both *oikonomia* and glory (his "bipolar" governmental machine; Agamben 2011: 114). Sovereignty must therefore be conditional not simply on the relations of humans but on the efficacious workings of a dense machinery. This is not the singular "leviathan machine" decried by Geertz (2004: 580), "a set-apart sphere of command and decision," but rather efficacious assemblages that establish the conditions of sovereignty precisely through their diffusion throughout social practices. But precisely how do things shape the conditions of sovereignty and what is at stake in subjecting sovereignty to conditions?

THE SOVEREIGN CONDITIONS

The current turn toward theorizing sovereignty as fundamentally "conditional" arises from two quite different sources. The first, advanced in large measure by human rights advocates, argues that sovereignty entails a "dual responsibility" (Evans and Sahnoun 2002: 102): a traditional Westphalian responsibility to recognize the sovereignty of other states and a concomitant "responsibility to protect" (R2P) those subject to authority.[16] An inability or unwillingness to fulfill this responsibility to protect necessarily abrogates claims to sovereignty and thus legitimizes "humanitarian intervention" by another power. Hence sovereignty is understood as conditional on fulfilling requirements. Not surprisingly, this R2P principle is soundly rejected by advocates of an inviolable conception of sovereignty, ranging from postcolonies of the global south suspicious of neoimperial agendas to world powers resistant to the suzerainty of Western conceptions of human rights. However, as a number of observers have pointed out (e.g., Glanville 2013) sovereignty has always been a conditional quality of the polity. Georges Bataille (1993: 221) sketched an early account of this sense of condition, arguing that sovereignty belongs to all individuals. Thus, its coalescence in a singular apparatus of rule is the product of a "conditional and temporary

[16] The International Commission on Intervention and State Sovereignty (ICISS) was established by the Canadian government in 2001 to answer a question posed by U.N. secretary general Kofi Annan in the wake of repeated failures by the world community to respond to state sponsored atrocities: "If humanitarian intervention is, indeed, an unacceptable assault on sovereignty, how should we respond to a Rwanda, to a Srebrenica—to gross and systematic violations of human rights that affect every precept of our common humanity?" Quoted in the ICISS Report p. 7. http://www.iciss.ca/pdf/ Commission-Report.pdf.

submission." If sovereignty rests upon a contractual set of obligations, it is necessarily conditional on the mutual fulfillment of requirements.

The second sense of conditional sovereignty emerges out of an understanding of "condition" as health or fitness. This sense of the term attends to perceived gaps between juridical and empirical sovereignty, between claims to authority and the capacity to enforce. This form of conditional sovereignty looms large in analyses of failing states whose claims to authority are often severely undermined by civil unrest, competing institutional powers, and nonstate actors. To illustrate, the Fund for Peace's Fragile State Index (FSI) for 2014—a kind of who's who of who's not—listed thirty-four countries on the brink of collapse, including sixteen whose governments operated under severe restrictions on their territorial sovereignty. But the FSI does not simply flag countries on the verge of unraveling; it also lists 144 other polities whose stability appears to be more assured. Thus, looked at in its entirety, the FSI is not simply an analysis of potential collapse; it is a condition report on sovereignty, a risk assessment of the likelihood of political reproduction. Chances are good (close to a sure thing) that when we wake up tomorrow Finland will still be ordered by its sovereign governmental apparatus; it is also likely (a good bet, but not a lock) that the U.S. government will still be authoritative; but it is much riskier to wager on the future of Somalia, for example.

The combined efforts to push sovereignty off its ontological pedestal by subjecting it to requirements, locating it "in practice" (Hansen and Steppu-tat 2006: 297), and setting it within a wide array of historical, cultural, and practical contexts (cf. Cattelino 2006), suggests that conditional sovereignty implies yet a third sense of condition at the heart of the sovereign project. As Khatchadourian (n.d.) has noted, condition understood as either a restriction upon or as an experience of subjectivization forces closer attention to condition in the sense of material surroundings. Such a view, as we shall see in part 2 of the book, implicates things not simply in constraining sovereignty, but in establishing a field of possibility, defining the material (pre) conditions that make sovereignty possible. Condition in this sense describes the circumstances indispensable to consequences.

An object-aware account of the political suggests that sovereign authority demands the reproduction of (at least) three key conditions:

1. a coherent public defined by relations of inclusion and exclusion that are materially marked and regulated;

2. the figure of a sovereign, cut away from the community by an apparatus of social and martial violence;

3. an apparatus capable of formalizing governance by transforming the polity itself into an object of desire, of care, and of devotion.

It is important to note that these conditions are historical and not teleological. That is, they need not emerge simultaneously, within a singular sequence, or form at all. But all three conditions are critical to the relations between humans and things that are fundamental to sovereignty. In order to explore one instance of the historical production of the machinery of sovereign authority, let us turn now directly to the "matter" at hand by delving into the Caucasus at the dawn of the Bronze Age.

PART II

Assembling Sovereignty

CHAPTER 3

The Civilization Machine in the Early Bronze Age

The true revolution in man's protohistory is not the Neolithic, since it may very well leave the previously existing social organization intact; it is the political revolution, that mysterious emergence—irreversible, fatal to primitive societies—of the thing we know by the name of the State.

(Clastres 1989: 202)

In 1688, officials of the Tokugawa Shogunate centered at Edo (modern Tokyo) issued the following decree targeting theater owners: "Puppet costumes must not be sumptuous. Gold and silver leaf must not be used on anything. But puppet generals only may wear gold and silver hats" (Shively 1955: 345). The regulations extended existing sumptuary laws regulating the consumption of luxury items to the finery worn by other objects. Sumptuary laws, a term taken from the extensive Roman *leges sumptuariae*, describe regulations placed upon the consumption of a wide range of goods, including garments, jewelry, food, alcohol, furniture, and funerary monuments. Sumptuary laws have long been as notorious for their extraordinary detail (witness, a 1463 English ordinance that limited to two inches "the extent to which the shoes of persons of rank could extend beyond their toes" [Beebe 2010: 812–13]) as for their almost complete ineffectiveness (to wit, a seventeenth-century Nuremberg ordinance complained that "both men and womenfolk have, in utterly irresponsible manner, driven extravagance in dress and new styles to such shameful and wanton extremes that the different classes are barely to be known apart" [quoted in Beebe 2010: 811]). Sumptuary rules are widely understood as legal instruments for preserving social hierarchies and enforcing moral orders, and, as such, they are quintessential political instruments of social reproduction, inhibiting changes in the material world—and our relations to it—that might undermine an existing order. This is certainly what Montaigne (1965: 197–98) read into Plato's sumptuary rules that refused "young men the liberty of introducing any change in their habits, gestures, dances, songs, and exercises, from one form to another; shifting from this to that, hunting after novelties … by which means manners are corrupted and the old institutions come to be nauseated and despised." But as Alan Hunt (2004: 599) has persuasively argued, sumptuary rules are also an effort to make identity legible in social worlds that are largely defined by interactions amongst strangers. They are in this sense tools for manufacturing—and stabilizing—a public. As the Tokugawa puppet law suggests, this public embraced not only an assembly of humans but also a complex material assemblage.

In this chapter, I examine the role of things in the reproduction of a public—the first condition of sovereignty defined in chapter two—during the Early Bronze Age in the South Caucasus. By a public, I mean a self-recognizing community that is not maintained exclusively through face-to-face interaction. It is thus in large part an assembly of strangers, in Michael Warner's (2005: 74) terms, who are made familiar to one another through an assemblage of publicity—forms of mass mediation and sites of encounter, such as those Benedict Anderson (1983) described as fundamental to the imagination of modern nations. The suggestion that material things are critical to the creation of a public follows closely Hannah Arendt's (1958: 22ff) conception of humanity as *Homo faber*. Where labor responds to the never-ending demands of biological subsistence, the work of *Homo faber* is located in the fabrication of artificial things that can be undertaken solely in the context of collective life. For Arendt, this fabrication produces the requisite spaces and tools that allow communities to come together to engage in political activity, to reproduce themselves not simply as individuals but as a collectivity open to governance. However, a necessary corollary to the manufacture of an "imagined community" is the simultaneous material inscription of exclusion that sets a collectivity off from its neighbors, who lie beyond command, beyond law, and, often, beyond the pale. The work of *Homo faber* is thus the production of a very specific kind of public, a spatially maximal sphere of mutual recognition of both familiarity and foreignness best described by that quintessentially archaeological term: "civilization."

Civilization in this sense refers neither to a perduring organic category of identification, as graphically represented in Edwin Blashfield's mural from the Library of Congress, nor to an apical stage of historical development, as defined by Lewis Henry Morgan's evolutionary schema and pictorially encapsulated in the tympanum from the Oriental Institute at the University of Chicago (fig. 8; cf. Bowden 2009; Elias 1994 Service 1975; Trigger 2003; Wengrow 2010). Rather, civilization here refers to a machine that re-

Fig. 8. Tympanum above the entry to the Oriental Institute, University of Chicago. (Photo credit: Elizabeth Fagan.)

produces the terms of inclusion and exclusion—work that both Blashfield's mural and the Oriental Institute's tympanum contribute to quite effectively as instruments in the reproduction of a particular understanding of world historical order. I adopt the term civilization here instead of potential alternatives because at present only this rather archaic term entails an inherent concern with the objects of both publicity and distinction. What civilization provides is a set of ready-made tools for defining relations of inclusion and exclusion among a spatially extensive and temporally enduring public. In contrast to traditional accounts of civilization (e.g., Breasted 1919, Childe 1925; Frankfort 1956), the civilization machine is a means, not an end, an apparatus of consolidation and segmentation, not a condition of existence. Let me illustrate the contrast by turning to the Caucasus.

In 1897, the Russian archaeologist Nikolai Veselovskii excavated a large *kurgan*, or burial tumulus, in the foothills of the northwest Caucasus, near the town of Maikop that, during the mid-twentieth century, inspired two radically different understandings of the nature of civilization in general, and of the ancient Caucasus in particular. The tumulus was more than 10 meters high and almost 200 meters in diameter. The contents of the tomb were nothing short of sensational. Mikhail Rostovtzeff (1922: 19–31) provided the first English-language summary of the inventory, describing turquoise and carnelian beads, stone tools, bronze weapons and cauldrons, gold animal appliqués, silver drinking vessels with zoomorphic decoration, and six silver rods with gold and silver bull figurine terminals. Not surpris-

Fig. 9. Decorated vase from the Great Kurgan at Maikop. (Source: Rostovtzeff 1922.)

ingly, the discovery stimulated interest in other large kurgans in the foot-hills of the North Caucasus—a landscape well represented on a decorated vase from the Maikop tomb (fig. 9)—allowing for the archaeological defini-tion of a material repertoire constitutive of a Maikop "cultural community" whose initial appearance is dated to the Late Chalcolithic period between 3800 and 3500 B.C.

Rostovtzeff set the Maikop assemblage within a wider art historical con-text that stretched from Egypt to Elam, but he concluded that the finds rep-resented the autochthonous flowering of a "very peculiar and very original" "civilization in the Caucasus" whose artistic traditions "owed nothing to for-eign centres" of cultural development (Rostovtzeff 1922: 32). Rostovtzeff's account of the Chalcolithic North Caucasus is particularly intriguing as it cuts against the grain of his larger analytical project, which cast early civili-zation in southern Russia not as a flourishing of isolated cultural develop-ment but as a product of cross-cultural elite collaboration. Rostovtzeff quickly became rather isolated in his interpretation of the Maikop materi-als. Just two decades later, V. Gordon Childe (1942: 132) reinterpreted Mai-kop assemblages as evidence not of regional autochthony but of the trans-formative impact of unspecified "influences" radiating outward from civilizations far to the south in the ancient Near East. For a preponderance of archaeologists since Childe, including Boris Piotrovskii (1973: 12), Aarne Tallgren (1922: 200), and Andrew Sherratt (1997: 458), to name only a few, the wealth, technology, and aesthetic sophistication of the Maikop tomb materials has been seen as a distant effect of processes set in motion in southern Mesopotamia. However, arguments for the derivation of Maikop material assemblages from southwest Asian models rest on precariously

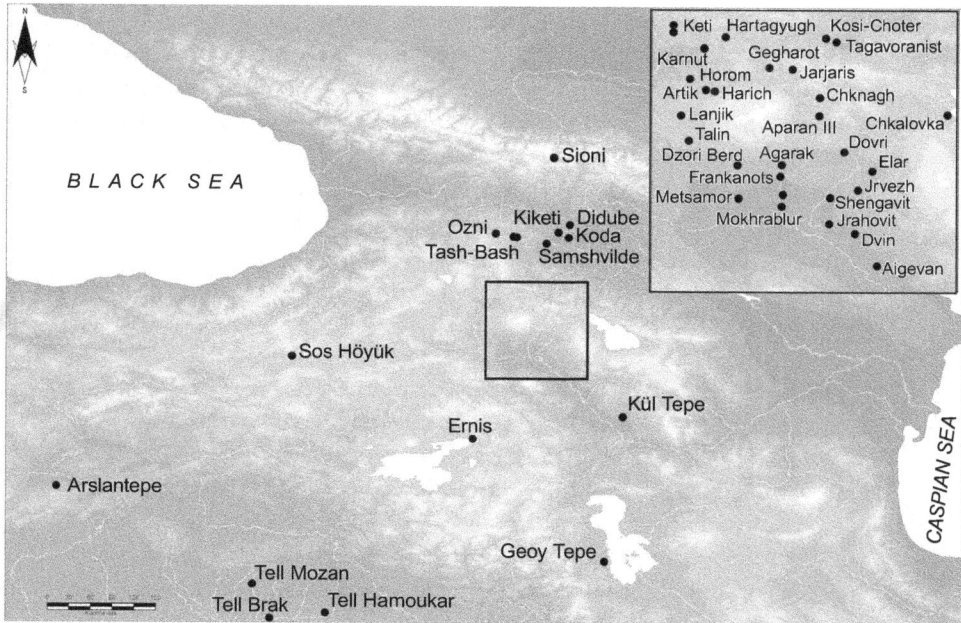

Fig. 10. Major Early Bronze Age archaeological sites of the Caucasus. (Map Credit: Adam T. Smith.)

thin evidence. The few ambiguous traces of possible iconographic similarity (see Trifonov 1994: 358) are overwhelmed by a wider quotidian material assemblage, including residential architecture and subsistence practices, that bears little resemblance to traditions in the alluvial plains of the ancient Near East (Kohl 2007: 82–84). What they do rest upon is a particular theoretical imagination of civilization derived, ironically, from Rostovtzeff himself, one that emphasizes the cosmopolitan origins of civilizations in the synthesis of techniques and technologies from a wide cultural catchment.

The cosmopolitan model of civilization, firmly rooted in the experience of European colonialism, is today so widely diffused as to constitute the hegemonic understanding of the concept (Wengrow 2010). However, cosmopolitanism is only part of the story of civilization, and arguably not the most relevant part, from a specifically political, rather than diffusely cultural, perspective. Civilizations are also exclusive clubs—communities that claim privileges, be they moral, technological, or political, over their neighbors and predecessors. Where is civilization without the excluded and denigrated barbarian? In this sense, civilizations as practiced are the exact opposite of the cosmopolitan self-image they cultivate. It is this instrumental sense of civilization that is critical to the development of sovereignty as it identifies, delimits, and legitimates a coherent public distinct from all others and open to claims of rule. Civilization, in other words, is a machine for manufacturing publics, stitching a community into an association that recognizes itself as a potential object of governance and thus providing the underlying logic of political association. As such, an archaeology of the civilization machine is an inquiry into the things that reproduce a public.

THE KURA-ARAXES

Just a few centuries after the initial appearance of the grand Maikop kurgans in the North Caucasus, communities in the South Caucasus and the Armenian Highland became closely tied into an expansive Early Bronze Age ecumene (fig. 10) that is today most often referred to as the Kura-Araxes horizon (Kuftin 1940).[1] The Kura-Araxes horizon has been most prominently identified with a distinctive suite of ceramic vessels (fig. 11f, g, l) with black and red-black burnished surfaces (Gopnik and Rothman 2011; Palumbi 2008; Sagona 1984). The origins of this red-black burnished ware are a matter of considerable debate at present. Radiocarbon determinations from a range of sites have helped to push its first appearance back into the Late Chalcolithic period in northeast Anatolia (at Sos Höyük; Kiguradze and Sagona 2003), the upper Euphrates (at Arslantepe and Tepecik; Frangipane and Palumbi 2007: 234), and the South Caucasus (at Areni-1; Areshian et al. 2012). However, as Giulio Palumbi (2008: 102) has pointed out, the Late Chalcolithic red-black burnished wares from Anatolian sites are usually a distinct minority amidst heterogeneous assemblages that indicate sustained interactions with regions outside of the Caucasus and Armenian Highland. For example, the Late Chalcolithic community at Arslantepe (level VII) was most closely tied to the Syro-Mesopotamian world. Red-black burnished wares represented only a negligible portion of the overall corpus of materials (never more than 2%; Palumbi 2008: 100). With the beginning of the Bronze Age around 3500 B.C., this situation changed dramatically.

A similar situation prevailed in the South Caucasus during the Late Chalcolithic period (ca. 4000–3500 B.C.). Early fourth millennium commu-

---

[1] The same archaeological repertoire has also been dubbed "the Shengavit culture" (Baiburtyan 1938), the "Early Transcaucasian Culture" (Burney and Lang 1972), the "Outer Fertile Crescent Culture" (Kelly-Buccellati 1980), and the "Culture of Northeast Anatolia" (Lamb 1954).

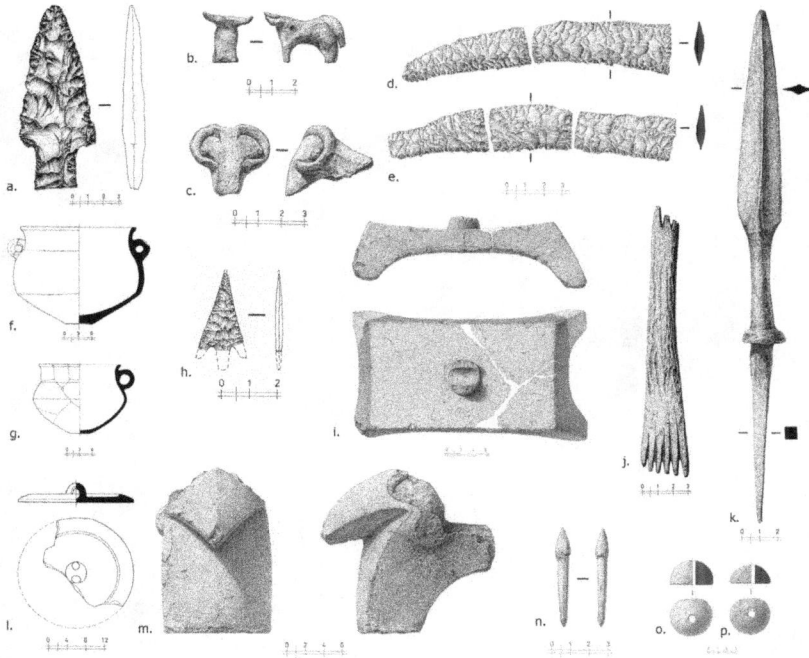

Fig. 11. The Kura-Araxes assemblage. (Source: Adam T. Smith.)

nities in the South Caucasus, such as those at Berikldeebi (level V) and Treli, utilized diverse ceramic assemblages that were dominated by chaff wares with untreated surfaces. Only a distinct minority of wares at these sites were characterized by technological features and stylistic elements that anticipated Kura-Araxes ceramics, including grit temper, firing in low temperature reducing atmospheres, painstakingly burnished surfaces, handles, and decorative knobs (Palumbi 2008: 34). But by the beginning of the second half of the fourth millennium, the heterogeneity of these sites had been expunged, overwhelmed by the full implementation of a distinctly Kura-Araxes homogenous ceramic repertoire.

In the centuries that immediately followed, communities in the South Caucasus at sites such as Elar and Mokhrablur (levels XI–IX) had wed these red-black burnished wares to the larger portmanteau of material culture that, taken together, defines the Kura-Araxes assemblage (Smith et al. 2009). This assemblage cuts across an array of materials and media, including rectilinear and circular residential architecture, ceramic zoomorphic hearths and animal figurines, bone implements including spindle whorls and awls,

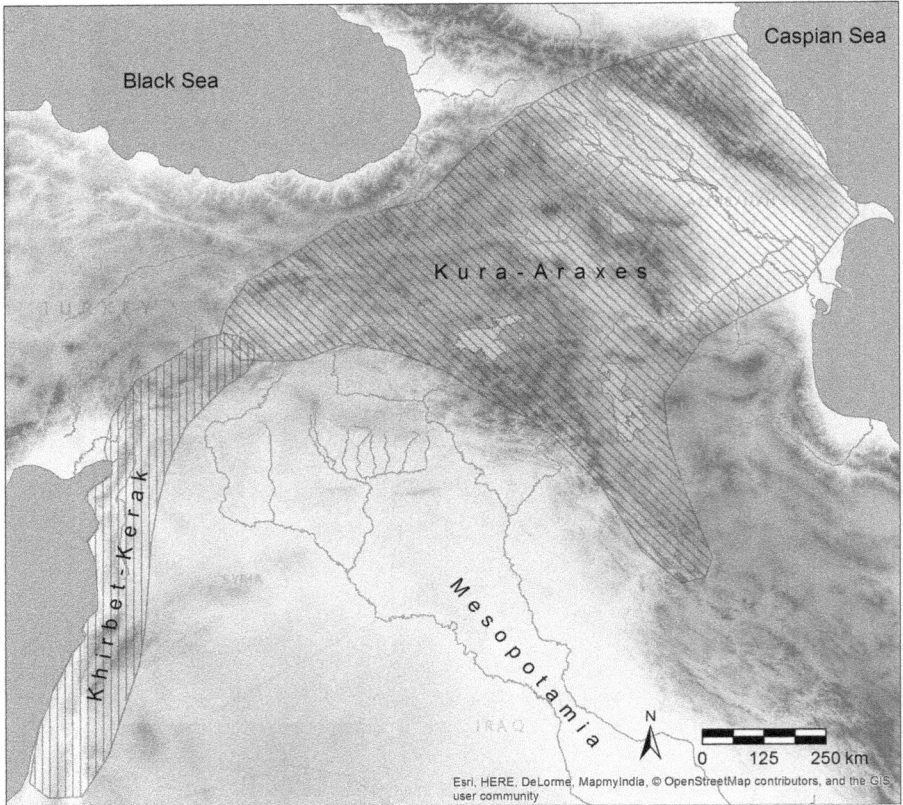

Fig. 12. Map of the maximum dispersal of the Kura-Araxes assemblage. (Map Credit: Adam T. Smith.)

bronze ornaments and weapons, and a lithic toolkit that favors flint for sickle blades and obsidian for scrapers and projectile points (fig. 11).

By the end of the fourth millennium, the Kura-Araxes assemblage had swamped the South and Northeast Caucasus (fig. 12), dramatically expanding the number of settlements and inexorably pressing the boundaries of the ecumene outward (Kelly-Buccellati 1974; Kohl 2007: 85ff; Rothman 2003). The metastasis of the Kura-Araxes assemblage rapidly spilled onto the Armenian Highland, and, by the beginning of the third millennium, a vast swath of southwest Asia was drawn together into a new kind of public whose practices and institutions were mediated by Kura-Araxes materials. At its height, the Kura-Araxes was arguably the most widespread archaeological horizon in the ancient Near East, extending from the Northeast Caucasus to the Levant to the central Zagros Mountains. As the Kura-Araxes assemblage expanded, it enforced a rigid material orthodoxy, dismantling old traditions and implementing the new repertoire.

Much archaeological research has focused on the sociology of the people who made the Kura-Araxes assemblage (Abay 2005; Rothman 2005)—did they belong to a unified ethnic group engaged in extended migrations? Or was the Kura-Araxes defined by a dispersed cluster of communities tied by bonds of interaction and exchange? What I am interested in here is not the sociology of the Kura-Araxes's unique public, but, inversely, what kind of public the Kura-Araxes assemblage produced. What role did this conspicuous new civilization machine of the Early Bronze Age play in establishing a new sense of community, new sentiments of attachment to a wider public, and a new sensibility of people and objects?

SENSIBILITY

As I argued in chapter 1, sensibility describes the dimension of human–object engagement most closely tied to the formal and material qualities of assemblages. The sensible embraces most immediately the physical flow of things—their circulation within and between distinct social locations (e.g., from mine to workshop, workshop to residence, residence to tomb)—and the transubstantiations that materials make—or do not make—as they move. One of the most distinctive dimensions of the Kura-Araxes phenomenon is the rigid regulation of material flows that appears to have governed relations between Kura-Araxes communities and their neighbors.[2] The precise geography and chronology of the Kura-Araxes expansion is at present only roughly sketched. But sometime around 2800 B.C., a widespread crisis gripped communities throughout the upper Euphrates, leading to widespread abandonments and numerous episodes of violent destruction.[3] Relations to regions south of the Taurus Mountains were largely severed, undermining local traditions linked to the Syro-Mesopotamian world and fostering engagement with the expanding highland public tied to the Kura-

[2] At present, our datasets are far more robust in detailing Kura-Araxes interactions (or lack thereof) with neighbors to the north and south. We lack a significant enough corpus of materials to evaluate potential ties to regions east and west of the Kura-Araxes ecumene.

[3] There is considerable disagreement on whether destruction episodes in the upper Euphrates Valley represent an often violent incursion by Kura-Araxes communities (as suggested by Lupton 1996: 97) or instead represent internal crises that created the conditions for new cultural connections to the Kura-Araxes world (as suggested by Palumbi 2008: 216). Our current understanding of Kura-Araxes communities suggests that the latter scenario is far more likely.

Araxes assemblage (Palumbi 2008: 215). New communities were established in the region with homes centered on three-leaf or horseshoe-shaped hearths and residential assemblages that repeated, albeit with some regional distinctions, the core repertoire of the Kura-Araxes portmanteau. In the northern Zagros, we see a similar pattern at sites such as Yanik Tepe (level L) and Godin Tepe where earlier traditions were abandoned in favor of the Kura-Araxes assemblage (Amiran 1965; Gopnik and Rothman 2011: 160ff).

Explanations for the Kura-Araxes expansion have largely presumed that the speed of cultural transformation indicates waves of human migration out of the Caucasus. These accounts have focused on a fairly limited set of "pushes" and "pulls" to account for such large-scale population movements. One of the most oft-cited pulls is the effect generated by the Late Chalcolithic expansion of southern Mesopotamian "Uruk" communities into Anatolia. Sherratt (1997: 468), for example, struggled to understand the Kura-Araxes as, like Maikop before it, a derivative effect of Uruk expansion. "The result of these [Late Uruk] contacts," Sherratt writes, "was to transform the Eneolithic cultures of Transcaucasia into a successful and independent bloc of highland peoples, the Kura-Araxes culture, which resisted incorporation into lowland polities but absorbed many of the characteristics of contemporary urban civilization." This image of the Kura-Araxes as a cluster of "complex settled northern polities" (Algaze 2001: 76) sparked by the intrusion of Mesopotamians into southern Anatolia has proven to be remarkably tenacious. Perimeter walls reported at the sites of Shengavit (Sardaryan 1967: 344), Mokhrablur (Kushnareva 1997: 74), Sos Höyük (Sagona and Sagona 2000: 59), and, most recently, Köhne Shahar (Alizadeh et al. in press) have proven to be particularly evocative, encouraging steady speculation on the complex labor coordination and the possibility of violence and warfare among Kura-Araxes communities.[4] Moreover, the inclusion of Kura-Araxes ceramics and metalwork in the inventory of the "royal" tomb at Arslantepe (period VI B), on the far western periphery of the Kura-Araxes ecumene, has also suggested to some that the Kura-Araxes may have been organized around hereditary leaders able to both concentrate wealth and demand human sacrifice as elements of mortuary ritual (e.g., Alizadeh et al. in press; cf. Kohl 1992a).[5]

---

[4] Few of the reported Kura-Araxes "fortification" walls have been securely dated and may well be later constructions or ad hoc structures related to the increase of violence during the transition between the Early and Middle Bronze Ages. Moreover, Sagona and Sagona (2000: 59) do not consider the "monumental" wall as Sos to be defensive in nature, suggesting instead that it served to spatially differentiate components of the community—an important reminder that not all large walls arise out of military calculations.

[5] This suggestion does not accord with the distribution of materials in the tomb. Marcella

However, the suggestion that communities in the late fourth-millennium Caucasus adopted elements of "urban civilization" is extremely difficult to countenance. The Kura-Araxes was in general a studiously village-based society centered on an egalitarian ideology that stood in stark contrast to the social worlds of Mesopotamia. The few examples of constructions that may have required more significant investments of community labor merely underline the rarity of such built environments within the larger Kura-Araxes assemblage. The sacrifice and conspicuous consumption of the Arslantepe tomb may find parallels in Maikop funerary traditions but are not elements of Kura-Araxes burial rituals (as we shall see below). Moreover, the spread of Kura-Araxes communities appears to have effectively overturned whatever cultural hegemony or economic privilege southern Mesopotamia enjoyed in the Armenian Highland during the Late Uruk period (cf. Algaze 1993; Stein 1999). Hence, a number of scholars (Kohl 2007: 83; Smith 2012a: 678) have suggested that it was likely the retreat of southern Mesopotamian investment in the region that created opportunities for the extension of the Kura-Araxes and its establishment as an alternative location of cultural production.

Antonio Sagona (1984: 138–39) has argued that pushes out of the Caucasus exerted a stronger force on Kura-Araxes expansion than pulls into neighboring regions. He suggests that population pressure in the South Caucasus triggered by climate change or overgrazing pushed waves of migrants into surrounding areas. Detailed paleoenvironmental studies are currently lacking for the region as a whole, but one palynological study of a sediment core from the Tsalka plateau indicates that the period from approximately 4000 to 2000 B.C. witnessed a rather stable "climatic optimum" (Conner and Sagona 2007: 35). Moreover, we do not see archaeological evidence for the kind of constriction in populations that might indicate a large-scale outmigration. At the site of Gegharot, for example, in the Tsaghkahovit Plain, the Kura-Araxes village expanded in the early third millennium, rather than contracted (Badalyan et al. 2008, in press). Indeed, the lack of evidence for population reduction in the Kura-Araxes heartland of the Lesser Caucasus throws cold water on the large-scale outmigration hypothesis as a whole. Population movements must have played a part in the rapid expansion of the Kura-Araxes assemblage, but it cannot have been the

Frangipane (2007–2008: 181) notes that the pottery within the lower chamber of the principal interred was largely associated with the Palace period wares of the Late Uruk occupation. Kura-Araxes wares were generally limited to the perimeter of the tomb, associated with the sacrificed adolescents. Hence it seems possible that Kura-Araxes communities in the area supplied sacrificial victims for the tomb (willingly or not), but were not genealogically tied to the principal figure (see also Palumbi 2008: 152).

primary mode absent evidence of wide-scale abandonments from sites in Armenia and Georgia—the scale of the territory covered by the Kura-Araxes at its height is simply too great. What else then could explain the unique flows of the Kura-Araxes assemblage across the northern Near East?

One clue to the forces driving expansion may lie in the rigid material orthodoxy of the public that was bound by the Kura-Araxes assemblage. As the assemblage expanded its reach, it foreclosed alternative material flows. Once communities were enveloped into the Kura-Araxes world, exchange with other ecumenes was largely severed. This insularity appears to have been an element of Kura-Araxes cultural practice from the earliest stages of its development. At the site of Godedzor in the Vorotan River valley of southern Armenia, for example, the latest stages of occupation (ca. 3500–3347 B.C.) are contemporary with the initial stages of the Kura-Araxes (Chataigner et al. 2010: 378). Though some decorative aspects of the Chalcolithic-period ceramics at the site may anticipate subsequent approaches to ornamentation within the Kura-Araxes tradition, not a single Kura-Araxes sherd has been recovered from the site's final phase of occupation despite the presence of contemporaneous early Kura-Araxes villages in the region (Badalyan pers. comm.).

At sites along the northern edge of Mesopotamia, such as those in the Khabur drainage of northern Syria, Kura-Araxes related materials are extremely rare despite the region's proximity to the Armenian Highland. After decades of excavation, only a handful of red-black burnished ware sherds have been found at sites in northeastern Syria (Kelly-Buccellati 1990: 123). At Tell Mozan, a small collection of "Transcaucasian"- style metals and perhaps a horseshoe-shaped hearth (Kelly-Buccellati 2004) are the only evidence for contact. Evidence for material flows in the other direction is similarly hard to find. Trade items from places outside the ecumene are exceedingly rare in Kura-Araxes sites. As Philip Kohl (1992b: 124) has aptly concluded, there is very little to suggest the movement of "materials or peoples" from northern Mesopotamia into the Armenian Highland and the Caucasus.

Indeed, what is most interesting about the relation between the world of the Kura-Araxes and its neighbors is just how little contact there seems to have been, suggesting a tightly regulated social boundary (Smith 2005). Even at the farthest margins of the Kura-Araxes world, such as the so-called Khirbet Kerak communities of the southern Levant, Raffi Greenberg (2007: 266) has noted a clear effort by households that utilized Khirbet Kerak wares to maintain rigorous social boundaries. At Bet Yerah, these boundaries were maintained by rigid spatial segregation from households that used the so-called common ware, even as the segregation of Kura-Araxes–related materials weakened at the end of the Early Bronze Age. Greenberg notes that the Khirbet Kerak households preserved a "technological separateness" that reinforced their distinction. The same insularity is also visible on the northern frontier of the Kura-Araxes world, where Maikop and Kura-Araxes communities constitute "totally distinct phenomena" with "very little evidence for direct contact" (Kohl 2007: 84).[6]

This highly restricted flow of materials was made possible by the sensible qualities of the Kura-Araxes assemblage, qualities that allowed the ecumene to be largely self-sufficient. Indeed, the Kura-Araxes assemblage appears to have worked quite diligently at being self-contained, needing little to nothing from neighboring communities. Metalwork provides a succinct case in point. Almost all of the extant Kura-Araxes metal artifacts are deliberately alloyed arsenical bronzes,[7] with concentrations of arsenic ranging from 2 to 8 percent that distinguish them from the increasing prevalence of tin bronzes in neighboring regions, most notably Anatolia and Mesopotamia (Chernykh 1992: 66; Courcier 2014; Kavtaradze 1999: 74). As a result, the Kura-Araxes public was largely excused from the developing exchange networks related to the tin trade, reinforcing both its solidarity and external distinction.

The expansion of the Kura-Araxes was not simply a matter of the adoption of a new style of making things on top of existing cultural, social, and economic practices. Quite the contrary, to become Kura-Araxes entailed a *conversion* to an entirely new way of life, one that swept away old traditions and excluded rivals. It was, in short, a civilizing moment, which demanded a rejection of past practices, an adherence to an orthodoxy enshrined in a self-contained material assemblage, and a recognition of the distinctiveness of a new way of life in contradistinction to neighboring communities. Recasting the Kura-Araxes expansion as a civilizing process, and not just a migration, necessarily shifts our explanatory focus away from a narrowly economic account of pushes and pulls focused on resource crises and incentives and towards an investigation of shifting social values mediated by objects. That is, while material flows appear to have created the conditions of possibility for a Kura-Araxes civilization machine, guarding its edges and main-

[6] A possible exception to this overall sense of social segregation comes from recent excavations at Köhne Shahar (Alizadeh et al. in press), where excavators found Kura-Araxes materials in close association with Ninevite V painted wares from northern Mesopotamia and a stamp seal and clay sealing similar to those found in the Late Chalcolithic level VI A at Arslantepe.

[7] As Peterson (2003: 32) notes, "sulphidic ores, which are typically rich in arsenic, are widely available in the Caucasus Mountains." Chernykh (1992: 60) counts "no less than 400 major deposits and ore bodies of copper, arsenic, antimony, gold, and other useful minerals" in the South Caucasus, many with clear evidence of ancient patterns of exploitation.

taining its internal mechanics, sensibility alone cannot detail the regimes of value that allowed the assemblage to be so remarkably efficacious in stitching together such far-flung communities into a coherent public. A concern with the values at the heart of the civilization machine necessarily pushes us beyond the domain of sensibility to consider the sensual dimension of the Kura-Araxes assemblage.

SENSE

Sense refers to those dimensions of the relationship between humans and things where the object world possesses not only operational capacities but also evocative potencies. Sense is a domain of semiosis, of signs and signification, a domain of value where assemblages circulate within dense layers of sedimented affects and aesthetics. The sensual thus attends to metamorphoses in values that objects make as they move—cloth becomes flag, seat becomes throne, house becomes home—and the transfigurations of human bodies as things position us within varying aesthetic fields. It is here that the ties that bound the public defined by the Kura-Araxes assemblage must lie.

Kura-Araxes assemblages are defined almost exclusively by two social contexts, the home and the tomb, locations critical to the reproduction of a coherent public. Let me provide a sense of these contexts by turning to the site of Gegharot in the Tsaghkahovit Plain of central Armenia (fig. 13), a major focus of the research of Project ArAGATS since 2002 (Badalyan et al. 2004a, 2008, in press; Smith et al. 2004). The archaeological remains of Early Bronze Age Gegharot (fig. 14) have been shaped by both the erosion of the outcrop and the construction activities of the later Late Bronze Age occupants of the site. However, because Late Bronze Age buildings were erected 3 to 5 meters from the circumferential walls that defined the citadel and terrace, Early Bronze Age constructions in the buffer zone, shown in gray, remained largely undisturbed.

The Early Bronze Age village at Gegharot was established on the summit and upper terrace of the hill around 3300 B.C., marked by an early Kura-Araxes ceramic group known as "Elar-Aragats," that boasts dimple ornaments and paired raised knobs (fig. 15). The initial Kura-Araxes occupation at Gegharot appears to have begun with the construction of several homes along the western edge of the citadel and the west terrace just below, on which was set a square stone crypt with an entryway, or dromos, in the southern wall (fig. 16). The tomb was constructed from local unworked granite with limestone blocks used for the northwest and southwest corner-

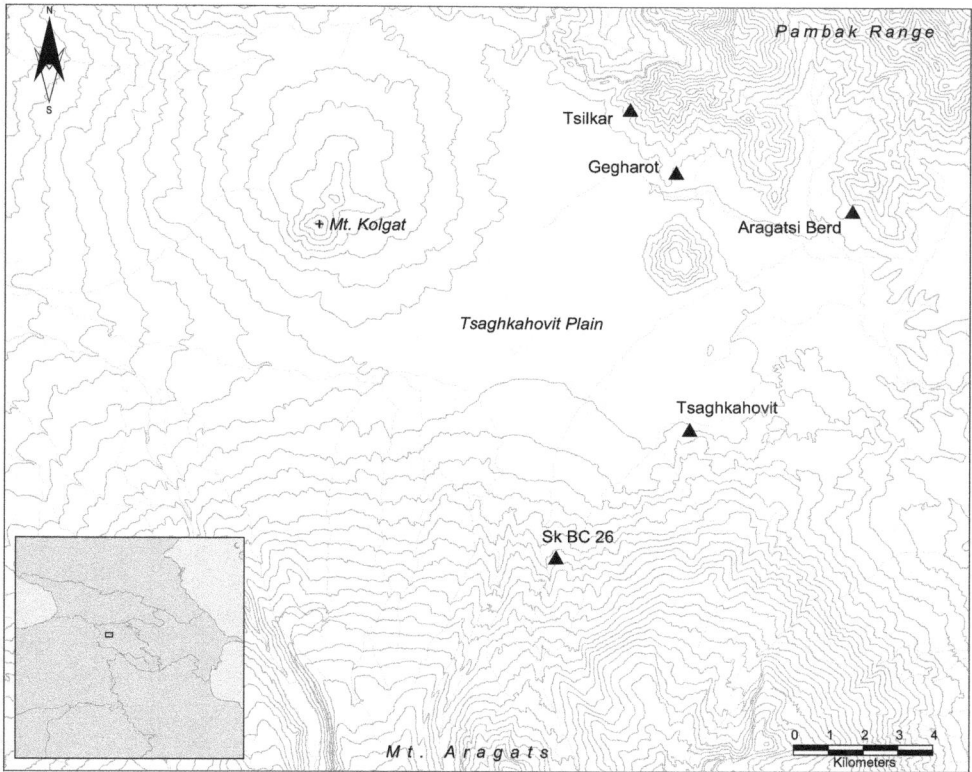

Fig. 13. Map of the Tsaghkahovit Plain in the Early Bronze Age. (Map Credit: Adam T. Smith.)

stones. Similar large blocks outlined the doorjambs and threshold of the dromos.

Closing the entryway was an upright slab with a flat base and rounded top. The roof of the tomb was built of three flat stone slabs. Inside the tomb were the remains of three individuals. The bones of two had been pushed into a pile against the northern wall, and the skulls of both were found in the northwestern corner. A large bowl had been placed between the two skulls. The skeleton of the third individual, presumably the last interred, was found fully articulated on the floor of the chamber. Collective tombs like this one in which burials were carried out in sequence over time were the primary form of Kura-Araxes interment. The artifact inventory of the Gegharot burial was relatively simple, including four ceramic vessels and seventy-nine cylindrical and discoidal beads made of white paste (fig. 17). A contemporary tomb from the site of Horom in the neighboring Shirak

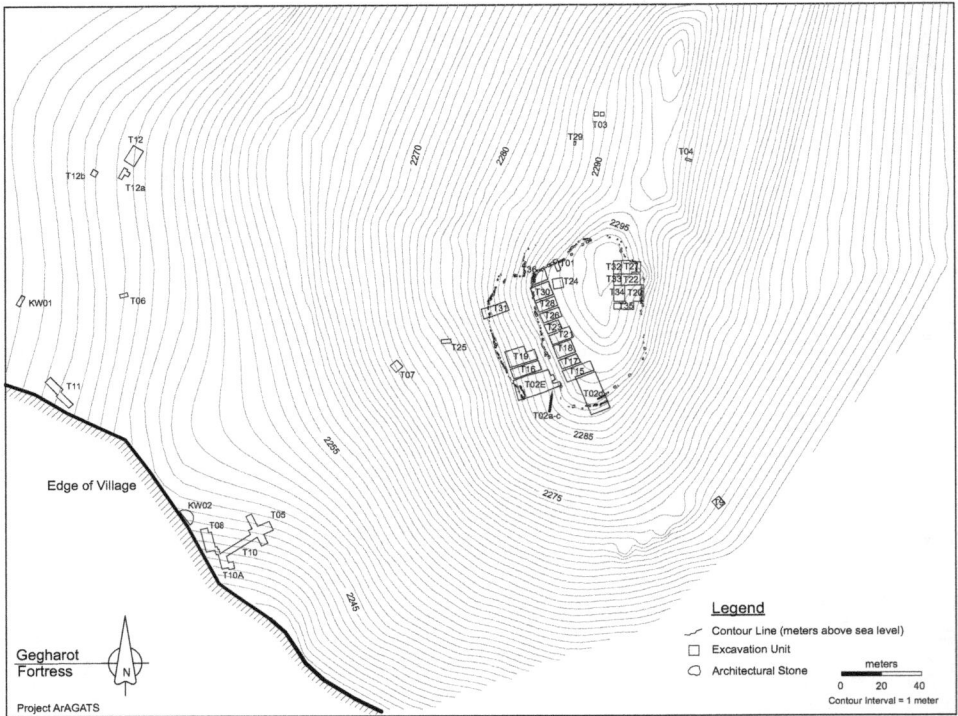

Fig. 14. Plan of Gegharot. (Map Credit: Adam T. Smith.)

Plain contained an almost identical inventory: three individuals, three vessels, and more than fifty beads deposited in a stone-walled mausoleum (Badaljan et al. 1993: 4). At Keti, Landjik, Chkalovka, Kiketi, Samshvilde, Balici-Zezvebi, and Koda, we see very similar small collective tombs with closely analogous artifact repertoires (Mirtskhulava 1975; Petrosyan 1989, 1996; Pkhakadze 1963, 1976). Two qualities of early Kura-Araxes burials warrant particular emphasis: their studied repetition and their relentless egalitarianism both within and across sites.

The residential spaces of the initial Kura-Araxes occupation at Gegharot were impeccably preserved thanks to a terminal conflagration that provoked a hasty abandonment. The best-preserved rooms of this period were found in operations set along the western edge of the summit (fig. 18). Here we uncovered a two-room rectilinear complex bound by single-faced, dry stone masonry walls. The rooms hosted a wide array of domestic activities. A small Kura-Araxes jar containing twenty-one fragments of obsidian deb-

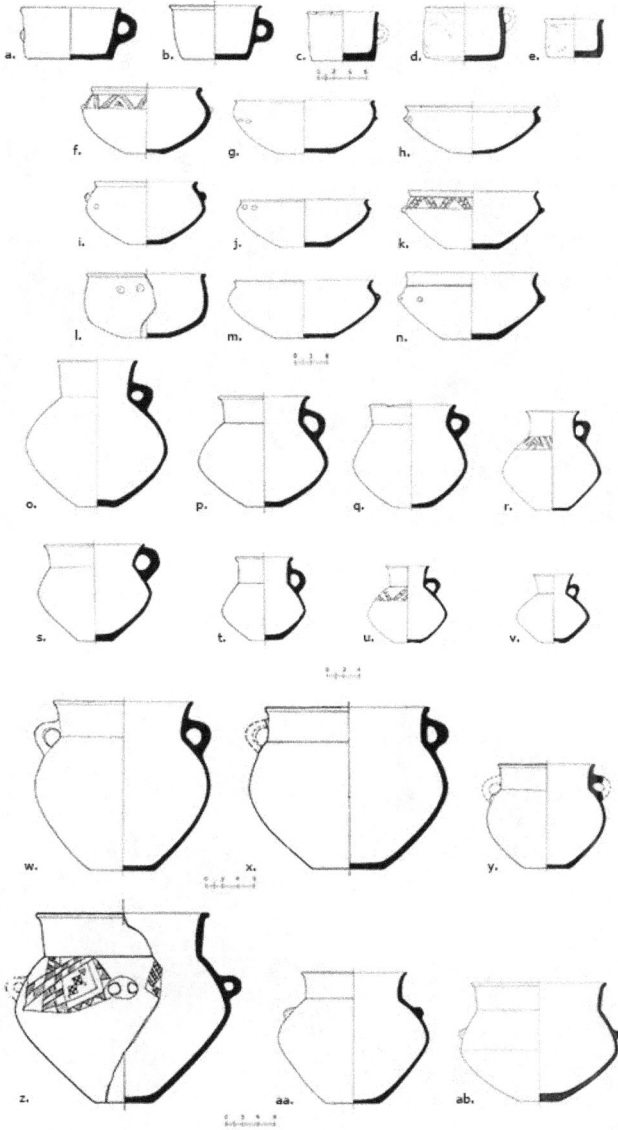

Fig. 15. Kura-Araxes Ceramics: Elar-Aragats group materials from Gegharot. (Source: Smith et al. 2009.)

Fig. 16. Photo of the Kura-Araxes tomb on the West Terrace at Gegharot. View through the dromos (door) of the collective tomb shows the articulated skeleton of the last individual interred. Behind is a pile of disarticulated remains from prior individuals placed in the tomb. (Photo Credit: Adam T. Smith.)

Fig. 17. Ceramic materials from the collective Kura-Araxes tomb on the West Terrace at Gegharot. (Photo Credit: Adam T. Smith.)

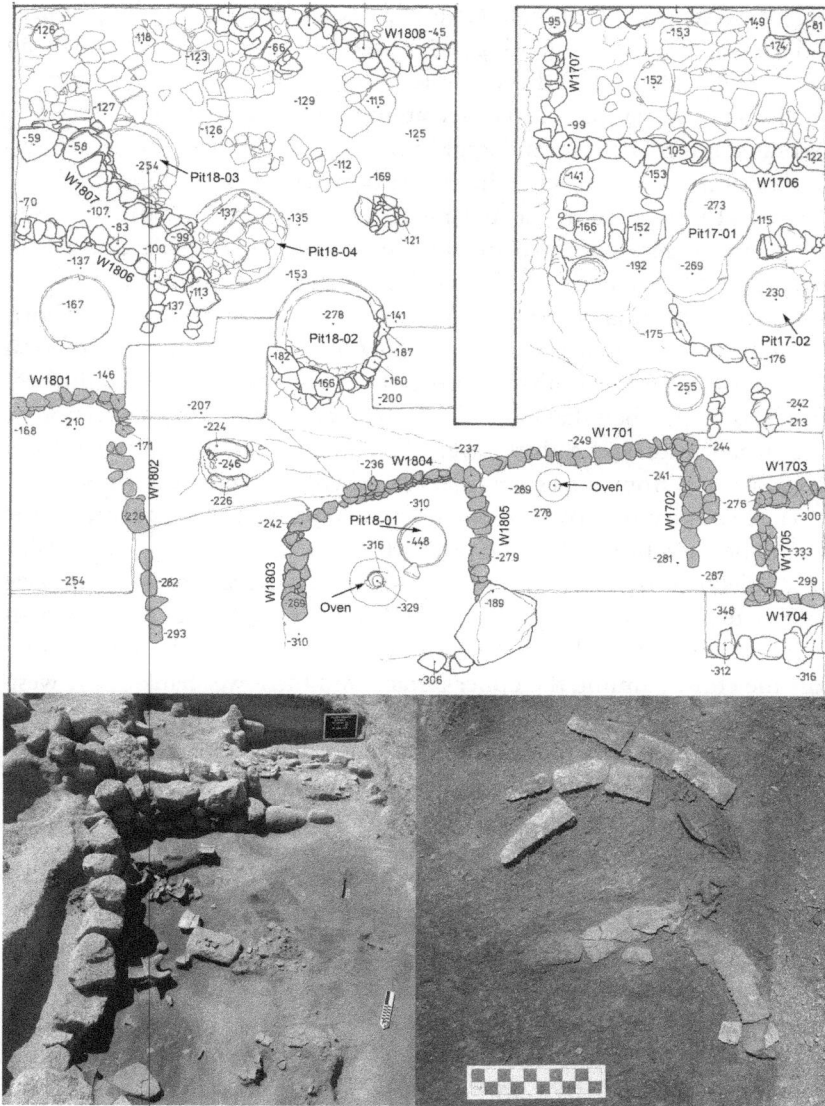

Fig. 18. Plan and photo of T17 and T18 on the West Citadel at Gegharot. Early Bronze Age domestic structures shown in gray in plan. Lower left: T17 room with materials in situ on floor including bronze spear and andiron. Lower right: T18 floor with sickle blades in situ. (Photo Credit: Adam T. Smith; drawing by Hasmik Sarkisyan, courtesy of Project ArAGATS.)

itage suggests stone tool manufacture; a decorated oven, grinding stones, and a range of vessels containing carbonized wheat remains testify to bread baking; clay andirons and a crucible found near a second oven suggest small-scale metalsmithing, an observation reinforced by the discovery of a decorated bronze bracelet and large bronze spearhead. The Gegharot spearhead finds its closest analogies in the period VI A palace complex (building III) and VI B "royal" tomb at Arslantepe (Frangipane et al. 2001: 108, 130). Additional weapons of obsidian and bone suggest hunting played a role in local subsistence, and five in situ sickles composed of thirteen flint blades testify to agricultural production. A large collection of bone spindle whorls and tools indicate domestic textile production, secondary products of local pastoralism. Near the southeast corner of the north room, cut into the bedrock, was a large bell-shaped trash pit that contained a large collection of carbonized seeds and a thick layer of smashed ceramics that included a range of wares from large storage jars to a small semispherical tripod cup.

The blaze that destroyed several residential structures at Gegharot at the end of the Early Bronze I period (ca. 2900 B.C.; see fig. 4) appears to have led to a brief hiatus in occupation. However, the Kura-Araxes assemblage quickly returned to the site during the Early Bronze II (fig. 19). This reoccupation entailed a substantial expansion of the earlier village to encompass the entire summit, the upper terrace, and the lower flank of the western slope. The later Kura-Araxes occupation at Gegharot is marked by "Karnut-Shengavit" ceramics (Smith et al. 2009: 47) with their distinctive belts of geometric ornaments incised on the collars of red-black burnished ware vessels. Gegharot's revitalized occupation established new residential structures on both the citadel and, notably, the western terrace atop the earlier collective tomb (fig. 20). The floor of the room that was built atop the collective tomb was littered with in situ ceramic vessels, including a broken jar neck that appears to have been reused as a pot-stand. Basalt grinding stones, ground-stone tools, and ceramic andirons, including a zoomorphic protome, complete the basic domestic repertoire. On the citadel, the later Kura-Araxes occupation included domestic rooms and extramural courtyards. One courtyard on the southern limit of the citadel yielded a cache of objects that included items typical of the Kura-Araxes assemblage, such as animal figurines of a ram and a bull, and more unique objects, such as a cache of stone, paste, and bronze beads (fig. 21). The tombs associated with this later occupation appear to have been moved down to the base of the hill. To date, we have documented three Early Bronze Age collective tombs of this later Kura-Araxes occupation (in the area denoted as KW02 in

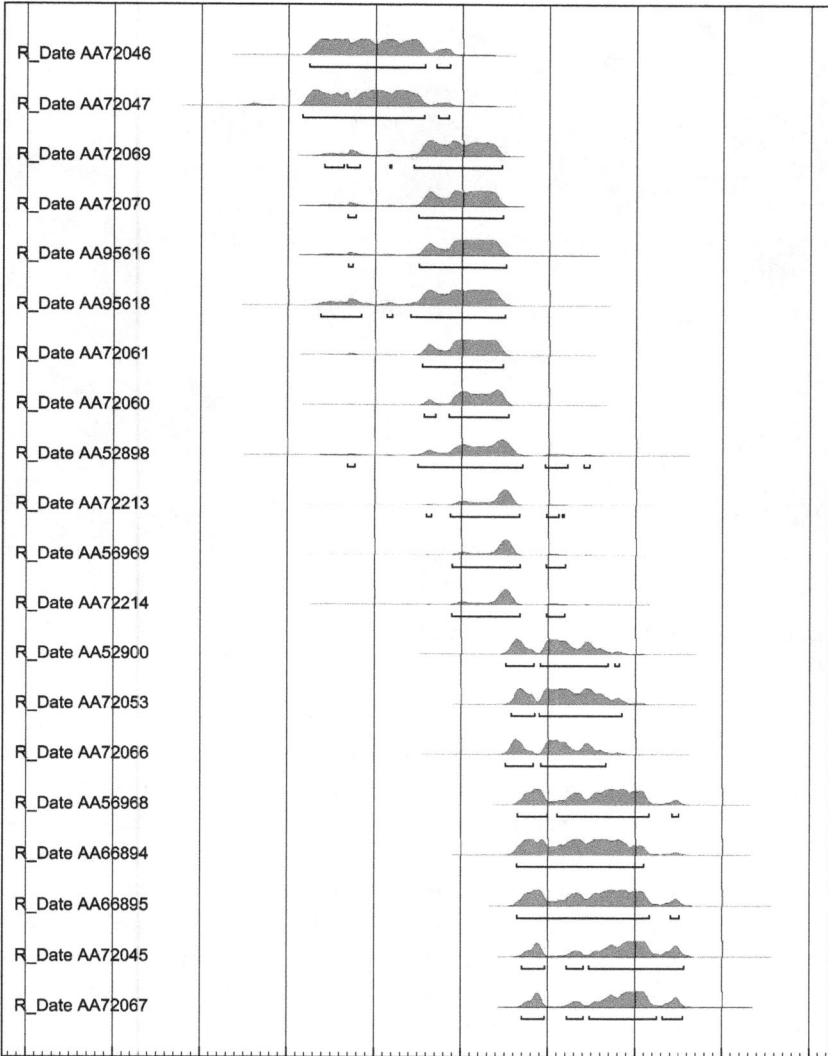

Fig. 19. Multiplot of radiocarbon determinations from the Early Bronze Age occupations at Gegharot. (Figure Credit: Adam T. Smith; data courtesy of Project ArAGATS.)

Fig. 20. Karnut-Shengavit Phase occupation floor on the West Terrace at Gegharot. (Photo Credit: Adam T. Smith.)

fig. 14). All three have been uncovered by modern construction activities along the lower escarpment where the site meets the modern village. As a result, the contents of the tomb were not well preserved, forestalling a census of the interred. However, the dimensions of the construction were largely similar to the earlier tomb discovered on the west terrace, and the surviving assemblage from one tomb—three vessels and a single lid—suggest that the later burials at the site departed little from the earlier model.

The most pervasive sensual quality of the Early Bronze Age assemblage at Gegharot and the Kura-Araxes world more broadly is grounded in its studied domesticity. Although Kura-Araxes homes deployed a range of materials—stone, mud brick, wattle and daub—and there is some variation in house and settlement plans—rectilinear and round, freestanding and agglutinative—the use of domestic space appears to be broadly similar. Hearths and ovens were the primary features, with storage pits or bins and occasionally small niches or benches. As Antonio and Claudia Sagona (2009: 537) have noted, there does not seem to be a rigid differentiation of an explicitly sacred space. Across the Kura-Araxes world, they point out, evidence for

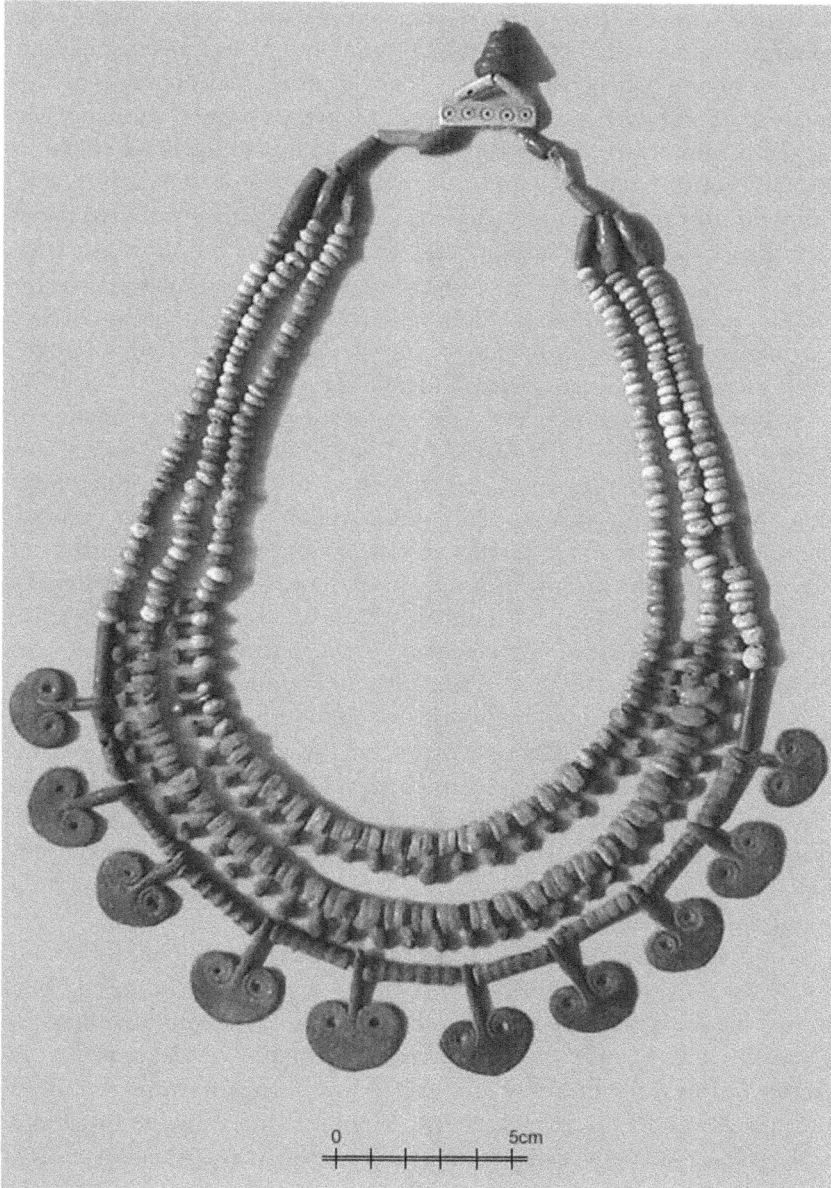

Fig. 21. Bronze and fossil coral bead necklace from late Early Bronze Age occupation at Gegharot. (Photo courtesy of Project ArAGATS; Photo Credit: Adam T. Smith.)

dedicated ritual buildings is, at present, not particularly compelling. Claims to sanctuaries at Pulur (Koşay 1976: 145–46) and Agarak (Avetisyan 2003: 54), for example, generally rest on a single unusual element—hearth or cache of figurines—within a more generally typical domestic assemblage). Gegharot appears to confirm the pattern noted by the Sagonas because we lack any construction that can be unequivocally described as a ritual focal point for the community as a whole, suggesting a highly distributed understanding of divinity and sacrality that was situated within the home itself. As the Sagonas (2009: 547) have cogently concluded, communication with the divine in the Kura-Araxes world involved a discrete material assemblage that embedded devotional ritual in the everyday space of the home, effectively sacralizing domestic spaces and assemblages.

A key material component in Kura-Araxes ritual practice appears to have been the hearth. Early Kura-Araxes hearths were rather homogenous features, circular depressions lined with clay and perforated with a central hole. But by the beginning of the third millennium, we find domestic complexes with decorated hearths, tri-lobed hearths, platform hearths, and a range of andiron forms, including horseshoes with anthropomorphic and zoomorphic protomes. Palumbi (2008: 312) observes that Kura-Araxes hearths became increasingly elaborate as the assemblage spread. At Sos Höyük, the Sagonas (2009: 539) note that herd animal figurines and stone and bone projectile points were scattered around hearths prior to reflooring episodes. Palumbi (2008) speculates that this process of aesthetic elaboration around the hearth reflects the increasing ideological role of animal husbandry in later Kura-Araxes society. I suspect he is broadly correct, but I want to reemphasize that what is critical is not simply the appearance of animal representations and the tools of hunting, but their specific incorporation into the hearth assemblage.

The articulation of the hearth and the flock addressed a key problem of social reproduction in Kura-Araxes societies, namely, how to tightly bind more mobile segments of an agropastoral public to the immobile space of value and divine intercession that was the home? The elaborated Kura-Araxes hearth assemblages accomplished this, I suggest, through a metamorphosis in value: as animals were brought into the house in the form of material representations, they gained a critical role in the ritual practices of domesticity, a phenomenon not unlike that which Ian Hodder (2006) describes at Çatalhöyük. The hearth assemblage helped to ensure social reproduction by reinscribing linkages between the interior of the home and the exterior pastures that tied increasingly far-flung communities to one another. The hearth assemblage thus was neither simply a cooking apparatus nor only a ritual focus of the home, but part of the civilization machine, a material apparatus for reproducing a self-conscious form of solidarity that situated each individual home within the wider ecumene.

When we place the sensual qualities of the Kura-Araxes home and tomb assemblage in the context of the wider early third-millennium Near East, we begin to see a relationship with developments to the south, but it is not the kind of relationship typically envisioned by the cosmopolitan understanding of civilization. Instead of interaction, the Kura-Araxes assemblage worked to repudiate the theory of sovereignty under development to the south in Mesopotamia so famously represented on the Standard of Ur (see chapter 2). Whereas the Mesopotamian public of the late fourth and early third millennium was increasingly segmented, riven by divisions of class, specialization, ethnicity, and urban affiliation reinforced by the aesthetics of distinction and subjection, the highland public was forged by a very different material order. The Kura-Araxes assemblage resisted processes of consolidation vital to the formation of centralizing institutions by tying the sacred to the space of the hearth and home; it forestalled the emergence of hereditary leadership positions and social inequality by collectivizing the deposition of the dead; and it worked against the formation of an apparatus of social distinction by obviating the need for imports across social boundaries.

In this sense, the Kura-Araxes appears to have been a paragon of what Pierre Clastres (1989) termed a "society against the state." Clastres argued that egalitarian communities should not be understood in terms of the absence of the political but rather as a highly developed understanding of sovereignty and its infringements—"the premonition of a socio-economic catastrophe" heralded by the advent of the state (Clastres 1989: 215). If the Kura-Araxes was simply a sphere of underdevelopment vis-á-vis neighbors in Mesopotamia, we would expect to see extensive flows of raw materials out of the highlands and foreign preciosities into the region. We see nothing of the sort. Instead, the sensual dimension of the Kura-Araxes assemblage suggests a palpable aversion to engagement with a Mesopotamian world that was moving headlong into a politics defined by enslavement, violence, and radical inequality. This aversion was developed and reproduced not only in the sense of things—the attachment of social values to assemblages of things tied to hearth and tomb—but also in an ingrained imaginary of how objects did social work. In turning to the imagination of things, we move from the domain of sense to a third point of articulation between humans and assemblages: sentiment.

SENTIMENT

Whereas sense entails the relation of form to value, sentiment describes the imagined capacities of things. This includes not only the sympathetic magic that allows qualities of objects to become qualities of subjects but also the capacities of assemblages to captivate us—to sublimate human action to the operation of material assemblages (see chapter 1). Sentiment hinges upon our imagination of the efficacy of things—the way we conceptualize their ability to intervene in, and transform, social life. If the spread of Kura-Araxes assemblages represented not simply a migration, but a process of conversion made possible by the operation of a civilization machine that secured the reproduction of values of domesticity and egalitarianism, then how did this remarkably compact material assemblage prove so effective in captivating communities across the Caucasus and northern Near East? Here, iconography provides our richest source of understanding.

As I noted earlier, ornamentation is rather rare on ceramics from the initial Kura-Araxes phases of the late fourth millennium. However, the iconographic repertoire of the Kura-Araxes exploded at the beginning of the Early Bronze II phase, around the turn of the millennium, just as the assemblage swamped the Armenian Highland. The new decorative traditions utilized a wider range of ornamental techniques, including incised bands, embossed emblems, and designs applied in relief (Smith et al. 2009: 47–51).

Early Bronze II iconography at Gegharot appears to be broadly similar across ware types, with little evidence for differentiation between jars, beakers, pots, and bowls. Decoration is typically organized in two registers: a band of incised geometric ornament at the base of the collar and a larger embossed or relief composition that extends around 180 to 270 degrees of the body surface (fig. 22). Sagona and Sagona (2009) have categorized Kura-Araxes ornaments into four general groups: random geometric, radial and sunbursts, tunnels and spirals, and composite shapes. To these we should add the more immediately anthropomorphic and zoomorphic representations and the double volute or anchor motif that occurs not only on ceramics but also in bronze (fig. 23).

The Sagonas (2009: 545; 2011: 405ff) have offered the most encompassing interpretation of Kura-Araxes iconography to date, arguing that the forms and figures relate to the trance states of shamanic ritual practitioners enhanced by natural hallucinogenics, such as the fly agaric mushroom. The striking decoration of Kura-Araxes ceramics and the dramatic use of color

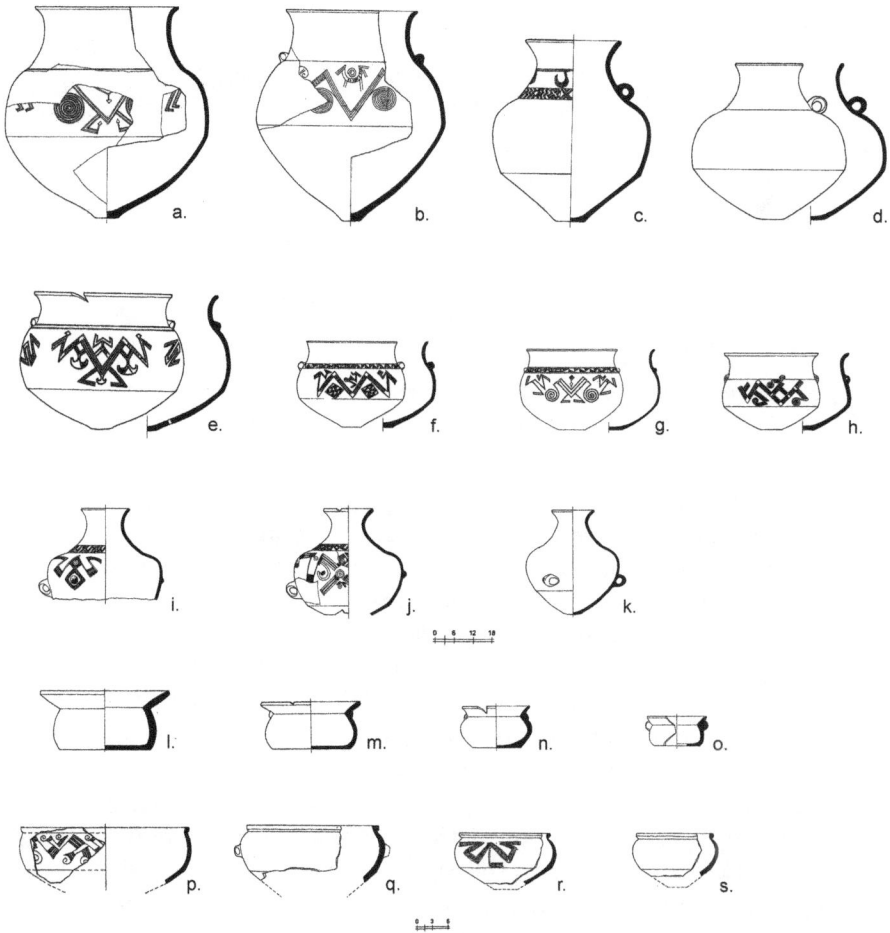

Fig. 22. Kura-Araxes ceramics: Karnut-Shengavit group decorated vessels from Gegharot and related sites: (a–f, i–s) Karnut, (g) Gegharot, (h) Frankanots. (Source: Smith et al. 2009.)

contrasts between lustrous black and red surfaces, they argue, articulated the pyrotechnic technology of ceramic manufacture with shamanic practices involving trance and pharmacologically induced hallucination.

There is much to recommend in the Sagonas' emphasis on the ritual sources of Kura-Araxes iconography. The figural images tend to emphasize the asymmetries of arms and legs akimbo suggestive of dance, and the composite animal forms evoke a rich mythological repertoire. The geometric

Geometric

Spirals

Radials

Anthropomorphs, Zoomorphs & Composites

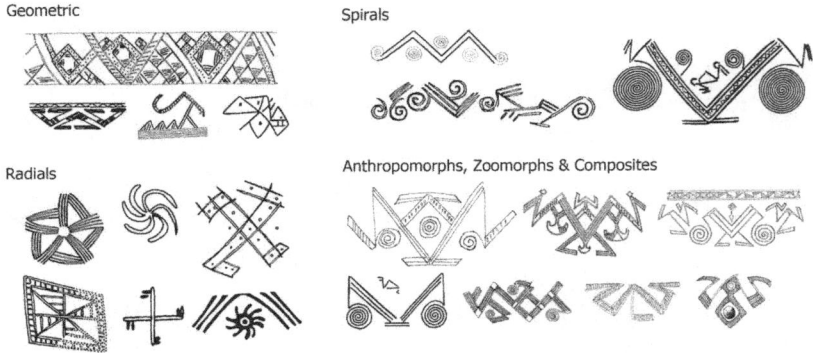

Fig. 23. Kura-Araxes geometric and figural iconographic repertoires. (After Sagona and Sagona 2009.)

bands appear to recall mountain landscapes, thus setting the figures in a specific environment familiar across the ecumene. In extending the Sagonas' argument, it is important to embed these images in the context of the home, where they were prominent elements of the domestic assemblage. At the site of Karnut (Badalyan 1984; Badalyan and Avetisyan 2007: 137–49), for example, an array of images was set on large storage jars placed in the corners of rooms. As elements of everyday life, they embedded a dense symbolic world into the fabric of domestic space.

The captivation of objects entailed in the Kura-Araxes iconographic repertoire is particularly notable in ceramic forms whose efficacy lay in establishing a highly visible symbolic lexicon—objects of publicity that mediated sentiments of captivation. The Sagonas, for example, call attention to a unique set of trays that they suggest were used to prepare hallucinatory substances. We can add to these trays small four-legged stands, such as one recovered from Gegharot (fig. 24a), that do not appear to relate immediately to practices of food preparation or craft manufacture. Still more convincing as media of aesthetic captivation, however, are the ceramic plaques recovered from Gegharot (fig. 24b) and many other Kura-Araxes sites, including Sos Höyük and Güzelova. These decorated panels echo the iconographic repertoire of the ceramic vessels and trays but in a form divorced from the functional apparatus of storage, serving, and preparation. The plaques thus provided a highly portable, and thus potentially exchangeable, medium for not only recording encounters with the divine but also transmitting the proper lexicon of signs for imagining the numinous. They were, in short, critical pedagogical tools of captivation, public media that

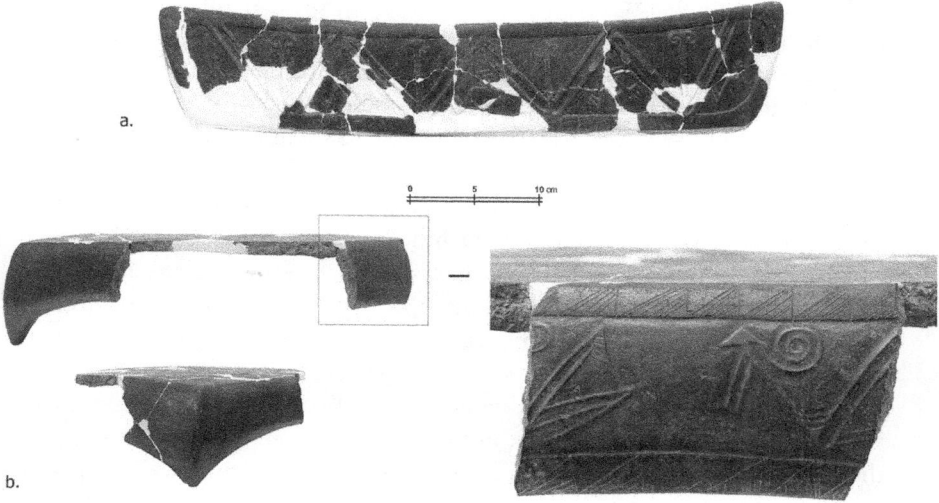

Fig. 24. Kura-Araxes (a) plaque (b) ceramic stand from Gegharot. (After Badalyan et al. in press; photo courtesy of Project ArAGATS.)

shaped and constrained the imagination of the divine, and thus powerful elements in the wider Kura-Araxes civilization machine that bound the highland public.

AN EARLY BRONZE AGE PUBLIC

The Early Bronze Age Kura-Araxes civilization machine was efficacious in at least three respects. First, it established a restricted domain of sensibility where flows within the ecumene were secured while connections to neighboring regions were discouraged or made superfluous. The result was a virtually self-contained repertoire. Second, it reproduced a sense of proper social life centered on the hearth, elevating values of domesticity and precluding the kind of social segmentation that was developing in neighboring regions, a social affirmation of egalitarianism on conspicuous display in the mortuary record. The collective tombs of the Kura-Araxes stand in stark contrast not only to the conspicuous consumption of the royal tombs of Ur and Maikop but also to the more modest tomb assemblages of neighboring regions from Syria (Schwartz 1986) to the Eurasian Steppe (e.g., Yamnaya, Novosvobodnaya, and Novotitorovskaya kurgans [Anthony

2007: 312, 332]). Third, the Kura-Araxes civilization machine disciplined the imagination of the divine, providing a shared iconography that constituted a common visual repertoire for understanding the numinous. This machine, in other words, accomplished the fundamental work of reproducing a civilization—a self-conscious set of networks, values, and worldviews publicized by a distinctive material assemblage.

By the time the Kura-Araxes world began to fray in the second half of the third millennium, the civilization machine had reproduced a remarkably consistent assemblage through highly dispersed locations of production for almost a thousand years. As southern Mesopotamia's colonial project waxed and waned, as rival dynasties of Sumer slaughtered one another in a quest for suzerainty, life in Kura-Araxes villages proceeded largely uninterrupted by autocracy or organized violence. The Kura-Araxes ecumene was not an underdeveloped backwater but a vibrant alternative cultural pole to the radical, in many senses horrific, transformations in human sociopolitical life gripping regions to the south in the places typically described as "civilized." And it was an alternative form of sociality that proved singularly enduring.

We would be hard-pressed to suggest that the spread and durability of the Kura-Araxes phenomenon were products of human will or design. Its expansion and reproduction was not the result of an imperial strategy or hegemonic program. The communities of the late fourth-millennium South Caucasus surely did not have an expansive material program in mind when they developed the Kura-Araxes assemblage. Yet the highland ecumene was indeed drawn together, guarded, and reproduced over almost a millennium. The efficacy of the machine lies in exactly this form of historical reproduction. Ironically, however, the Kura-Araxes civilization machine also set in motion processes that would ultimately draw the Caucasus into a political order of sovereign power. The public manufactured by the civilization machine was open to mobilization and subject to competing claims that would come to undermine the coherence of the whole. But this work of segmenting the public, of dividing it against itself, is not embedded in the logic of a civilization machine. Instead, it reflects the operation of a different kind of machine, what I will call a war machine, whose development during the Middle Bronze Age is the subject of the next chapter.

The War Machine in the Middle Bronze Age

As for the War Machine in itself, it seems to be irreducible to the State
apparatus, to be outside its sovereignty and prior to its law: it comes
from elsewhere.

(Deleuze and Guattari 1986: 2)

At the height of Italy's medieval communes, the painter Ambrogio Lorenzetti was commissioned to decorate Siena's Sala dei Nove, the private coun-
cil chamber of the Nine Governors and Defenders of the Commune and
the People (Starn 1994: 1), with an allegorical mural cycle on good and bad
governance (fig. 25). In one pair of images, we see the malevolent figure of
Tyranny—portrayed with braided locks, goat horns, and a chalice in her left
hand—presiding over a court of vices: Fraud, Treason, and Cruelty to her
right; Furor, Division, and War to her left. Justice lies bound at her feet
while Avarice, Vainglory, and Pride gaze down from above. The adjacent
cityscape reveals the consequences of tyrannical rule: a closed city beset by
violence, watched over by Fear. The second image pair, covering the north
and east walls, depicts good governance and its effects. The city and countryside shown on the eastern wall are safe, prosperous, and happy. Dancers
at the center of the city celebrate the fecundity of the countryside that flows
unimpeded into the stalls of the market. The scene is observed by the figure
of Peace on the adjacent northern wall. She reclines on the end of a couch,
her suit of armor neatly put away, as part of an ensemble of civic virtues that
flank an outsized figure with a white beard, holding a scepter and rope in
his right hand and a shield in his left. Magnanimity, Temperance, and Justice sit on his left; Prudence, Fortitude, and Peace on his right. Faith, Hope,
and Charity gaze down on the assembly from above.

Interpretations of Lorenzetti's understanding of just governance have
generally centered on the bearded figure at the center of the ensemble of
civic virtues. This figure has variously been interpreted as an image of "the

Fig. 25. Ambrogio Lorenzetti, *Allegory of Good and Bad Government*, Sala dei Nove, Sienna, Italy. Above: Good government; below: Tyranny enthroned. (Photo Credit: Scala/Art Resource.)

Aristotelian concept of the common good" (Rubinstein 1958: 184) and as a depiction of the kind of ruler required "if the dictates of justice are to be followed and the common good secured" (Skinner 1999: 10). However, what makes the figure so distinct from the personification of tyranny is his articulation with the clusters of figures below him. The rope that he holds in his hand originates on the far left side of the mural, where Justice is enthroned with scales that balance winged figures representing the Aristotelian subcategories of commutative and distributive justice. Below her, Concord, with a carpenter's plane in her lap for smoothing discord, joins together threads from both scales, passing the entwined rope along to the twenty-four representatives of the *populo grasso*, Medieval Sienna's elite citizenry from which the nine governors were elected. The rope then rises to the right hand of a hirsute personification of sovereignty, underscoring the argument of the allegory as a whole that good governance emerges out of the bond between rulers and ruled.

This affirmation of the solidarity of the civil community is made explicit in the inscription below the *populo grasso*:

> Wherever this holy virtue of Justice rules
> She induces many souls to unity
> And those brought together in this way
> Create through their *signor* [sovereign] a common good for themselves.[8]

Although Lorenzetti's images on the walls of the Sala dei Nove are often referred to as the war and peace murals because of the scenes of chaos that accompany Tyranny (e.g., Polzer 2002), the rule of the *signor* is not bloodless. Good governance deploys two forms of violence, anticipating Agamben's (1998: 39) account of sovereign power (see introduction): the constituted violence of law in the upper left, where a servant of Justice beheads a man, and the constituting violence of martial force in the lower right, where soldiers and cavalry parade captured enemies of the commune. The weapons of martial and legal violence thus bracket the rope that binds the political community together, forming a political assemblage that at once separates the sovereign from the body politic and reaffirms his tie to it. What marks tyranny is not simply the presence of vice but the absence of the tie that articulates the one to the many. Good governance, in contrast, emerges not simply in the assembly of an array of virtues around an elevated figure of rule, but in an apparatus that simultaneously severs the sov-

---

[8] Translation in Skinner 2002: 99. My rendering of *signor* is in brackets; however, this term might also be translated as "lord," "lordly power," or, as Skinner prefers, "supreme judge" (100).

ereign body from the rest of the social community while also drawing it back in to reproduce the solidarity of the polity. Lorenzetti's murals thus illustrate the machinery behind what political theorists have long referred to as the *aporia* of the one and the many, the puzzling unity of communities predicated on difference and segmentation.

As we saw in the previous chapter, publics can and have been powerfully, and enduringly, reproduced on a significant scale without radical segmentation thanks to the operations of the civilization machine. Hence, the production of the "one" from the "many," the cutting of the social body into discrete components, must be accomplished elsewhere, in another apparatus that, in its most basic operation, works to reproduce the separation of sovereign from subjects. As an instrument of social cleavage, this machine is fundamentally an apparatus of both real and symbolic violence, capable of dissecting the social body reproduced by the civilization machine without undermining its coherence. Deleuze and Guattari (1986) have termed this assemblage "the war machine."

The war machine lies outside the state apparatus, assembled by those that Deleuze and Guattari (1986: 50ff) refer to enigmatically as "the nomads". The qualities of the war machine, they argue, were initially formulated in contradistinction to the regimented rationality of centralizing institutions. Where the emergent state invests in sedentarization, the war machine of the nomad is a vagabond that uses speed and violence to mobilize and dissect its public. The early polity, they argue, had no war machine of its own but instead appropriated it from those on its margins. Through this appropriation, the smooth space of the nomad was transformed into the striated territory of the sovereign imperium (Deleuze and Guattari 1986: 14–15; cf. Clastres 1989). The close articulation of mobility and violence in the apparatus of Deleuze and Guattari's war machine bears an uncanny resemblance to the situation in the Caucasus during the Middle Bronze Age, so let us return to the region at the moment when the civilization machine of the Kura-Araxes fell into crisis.

THE CAUCASUS IN TRANSITION

We left the Caucasus at the end of the last chapter during the final phase of the Early Bronze Age, a moment of significant historical transition. The beginning of the Middle Bronze Age is marked by the formation of a radically new social order across the Kura-Araxes world. In the South Caucasus, this new era was heralded by the widespread abandonment of settled villages and the appearance of a new highly mobile way of life. As far as we now know, it appears that this transformation began sometime around 2600 B.C., when the public assembled by the Kura-Araxes civilization machine began to unravel as communities across the region abandoned the villages that they had occupied for centuries. New material forms and aesthetics in media as diverse as ceramic, metal, and stone replaced long-held traditions (Aliev 1991; Kushnareva 1997; Kushnareva and Markovin 1994: Rubinson 1977, 2005). And new tumulus graves, known as kurgans, erupted across the South Caucasus, replacing the traditional collective crypts of the Early Bronze Age.

At Gegharot, in central Armenia's Tsaghkahovit Plain, the end of the Kura-Araxes occupation appears to have been rather hurried (Badalyan et al. 2008, in press). Excavations of room complexes of the late Early Bronze Age from across the site revealed domestic contexts with extensive in situ remains, including floors littered with complete pots, jars, andirons, ovens, and hearths. In addition, other Kura-Araxes settlements in the Tsaghkahovit Plain appear to have been abandoned at the same time, including what appears to have been a sizable contemporary village at Aragatsiberd (fig. 13; Greene 2013). The abandonment of the Tsaghkahovit Plain during the twenty-sixth century B.C. marked the beginning of a thousand-year hiatus in substantial human occupation of the region. The breakdown in regional settlement patterns at the end of the Early Bronze Age is not unique to the Tsaghkahovit Plain. Kura-Araxes sites across the South Caucasus were suddenly abandoned (see Kushnareva 1997: 81), leaving an archaeological landscape composed primarily of mortuary sites anchored by only a small handful of dispersed, often ephemeral, settlements (fig. 26).

The causes behind the abandonment of villages like Gegharot and the breakdown of the Kura-Araxes civilization machine more broadly are not well understood, but two principal theories predominate. The first looks to transformations in local ecology and the productive economy. Pavel Dolukhanov and Gregory Areshian have both argued that the desiccation of local environments from forest clearance and soil salinization undermined the carrying capacity of Kura-Araxes dry-farming practices. However, the collapse of the Kura-Araxes does not appear to be synchronized with a known phase of widespread aridization, nor do we have a palynological record that might attest to extensive forest clearance. Indeed, the rather restricted scale of bronze production in the Early Bronze Age Caucasus suggests that demands upon forests for fuel would not have been exorbitant.

A second, more convincing, account of the Kura-Araxes collapse looks to evidence for the arrival of new populations in the region. Half a century

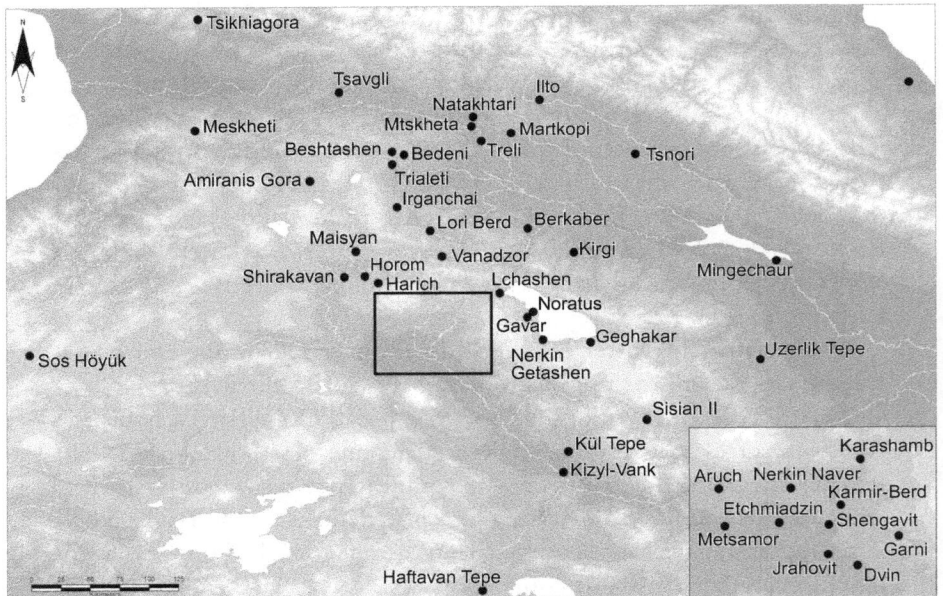

Fig. 26. Major Middle Bronze Age archaeological sites in the South Caucasus. (Map Credit: Adam T. Smith.)

ago, Giorgi Melikishvili (1965; Puturidze 2003: 114) argued that the lack of unambiguous material links between Kura-Araxes and succeeding "Early Kurgans" phase (fig. 4) assemblages indicates the arrival of a new population, one which he assumed arrived as migrants from the south. However, based on parallels between kurgan assemblages from the North Caucasus, Kohl (2007: 119) has perceptively argued that the evident material rupture between Kura-Araxes and later traditions was more likely the result of an influx of cattle-herding pastoralists from the southern Eurasian steppe. Kohl (2007: 121) suggests that a process of hybridization followed the arrival of the new migrants, visible in the mixed, or perhaps better "entangled" (Hodder 2012), material assemblages of the earliest kurgan burials.[9]

The most conspicuous evidence for the entanglement of material traditions during the transition from the Early to Middle Bronze Age comes

---

[9] Kohl's (2007) understanding of hybridization is a straightforwardly material one, referring to the admixture of features from previously distinct traditions to form new morphological and decorative styles (cf. Bhabha 1994).

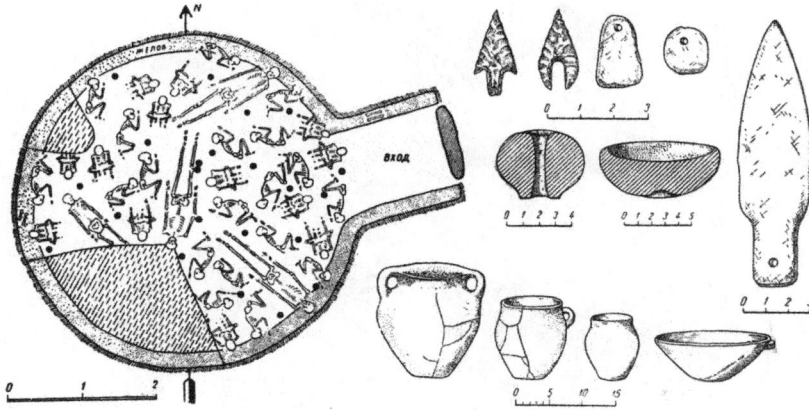

Fig. 27. Plan of kurgan number 119 at Stepanakert. (After Gummel 1948.)

from kurgan number 119 at Stepanakert (Gummel 1939, 1948), where the conjoining of the new burial form with an earlier practice of collective burial was reinforced by an assemblage that mixed distinctly Early and Middle Bronze Age elements (fig. 27). Although partially destroyed, the kurgan contained at least forty to forty-five intact skeletons of both adults and children. Most had been interred in a flexed position on their side with hands raised to the face. But four individuals, including one beneath the center of the mound, were laid out in an extended position on their backs. Next to the central skeleton was a mace, a dagger, and two mortars. The other three extended skeletons were complemented by "arrowheads, spindle whorls, beads covered with gold foil, and stone pendants" (Kushnareva 1997: 228). What is most compelling about the Stepanakert kurgan (and a similar collective tomb from Tkviavi [Makalatiya 1943]) is the conjoining of traditional Kura-Araxes traditions of collective burial to new practices that emphasized the social distinction of a small group of individuals. Nevertheless, the transitional era of hybridization in the South Caucasus appears to have been relatively short-lived.[10] By 2200 B.C. or so, the faint lingering traces of the Kura-Araxes material world in this region had disappeared.

The contrast between the material assemblages of the late Early and initial Middle Bronze Ages in the South Caucasus is simply startling. Take for example a typical terminal Early Bronze Age burial from the upper level at

[10] But see Sagona (2000: 340) for suggestions that "vestigial" Kura-Araxes traditions lingered well into the second millennium at the site of Sos Höyük.

Fig. 28. Burial from the upper level at Shengavit. (Source: Sardaryan 1967. Reproduced courtesy of the Institute of Archaeology and Ethnography, Republic of Armenia)

the site of Shengavit (fig. 28; Sardaryan 1967). It bears all the hallmarks of the Kura-Araxes civilization machine—collectivism in the array of scattered skeletal material and egalitarianism in the studiously limited mortuary assemblage. Contrast that interment with kurgan number 1 from the Tsnori group in the Alazan valley of eastern Georgia (Dedabrishvili 1979), one of the earliest of the Early Kurgans (fig. 29a). The mound of the kurgan covered more than 3 hectares, an area Kohl (2007: 114) points out was larger than most Kura-Araxes villages. The oval mound was 168 meters long, 136 meters wide, and more than 11 meters high. More than 51,000 cubic meters of earth and 8,000 cubic meters of stone went into the mound's construction. Evgenii Chernykh (1992: 101) estimates that the kurgan demanded 23,000 person/days of labor. Below the center of the mound was a cobble embankment, 80 meters in diameter and 2 meters thick, that covered the remains of a 166-square-meter burial chamber, 3 meters deep, constructed of thick beams supporting a wooden roof covered by a large rug. In the center of the chamber was a huge wooden funeral bed upon which lay the principal interred. Although robbed soon after its construction, the tomb appears to have included ceramic vessels, bronze weapons, gold ornaments, and the bodies of several human sacrifices.

The burial chamber of kurgan 2 at Tsnori, found just over half a kilometer from number 1, was slightly smaller, just 100 square meters and 2.5 meters deep, but it was intact and so provides a more complete sense of the

Fig. 29. Middle Bronze Age kurgans at Tsnori: (a) general view of kurgan 1, (b) gold lion from kurgan 2, (c–g) ceramics from kurgan 2, (h, i) the burial chamber of kurgan 2. (After Dedabrishvili 1979.)

earliest kurgans (fig. 29h, i). In the center of the pit was a large four-wheeled wagon, loaded with part of a funerary assemblage that included about forty ceramic vessels (e.g., fig. 29c–g), a plate, obsidian arrowheads, a leather shield with bronze umbo, and assorted objects of gold, including a lion figurine (fig. 29b). Amidst the conspicuous accumulation of wealth were two bodies. Near the center of the chamber was an adult male approximately forty years of age adorned with gold and silver jewelry, including beads, bracelets, and a pin. Off to one side was the skeleton of a female, approximately thirty years of age, who the excavators suggest was sacrificed as one more part of the funerary assemblage.

The contrast between the Shengavit crypts and the earliest kurgans, such as those at Tsnori, and similar finds from Bedeni and Martkopi (Dzhaparidze 1993, 1998; Puturidze 2003) could not be starker. In place of the studied egalitarianism of Kura-Araxes mortuary ritual, we find a material apparatus of political violence dedicated to the manufacture of social distinction—the conspicuous consumption of wealth, the monopolization of collective labor, the valorization of singular individual bodies, and their emplacement within a material framework newly populated by arms and armament. This apparatus proves quite consistent throughout the Middle Bronze Age (Esaian 1966; Picchelauri 1997).

By the last century of the third millennium, the localized variability of ceramic assemblages that underlay the Early Kurgans complexes yielded to a more homogenous regional assemblage that defines the Middle Bronze II phase (Smith et al 2009: 55ff). The advent of this so-called Trialeti-Vanadzor complex marks not only a new archaeological phase but also a resurgence in the region's civilization machine, defined by a new regionally distributed material assemblage, that reinstated traditional aspirations to coherence across the South Caucasus. Initial Trialeti-Vanadzor ceramic styles appear to have developed as an elaboration of Early Kurgans antecedents (fig. 30a–c; Dzhaparidze 1994; Kushnareva 1994a). Subsequently, however, Trialeti-Vanadzor ceramics developed into new painted wares with an original decorative lexicon composed of loops, chevrons, and zoomorphs rendered in black or brown on black, brown, and red-slipped surfaces (fig. 30d–f). Trialeti-Vanadzor ceramics were widely distributed across the highland South Caucasus, in tombs both great and small and in the few known occupation sites. Moreover, these wares were folded into a larger assemblage that reflected broadly shared technological and aesthetic practices, suggesting that, by the last century of the third millennium, a rebuilt civilization machine had reconstituted itself as a material apparatus for reproducing a broad sense of a coherent public.

Paradoxically, however, the revived civilization machine of the Middle Bronze Age and its newly configured public emerged alongside the new material apparatus dedicated to social segmentation and violence. This apparatus, a war machine dedicated most fundamentally to sustaining forms of violence, reproduced new sensibilities of social segmentation, new sentiments of subjection, and new senses of distinction that enabled the sustained reproduction of an emergent, charismatic form of sovereignty.

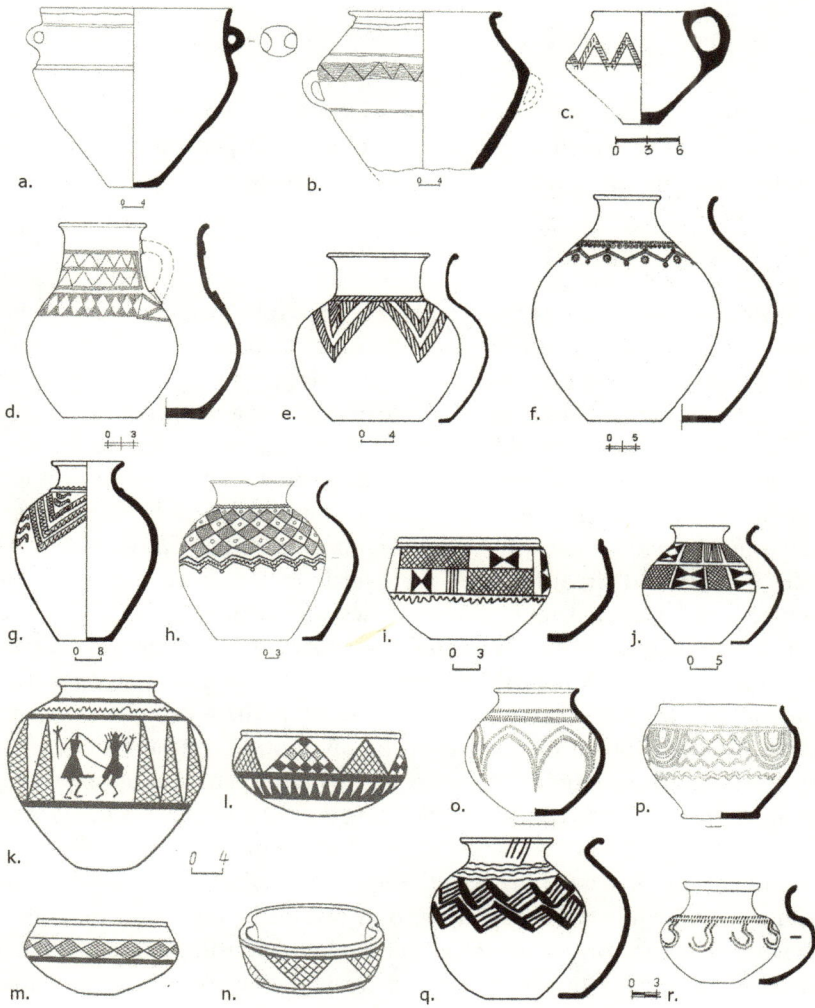

Fig. 30. Ceramic traditions of the Middle Bronze Age: (a–c) Early Kurgans, (d–f) Trialeti-Vanadzor 1, (g, h) Trialeti-Vanadzor 2, (i, j) Karmir Berd, (k–n) Karmir Vank, (o–r) Sevan-Uzerlik. (After Smith et al. 2009.)

SENSIBILITY

Let me begin to describe the operation of the war machine in the domain of sensibility, the dimension of human–object engagement most closely tied to the formal and material qualities of assemblages.

Flows

As I noted in the previous chapter, despite the rapid dissemination of the Kura-Araxes assemblage during the late fourth and early third millennia and the breadth of territory it ultimately enveloped, a rigorous policing of social boundaries ensured that very little material flowed either into or out of the ecumene. The assemblages of the Kura-Araxes entailed very little, which is to say they made few demands upon wider exchange networks for significant movements of goods. Material flows in the Early Bronze Age were thus defined by a relatively self-contained domestic economy, a symbolically powerful ritual focus on the hearth, and a severe restriction on connections across civilizational boundaries (see chapter 3).

The Middle Bronze Age, in contrast, was marked by a relentless flow of things and people. The dearth of long-term settlements and the considerable number of ephemeral occupation surfaces (perhaps campsites) dating to the Middle Bronze Age testifies to highly mobile communities predicated on pastoral economies that were, for the most part, in motion. An expansive apparatus dedicated to reproducing flows made this relentless mobility possible. The grand tombs of the Early Kurgans phase provide a glimmer of this new assemblage, with the interred lying atop wagons set on solid wheels. However, the wagon was only one element in a diverse assemblage that centered on the movement of humans and things. By the second phase of the Middle Bronze Age, the increasingly diverse field of two- and four-wheeled vehicles interred in the largest kurgans of the Trialeti-Vanadzor complexes was joined by the sacrificed bodies of draught animals, including oxen and horses. Moreover, burials from sites such as Trialeti (group II; Gogadze 1972), Lori-Berd (Devedjian 1981), and Aruch (Areshian et al. 1977) all testify to a material apparatus that was impossible absent large-scale flows of raw materials—animals, wood, textiles, bronze, gold, silver, ceramics, obsidian, carnelian, shell—and finished products—carpets, weapons, tools, vessels, milk, meat—all as a condition of sociopolitical reproduction. In one sense, these flows were quite prosaic, sociotechnical entailments demanded by the sensible qualities of things: weapons require furnaces and forges, molds and hammers, ores and alloys. But in another sense, the flow of materials across the Middle Bronze Age Caucasus was regionally unprecedented in its scale and diversity (Rubinson 1976: 227–28; Shanshashvili et al. 2010). The most conspicuous of the entailed flows was undoubtedly the influx of tin into the region beginning in the initial Middle Bronze Age.

In general, tin bronzes appear in only limited quantities in late Kura-Araxes contexts, such as those recovered from the early to mid-third-millennium collective catacomb tombs at Velikent in Dagestan (Kohl 2003: 18). The initial phases of the Middle Bronze Age, in contrast, witnessed a significant increase in the proportion of bronzes utilizing tin as a key ingredient in an increasingly complex set of bronze "recipes" (Chernykh 1992: 106). At present, despite the wide variety of ore bodies in the Caucasus (Courcier 2010), there are no known native tin sources in the region, so its appearance in Middle Bronze Age metalwork can only be the result of exchange (Abramishvili 2010).[11] Indeed, the introduction of tin at a significant scale during the initial Early Kurgans phase is a key marker of the breakdown of the rigidly enforced boundaries of the Kura-Araxes. The new tin bronzes appeared in kurgans across the South Caucasus during the initial phases of the Middle Bronze Age, including burials at Martkopi, Tsnori, Stepanakert, Sachkhere, Trialeti, and Vanadzor (Kirovakan) (Chernykh 1992: 107ff). Moreover, the repertoire of tin-alloyed items was quite broad, including personal adornments, tools, and, most indelibly, weapons.

The armaments of the Middle Bronze Age included a truly fearsome array of devices, from rapiers and daggers to socketed spears and axes—items that were either rare or unknown in Kura-Araxes assemblages. As demand for weaponry increased amidst the growing violence of the era so too, apparently, did the demand for tin, which provided greater rigidity than arsenic-copper or even arsenic-tin-copper alloys. Kavtaradze (1999:84) notes a general increase in the proportion of tin included in Early Kurgans phase alloys, rising from roughly 1 to 5 percent in bronzes from initial Middle Bronze contexts, such as the Martkopi kurgans, to 8 to 15 percent in the slightly later Bedeni kurgans. Tin alloys also prevail in the second phase of the Middle Bronze Age, with tin content generally ranging from 4 to 14 percent (Kavtaradze 1999:85). However, there are also signs that tin resources came under local pressure as demand surged.

By the early second millennium, metalsmiths in western Caucasia appear to have begun exploiting local antimony ores to create copper-arsenic-

---

[11] For a discussion of possible tin sources, see Boroffka et al. 2002.

antimony alloys for cultic items and personal adornments, presumably allowing the available tin to be reserved for weapons and tools (Chernykh 1992: 113; Kavtaradze 1999: 86–87). Although this shift appears likely to have been a widespread response to shortages in imported tin, the metal-production process itself appears to have been highly dispersed. Chernykh argues, based on variation in alloy recipes and smithing techniques, that a large number of workshops were involved in bronze production during the Middle Bronze Age, each with distinctive casting and forging methods. What does seem apparent from the negative evidence of undocumented settlements is that some of these workshops must have been mobile, moving alongside the flows of people and things across the transhumant routes of the South Caucasus. Hence, key forms of transubstantiation—the alteration of material states, including ore into metal and metal into goods—took place within, rather than outside of, the wider flow of people and things.

Although evidence for the flow of South Caucasian materials outward is not robust, local obsidians have been documented in assemblages from contemporary late third- and early second-millennium sites from southern Iran (e.g., Tal-i Malyan) to western Anatolia (Badalyan et al. 2004b: 464). It is possible that much of what was moving out of the Caucasus within economic relations of exchange were items such as textiles, horses, pastoral animals and products that would be difficult to detect or track archaeologically. Flows of materials from neighboring regions into the Caucasus were certainly more extensive than in the Early Bronze Age. Finds of necklaces with shell beads made from sea molluscs native to the Persian Gulf testify to far-reaching exchange ties, even though they give us little to go on in estimating the scale of trade (Kavtaradze 2004: 549). Although the evidence for interregional long-distance trade is at present underdeveloped, it is nevertheless apparent that a sizable assemblage was indeed moving out of Middle Bronze Age communities: not into the profane network of economic exchange but into the sacred world mediated by tomb and grave assemblage.

The kurgan field at Trialeti, the best studied of the Middle Bronze Age mortuary complexes, appears to have been constructed as a grand highway linking this world to the next (Dzhaparidze 1969; Gogadze 1972; Kuftin 1941; Rubinson 1976). Goderzi Narimanishvili (2003) has documented a series of straight, broad, cobblestone roads that lead to the eastern gate of the largest kurgans (fig. 31). These roads varied in size, but the largest were more than 350 meters long and up to 6 meters wide. The paths are traditionally described as processional ways, routes taken by the community of

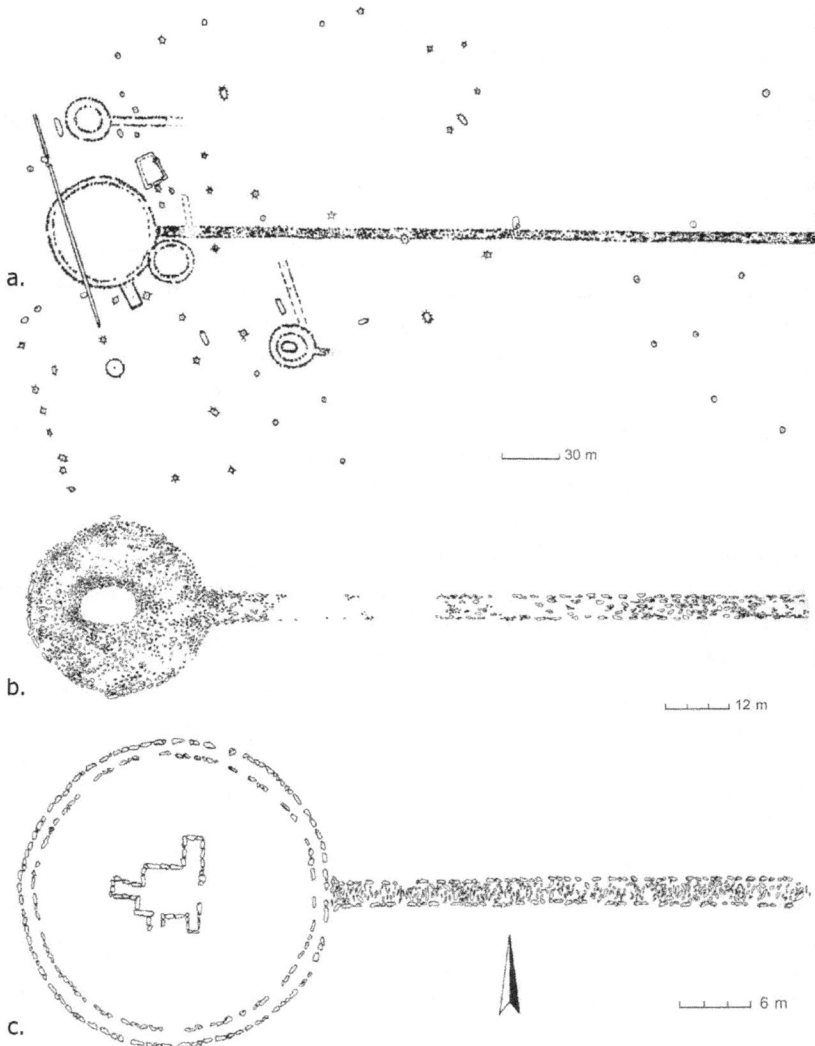

Fig. 31. Kurgans at Trialeti and their "ritual roads": (a) kurgan 47, (b) kurgan 17, (c) kurgan 3. (After Narimanishvili 2003.)

mourners during rituals of interment. However, the processional ways not only lead toward the kurgan, but also away from it. Indeed, it is not clear from the available evidence that the routes consistently lead to the dromos, or doorway, of the kurgan. The most consistent dimension of the pathways is that they radiate due east from the kurgan. Although we lack historical or even ethnohistoric data that might frame the significance of east–west orientations, it is nonetheless no less plausible to understand the Trialeti roads as egresses from this world to the next than as processional ways for grave rites. Whether entries or exits, the roads, wagons, and draft animals that were elements in many kurgan assemblages do suggest that the tomb was not intended to be a terminus but rather simply another way station in the continuing flow of things and bodies.

It is critical to note that the materials that flowed between this world and the next were highly asymmetric in their distribution across Middle Bronze Age mortuary assemblages. Marina Puturidze (2003: 126) has identified four major social groups interred in Trialeti-era kurgans that are distinguished by significant differences in grave goods. Roads, wagons, and draught animals, for example, appear only in a small subset of tombs of the upper social strata. In developing a sociological account of Trialeti mortuary practice, we should not lose sight of the role of things in meditating ties between the earthly and the otherworldly. By drawing earthly objects into the world of the sacred, the tomb assemblages from Trialeti and similar Middle Bronze Age complexes extended distinction from this world into the next, naturalizing inequality in reference to the fundamental order of things. The kurgan assemblages thus turned an earthly machinery for the reproduction of social difference into a cosmic order that pulled emergent sovereigns away from the Middle Bronze Age public and into the transcendent sphere of the deities. In Agamben's (1998) terms, such a shift would have been critical to combining a constituted power to deploy ordered violence with a constituting power to define exceptions.

Transubstantiation

The material flows of the Middle Bronze Age war machine promulgated key transubstantiations in objects as they entered and left assemblages from the loom to the smithy. But the most fundamental transubstantiation at work in the war machine attended the production of a significant new arsenal of stone and bronze weapons. Bronze weaponry typically receives the most attention, but the shift in the nature of socially deployed violence is arguably most emblematically visible in the understudied lithic assemblage of the Middle Bronze Age. Early Bronze Age projectile points were generally made of obsidian, with a straight stem beneath a triangular blade (fig. 32a). This form was repeated in both arrow and spearheads (Picchelauri 1997). In contrast, Middle Bronze Age projectile points were significantly smaller and lanceolate in shape, having a bifurcated auriculated base with

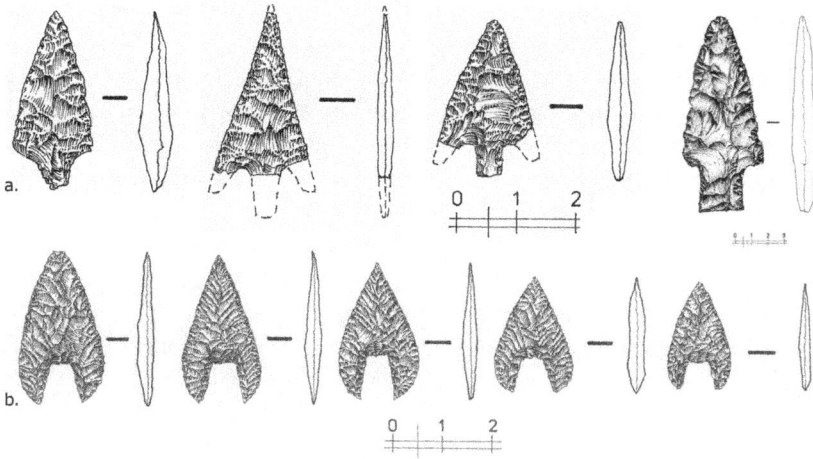

Fig. 32. Obsidian projectile point traditions of the (a) Early Bronze Age (Gegharot) and (b) Middle and Late Bronze Age (Gegharot kurgans). (courtesy of Project ArAGATS.)

sharpened barbs (fig. 32b). Considerably more research is certainly warranted into the technological properties of the two forms, but there appear to be three fundamental physical properties of the Middle Bronze Age obsidian point that contrast with Early Bronze Age antecedents.

First, it was open for mass production because it demanded far less raw material, skill, and time in production than earlier projectile points. As a result, these small stone points remained the weapon of choice in the South Caucasus well into the Iron Age. Second, the thinner, more compact, form and reduced weight of the point would have simultaneously created greater accuracy (by decreasing drag and thus flattening the trajectory of the shot) and enhanced the weapon's penetrative power (by reducing cross-sectional area and thus decreasing resistance from the target surface). The thicker design of Early Bronze Age projectile points would have made for considerably more drag and necessitated a higher, more arcing, shot with less force exerted at the point of impact. But why did increased penetrating power emerge as a critical affordance of projectile points in the South Caucasus only at the dawn of the Middle Bronze Age (cf. Erdal and Erdal 2012)? What entailments within the assemblage drove the promulgation of a very different material form? The changes in projectile technology appear to have shadowed alterations in other elements of the South Caucasian martial assemblage, most notably new forms of body protection, such as shields and armor (Reinhold 2003: 33). These materials would have severely degraded the effectiveness of Kura-Araxes obsidian projectile points. Since we presume that the hides of game animals were no thicker in the Middle than the Early Bronze Age, it is likely then that enhanced penetration was promoted not by new hunting requirements, but rather by new military practices (cf. Márquez et al. 2009). Third, and perhaps most significantly, the hafting of the Middle Bronze Age arrows, likely using a simple adhesive to fit the head to the shaft, allowed for separation on impact. Separation would have reduced the chances that an arrow might be extracted prematurely, thus maximizing damage to the target. Extraction of an embedded point is less a concern in hunting than it is in warfare.

In sum, the affordances of the Middle Bronze Age lithic projectile points appear to signal a martial assemblage driven primarily by the material logics of violence directed against humans rather than changing demands in hunting practices. As not simply a technology, but an apparatus of transubstantiation within the emerging war machine, the real efficacy of the new obsidian points lay in the social reproduction of violence along three key axes. First, the new points greatly reduced the material cost of conflict by shifting production to a rapid-manufacture, deskilled technology. Second, the discovery of points in a wide range of mortuary contexts, from grand kurgans to more limited funerary assemblages, contrasts markedly with their more restricted appearances in Early Bronze Age sites. This suggests a proliferation of the apparatus of violence during the Middle Bronze Age as the tools of conflict were distributed across a far wider social field. Third, the design of the points likely escalated the intensity of physical damage. The formal transubstantiations underlying the apparatus of violence in the Middle Bronze Age—the knapping of stone, the smoothing of arrow shafts—were paralleled by a fundamental shift in values, most notably those surrounding the social framing of violence against humans. In moving to the realm of value, we also move away from the sensible and toward the domain of sense.

SENSE

Metamorphosis

Although the grand kurgans tend to preoccupy archaeological attention, it is important to keep in mind the diversity of Middle Bronze Age tomb assemblages. The well-documented tombs from Lori-Berd in northern Armenia provide a succinct case in point (Devedjian 1981, 2006). The excavator, Seda Devedjian, aptly describes the necropolis as the burial ground of the region's elite, but of twenty-four excavated Middle Bronze Age kurgans at the site, half include relatively modest grave inventories, typically composed of two to ten ceramic vessels, augmented in five cases by the head and forelimbs of a pair of horses. Five of the largest kurgans more closely resembled the garish assemblages of the Early Kurgans sites, with extensive inventories of personal adornments of bronze, precious metal, carnelian and paste; weapons, including rapiers, daggers, and projectile points; tools, such as awls and hammers; vessels of ceramic and metal ranging from large storage jars to buckets to small cups (fig. 33). These and the other so-called grand kurgans from sites such as Vanadzor (Kirovakan; Martirosyan 1964: 64ff), Karashamb (Oganesian 1992a), and Nerkin Naver (Simonyan 2004) were, in a sociopolitical sense, sites of conspicuous consumption par excellence, attesting not only to what Veblen (1994) called the "pecuniary strength" of the deceased but also the predatory politics of emergent social differentiation.

This sense of predation can be seen in two dimensions: first in the capacity to command labor, and second in the removal of wealth from circulation, which necessarily enforced "continence" (Veblen 1994) on the nonelite population. Elite differentiation was not simply reflected by the interment of high-status goods; the entire social order of haves and have-nots was reproduced through the removal of luxuries from general circulation, which forced the abstention of the nonelite. As such, kurgans operated as a complex apparatus for generating value through scarcity, metamorphosing things into objects of desire. This form of metamorphosis is quintessentially the work of an assemblage, a process of mass mediation where wealth is reproduced not in any single object or any one material but through the intimidation of accumulation. The creation of value across a necropolis was thus accomplished not only by the conspicuous presences of elaborate funerary inventories, but also the consequent, and no less notable, absences in the remaining tombs. Kurgan assemblages, through their capacity to metamorphose earthly things into metaphysical objects of desire, thus operated as critical components of the war machine, manufacturing social distinction and cleaving the social body. At the center of this sensual process were sovereign bodies, both living and dead, and hence some kind of transfiguration must have been at work in the Middle Bronze Age war machine, an "apparatus of glory" (Agamben 2011: 245) that altered the human body into a majestic body.

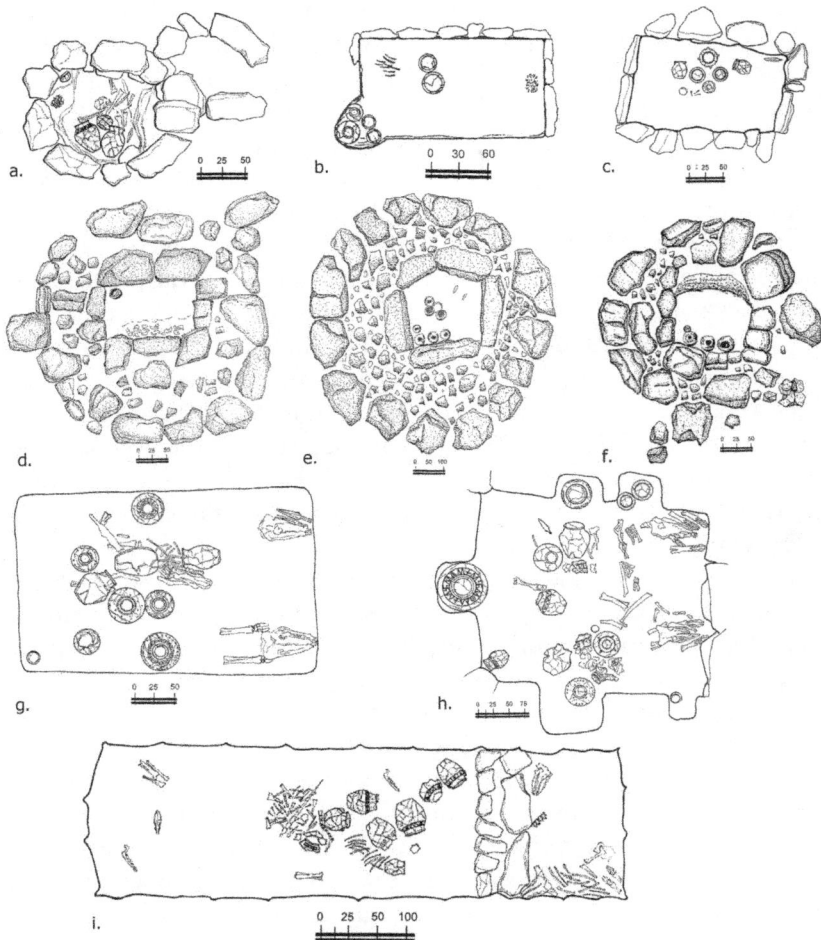

Fig. 33. Middle Bronze Age tombs from Lori Berd: (a) tomb 66, (b) tomb 82, (c) tomb 92, (d) tomb 87, (e) tomb 89, (f) tomb 90, (g) tomb 74, (h) tomb 61, (i) tomb 65. (After Devedjian 2006.)

Transfiguration

Arguably the most analytically perplexing element of the Middle Bronze Age "grand" kurgan assemblage is not the grave furnishings but the human bodies. Variability in the treatment of dead bodies over the course of the Middle Bronze Age is quite striking. Though many of the earliest large kurgans, like those from Tsnori and Bedeni, appear to have been virtual death pits, with human sacrifices surrounding the body of the principal figure, the frequency of human sacrifice in elite tombs diminished considerably in the succeeding Middle Bronze II period. Indeed, the elite Middle Bronze I kurgans contained a surfeit of bodies, while the grand kurgans of the Middle Bronze II phase experienced a severe shortage! The large Middle Bronze II Trialeti and Zurtaketi mounds contained no human bones (Dzhaparidze 1969: 275; Kushnareva 1997: 93), a finding which the excavator, B. A. Kuftin (1941), attributed to new rites of cremation. Kurgans from contemporary sites, such as Kirovakan, Aruch, and Lori-Berd, included large inventories of a diverse array of things in chambers surmounted by huge piles of rock and earth (Devedjian 2006; Kuftin 1941; Kushnareva 1994b: 112). But the human body was conspicuously absent. The sacrifices of the initial Middle Bronze Age were thus succeeded by a phase of radical decorporealization as the body of the deceased was transfigured prior to interment.

However, this approach to mortuary ritual was oddly short-lived. During the third and final phase of the Middle Bronze Age, the body of the deceased returned just as the lavishness of tomb furnishings moderated considerably. For example, the most highly elaborated of the kurgans from the Middle Bronze III burial fields at Karmir-Berd (Areshian 1970), Verin-Naver (Simonyan 2006), Kizyl-Vank (Abibullaev 1982), and Shirakavan (Torosyan et al. 2002) were composed largely of individual interments and included very few artifacts of bronze or precious metal. How are we to understand the shifting treatment of the body of the deceased within the context of Middle Bronze Age tomb assemblages? What seems quite clear is that mortuary rituals were deeply concerned with the transfiguration of a physical body into a metaphysical one. Within the Middle Bronze I regimes of conspicuous consumption, the interred body was surrounded by a dense assemblage of desired objects, as things operated to transfigure the dead body into an extraordinary body. In the cremation practices of the Middle Bronze II, we see a new approach to the same problem as the process of transfiguration was removed from the tomb and emplaced within the rites of cremation. Lastly, the return of the body suggests a reemplacement of the process of transfiguration back within the confines of the tomb, out of view of the participants in funerary rites.

This shifting approach to mortuary practice suggests that during the Middle Bronze Age the fundamental work of the kurgan was the transfiguration of dead bodies into something more than inert flesh. In this respect, the mortuary assemblages of the Middle Bronze Age proved to be efficacious machines, pulling the bodies of erstwhile sovereigns away from the wider social corpus by according them forms of value that were not simply larger but largely incommensurable with the interred bodies of the wider public. The tombs of the emergent sovereigns of the Middle Bronze Age were not simply bigger, richer, or more garish, they were fundamentally different in their operation, securing not simply a well-appointed afterlife but also reproducing the central paradox at the heart of sovereignty—the ruler lies both within and outside the polity, subject to its rules yet beyond its order.

The grand kurgans were thus quintessential spaces of exception where general premises of order yielded to the intense subjection of sacrifice. Certainly sacrifice can include the sacrifice of things demanded by the concentration of wealth that enforced continence on the rest of the population, but the most conspicuous forms of sacrifice were the human sacrifices contained in the earliest tombs. Human sacrifices are, to use Agamben's (1998) terminology, the ultimate foundation of sovereignty because they entail the reduction of a human life to what he calls "bare life," mere biological existence stripped of the rights and obligations of being subject. It thus entails an insertion of the human body within an assemblage not as subject but as object. The inclusion of human sacrifices thus signals the transfiguration of a sovereign's body into one that lies beyond the polity and the transfiguration of subject bodies into funerary objects. In probing the imagined relationship between body and object, we move away from the domain of sense and into the world of sentiment.

SENTIMENT

In various dimensions of the Middle Bronze Age kurgans, we have already seen aspects of prevailing sentiments. The very idea of grave inventories as "tournaments of value" (Appadurai 1986: 21) entails a powerful form of captivation, one that demands the presence of objects not simply as functional equipment for the afterlife but as talismans that work to reproduce the distinction of the sovereign. Additionally, the involvement of collective labor in kurgan construction also hints at the possibility of a highly politicized version of what consumer psychologists have labeled the Ikea effect: the enhanced affection for objects created by the investment of personal labor (Norton et al. 2012).

At present, our best window onto the sentiments that shaped the imagined efficacy of things in the Middle Bronze Age comes from a large kurgan at the northern end of the burial ground at Karashamb, on the west bank of the Razdan River, dating to the Middle Bronze II phase (Oganesian 1992a).

Fig. 34. The Karashamb goblet, photo (inset) and annotated roll out drawing. (Photo credit: Courtesy of Institute of Archaeology and Ethnography, Republic of Armenia; roll out after Kushnareva 1997.)

The architecture of the Great Kurgan at Karashamb and its inventory was generally similar to that from tombs at Vanadzor (Kirovakan) and at Tria-leti (Oganesian 1988: 145). The kurgan was a raised earthen and stone mound built atop a funerary area delineated by a ring of stones. Within the tomb chamber, the excavators uncovered numerous animal bones, weap-ons, ornaments, and utensils, but, typical for the era, no human skeleton.

Among the finds in the Great Karashamb Kurgan was a remarkable silver-plated goblet (fig. 34), its exterior surface divided into six registers, separated by raised bands, each decorated with images in relief (Oganesian 1992b: 86). The top and bottom registers depict a boar hunt and a parade of lions and leopards (1, 4, 6). But the second and third registers most directly interest me here. The second register depicts a battle (a), a parade of a cap-tive (b), and a feast (c), most likely providing a narrative order in which the scenes are to be read. The battle scene is composed of two sets of two foot soldiers fighting with spears and daggers. In the adjacent procession, three soldiers trail behind a single unarmed captive pressed forward by a spear in its back. At the center of the scene, two attendants fan a seated figure, the erstwhile sovereign, who sips from a cup as servants attend to offerings set atop two large tables (Oganesian 1992b: 86). The third register presents a group of scenes related to conquest and its aftermath, including images of human sacrifice (f, h), ambulatory headless bodies (d), and a seated figure sharpening an axe next to a pile of decapitated heads, shields, spears, swords, and armor (g).

I should note that the Karashamb goblet was not an isolated production. Similar metal drinking vessels are known from kurgans 5 and 17 at Trialeti, from a contemporary burial at Maikop, and from the kurgan at Vanadzor (Kirovakan) (Kuftin 1941: 8, 90; Dzhaparidze 1988: 8). Moreover, as Karen Rubinson (2013) has cogently pointed out, Kura-Araxes communities had a durable tradition of anthropomorphic and zoomorphic representation, so the appearance of figural imagery is not new to the South Caucasus. However, what is unique is the encompassing view that the goblet presents of the sentiments fundamental to the reproduction of the Middle Bronze Age war machine.

In a purely representational sense, the scenes on the Karashamb cup portray the practices central to the reproduction of sovereign distinction: war and conquest, feasting and celebration, punishment and ritual, and hunting. These practices are indelibly linked by an assemblage of violence, which glorifies the putative sovereign, expropriates goods as tribute and treasure, and kills any who resist or compete. In a thematic sense, the image is thus a succinct encapsulation of Weber's (1968: 51–53) description of charismatic authority, wherein prestige rests upon the physical segregation of the leader as a sacral figure (as he presides over the feast) and the provision of needs through the spoils of violent conflict. In a more metaphorical sense, the images on the cup work to legitimize social violence by naturalizing it in relation to the hunt. Just as the tools of the hunt mediate the tie between ruler and the wild, affirming his charisma as a warrior and extending his putative dominion over the untamed wilderness, so do the instruments of war mediate relations between ruler and foe.

But the most significant argument at work on the Karashamb goblet is a primordial rendering of the *aporia* of the one and the many at the heart of sovereignty, an ancient anticipation of Lorenzetti's murals in the Sala dei Nove. Just below the seated figure of the sovereign at the feast is a winged figure (e) that is typically described as a supernatural being. By its positioning directly below the seated sovereign, the figure is clearly paired with him, but the relation is not readily describable as contrastive since violence threads its way through the scenes in both registers. Instead, the relation between the second and third registers seems to be one of complementary forces of sociopolitical reproduction. As sovereign power demands the feast, so too must it demand combat to supply the table, creating an unceasing cycle of consumption and destruction. This constituted power of an emergent sovereign here literally rests atop a constituting power grounded in the originary violence of human sacrifice. The supernatural figure in the lower register is not distinct from sovereignty and its practices, but enveloped within its paradox. To use Kantorowicz's (1957: 78ff) terms, I suggest that the winged figure represents what Tudor-era lawyers would later call the "eternal majesty" of the sovereign, marked iconically by a form of "haloing" created by the juxtaposition of organic and supernatural bodies. But unlike the exclusively corporeal account of the Tudor sources, both the organic and eternal bodies are defined on the Karashamb cup in reference to the operation of a dense material assemblage.

This is most clearly visible in the scene on the cup that typically elicits the sternest reaction from modern viewers: the pile of decapitated heads in the third register. I have previously (Smith 2001: 165) suggested that the pile of arms and armor represented spoils of war, but I now think this incorrect because the scenes surrounding the majesty of the eternal sovereign bear less on combat (depicted in the register above) than on human sacrifice. With death as the focal theme, the pile of weaponry and heads bears more than a passing resemblance to key features of the kurgan inventory, an assemblage that reproduces the majesty of the sovereign in the afterlife. Hence, just as we see in the second register the organic sovereign and the means of reproduction of constituted power, in the third we see the supernatural sovereign and the means of reproducing his constituting power. These "things" are thus not "mere" instruments but the vital matter of the polity. They captivate not because they represent sovereignty, but because the charismatic form of proto-sovereignty in the Middle Bronze Age was unimaginable without them.

TERRITORIALIZATION AND CONTRADICTION

The conjoined operation of the civilization and war machines is predicated on a paradox—the assembly of a public as a coherent body and its segmentation into sovereigns and subjects. This paradox reached a critical impasse by the final phase of the Middle Bronze Age when the violence of elite competition appears to have encouraged new forms of territorialization. The extensive Trialeti-Vanadzor horizon that embraced most of the highland South Caucasus and adjacent regions of eastern Anatolia in the Middle Bronze II period fragmented into (at least) four distinct, yet geographically overlapping, ceramic groups. The Karmirberd horizon, which largely prevails in the highlands of the central South Caucasus, is principally de-

fined by a monochrome painted pottery tradition most iconically represented in the materials from the site of Verin Naver (Simonyan 1984). In
contrast, a polychrome painted pottery tradition known as the Karmir-Vank
horizon is best known from eastern Anatolia, Nakhichevan, and northwestern Iran (Özfirat 2008). Lastly, the Sevan-Uzerlik horizon tends to predominate in the western steppe of Azerbaijan, the Nagorno-Karabakh highlands,
and southeastern Armenia (Kushnareva 1997: 129ff). Sevan-Uzerlik ceramics are predominantly black polished vessels with incised and punctate
decoration.

The geographic differentiation of ceramic styles cannot be taken as
indicative of a rigid new cultural mosaic. In Georgia, though Trialeti-
Vanadzor traditions persist, it is also possible to detect the expanding influence of Sevan-Uzerlik complexes. Sites in Armenia often boast mixed assemblages that combine Karmirberd ceramics with Sevan-Uzerlik (Verin
Naver), Karmir-Vank (Aruch, Karashamb), and Trialeti-Vanadzor (Harich)
wares, and settlements in northwestern Iran, such as Haftavan Tepe, include both monochrome Karmirberd and polychrome Karmir-Vank ceramics (Avetisyan and Bobokhyan 2008; Burney 1975). Although the distribution of wares does not neatly map emergent identity categories, the
shifting ceramic assemblages of the terminal Middle Bronze Age were at
work generating a new form of social segmentation that cut across the
operation of the civilization machine not through distinction but through
territorialization.

Territorialization, as Deleuze and Guattari (1986: 115ff; 1987: 419) noted,
is one consequence of the operation of the war machine wherein the violence of elite competition encourages regional segmentation. With the proliferation of the assemblages of the war machine across the region, conflict
would have descended into a series of stalemates enforcing geographic segmentation. Hence the war machine's operation effectively parasitized the
workings of the civilization machine, fragmenting the South Caucasian
public in evidence during the Trialeti-Vanadzor phase into smaller and
smaller segments. Communities at the end of the Middle Bronze Age thus
found themselves caught in a paradox in which the war machines of erstwhile sovereigns threatened the operation of the civilization machine and
hence the dissolution of the very community of subjects that sovereignty
requires. Moreover, as political violence increased, the rising demand for
key resources, particularly metals, demanded a reduction in the opulence of
the grave assemblages. Thus, the extension of the war machine's capabilities
to conduct violence through warfare placed significant constraints on its
capacity to reproduce radical social distinction in mortuary practices.

Given such a state of contradiction, it is perhaps not surprising that the end of the Middle Bronze Age was marked by the emergence of a new machine capable of resolving the *aporia* created by the concerted operation of the civilization and war machines. This shift was not a moment of collapse but rather of extension, when sometime around 1500 B.C. large-scale permanent settlements returned to the South Caucasus in the form of stone masonry fortresses perched atop tall rock outcrops. These fortresses were the site of a critical new machinery that regularized the authority of the sovereign through the operation of an apparatus of routinized distinction and administration. It is to this new machinery of fully realized sovereignty that appropriated the war machine of "the nomads" that we turn in the next chapter.

The Political Machine in the Late Bronze Age

In short, it is at one and the same time that the State apparatus appropriates a
war machine, that the war machine takes war as its object, and that war
becomes subordinated to the aims of the state

(Deleuze and Guattari 1986: 113).

One of the most compelling representations of things engaged in the work
of sovereignty comes from a pair of painted Moche jars reportedly from the
Chicama valley of northern Peru, dated to the early first millennium A.D.
(fig. 35).[1] A number of scholars have argued that the scenes on the two jars
depict a version of "the revolt of objects" (Jackson 2008: 144ff; Krickeberg
1928; Quilter 1990), a mythic theme of things in rebellion that was widely
disseminated across the pre-Columbian New World.[2] In a Peruvian version of the tale recorded by Francisco de Avila in the early seventeenth century, household objects and domesticated animals, awakened by a celestial
event (such as an eclipse), rise up against humans: "Mortars and grinding
stones began to eat men.... Llamas began to drive humans" (quoted in
Quilter 1990: 46). The images on the Moche vases seem to portray a similar
event; however, as Patricia Lyon (1989) has noted, the majority of the animated objects on the Moche vessels are not everyday objects but an assemblage of sovereign power: weaponry and regalia instead of mortars and
grinding stones. Thus the images appear to advance a theory of the political
emplaced within the tropic field of a larger mythic theme.

---

[1] Currently one vessel is in the Museum für Völkerkunde in Berlin, the other is held in the
Museum für Völkerkunde in Munich. Animated things appear in a number of Moche compositions, including a mural from the Huaca de la Luna (Quilter 1990) and a spouted jar in the
collections of the Art Institute in Chicago (Donnan and McClelland 1999: fig. 4.71), among
others.

[2] In *The Raw and the Cooked*, Levi-Strauss (1969: 299) provides a brief comparison of the
theme of the revolt of objects in mythologies from the Arctic to South America.

Fig. 35. Two Moche vessels bearing fine line images of "the Revolt of Objects": (a) the Munich vase, (b) the Berlin vase. (Drawing by Donna McClelland. The Christopher B. Donnan and Donna McClelland Moche Archive, Image Collections and Fieldwork Archives, Dumbarton Oaks, Trustees for Harvard University, Washington, D.C.)

The images on both vessels depict a variety of animated things engaged in conflict with human figures. On the vessel now in the collections of Berlin's Museum für Völkerkunde (fig. 35b), a skirted human figure stands alone inside a gabled structure, while, outside, two naked human captives, bound by ropes, have been subdued by animated shields, clubs, and helmet crests. On the second vessel, now in the collections of Munich's Museum für Völkerkunde (fig. 35a), a more elaborate image depicts anthropomorphized weapons and regalia subduing human figures. In the lower register of the composition, humans are shown in various stages of defeat and capture as objects grab their victims and bind them naked with ropes.

Christopher Donnan (1976) has argued (contra Kroeber 1951) that Moche art was fundamentally an approach to representation structured by religious themes, its iconic repertoire charged with dense symbolic content. But as Quilter has pointed out, the density of Moche religious symbology does not preclude their role in maintaining a wider set of political and social institutions invested in the maintenance of order, both cosmic and quotidian. Quilter (1997) has argued for a narrative approach to the "revolt of objects" compositions, allowing them not only to represent a key element in "the mythic corpus of Moche ideology" (Quilter 1990: 58) but also to argue for the reproduction of the existing order, an order defined by the disciplining of things. In this interpretation, the "revolt of objects" images advance an ethical account of the Moche polity (Ankersmit 1996), an injunction to subjection built upon a rhetorical assessment of interests. In Quilter's terms (1990: 59), "The maintenance of the current status quo, however unequal or unfair, is justified by the argument that the alternative is chaos—a world turned upside down."

It is also possible to interpret the images as advancing an aesthetic account of Moche sovereignty. In this reading, although the images may well reference a past mythic event, they also represent the Moche experience of the political, one dominated by seemingly autonomous activities of the instruments of sovereign violence. To adopt Ankersmit's (1996: 45) account of the political aesthetic, actions undertaken in one medium (i.e., the sovereign) are "made visible and present in another medium" (i.e., the assemblage of rule). Whereas an ethical account reads the Moche images as cautionary tales about what happens when order fails, an aesthetic account understands the images as representations of the machinery of political reproduction. The images in this aesthetic sense reify the political, occluding the sovereign body and highlighting instead the apparatus of rule. The objects portrayed on the Munich and Berlin vessels in this sense are not in revolt; they are, quite oppositely, engaged in guaranteeing the reproduction of the existing order of things by doing what they do all the time—binding, disciplining, captivating. As such, the images underscore Hobbes's (1991) understanding of sovereignty as vested not in a human body but in an automaton, not in the ethical consent of subjects to subordination but in their captivation by an aesthetic project maintained by a machinery of rule.

Friedrich Schiller (1982: 13) described this political machine as a "terrifying empire of force." The ethical state was held together by the "sacred empire of law," but the aesthetic state was reproduced by taste and by the correct "moral orientation" that it provided (Schiller, quoted in Ankersmit 1996: 22). Subjectivization within the aesthetic state is not simply a following of moral law but the cultivation of the taste to recognize the pleasure of conformity (Schiller 2005; cf. Eagleton 1990: 114). It is this sense of the political aesthetic that I have described elsewhere as a "pleasure of position" (Smith 2006), a sublime experience of location within what Adam Smith (1982: 316) called a great "immense machine whose regular and harmonious movements produce a thousand agreeable effects." Claude Lefort (1988:

215–16) has described this work of positioning as "a hidden part of social life, namely the processes which make people consent to a given regime—or, to put it more forcefully, which determines *their manner of being in society*—and which guarantee that this regime or mode of society has a permanence in time." I should be clear that aesthetics in this sense is meant not as a form of disinterested judgment (which Bourdieu [1984] pointedly rejected as a philosophical illusion), but as a recognition of the machinery of sovereignty, of the assemblages that reproduce political community not by mere coercion or consent—the limited apparatus of the ethical state—but through the pleasures that follow from making sovereignty itself into a kind of object. The transformation of the sovereign from a body to an object—what Peter Weibel (2005: 1012) has described as the "artificialization of the state"—represents the work of a different kind of machine than either the civilization or war machines that we have studied in the previous two chapters. This re-presentation of authority is accomplished through what is best described as a political machine, whose operation reifies sovereignty, giving it the solidity, durability, and form that makes possible the aestheticization of political association. In other words, it is this machine that manufactures "formal" sovereignty by rendering the political aesthetic and securing not simply a willingness to be governed but a desire to be ruled.

THE CAUCASUS AT THE BEGINNING OF THE LATE BRONZE AGE

In opening an inquiry into the political machine in the South Caucasus, let us return to the region at the moment we left it at the end of the previous chapter, the waning years of the Middle Bronze Age during the seventeenth and sixteenth centuries B.C. At that time, the landscape of the Middle Bronze Age was shaped by widespread mobility, with vast kurgan cemeteries anchored by archaeologically ephemeral settlements. The extension of the war machine's capabilities to conduct violence, so graphically illustrated on the Karashamb goblet (see chapter 4), had produced not only radical social inequality, as seen in the conspicuous funerary assemblages of sites like Tsnori, Trialeti, and Lori Berd, but also increasing territorialization. This territorial segmentation is most visible in the diverging assemblages of the final Middle Bronze III phase that undercut the widely shared material assemblage of the earlier Trialeti-Vanadzor horizon. The proliferation of the war machine thus pushed the aspiring charismatic sovereigns of the late Middle Bronze Age into a potentially destabilizing state of contradiction as segmentation and territorialization threatened to undermine the operation of the civilization machine and hence the cohesion of the very community of subjects they sought to rule. And indeed we see in the final phase of the Middle Bronze Age a severe reduction in the conspicuous consumption of mortuary assemblages—the critical matter of charismatic distinction—at sites such as Shirakavan (Torosyan et al. 2002) and Karmir-Berd (Simonyan 1982). The contradiction at the heart of the *aporia* of the one and many, manufactured by the simultaneous operation of a war machine and a civilization machine, thus appears to have begun to pull the one—aspiring sovereigns—back into the fold of the many, undoing the principle of radical distinction fundamental to charismatic sovereign authority.

However, by the middle of the second millennium we see evidence of a new machine at work in the region, one dedicated to the manufacture of an institutionalized apparatus of governance set within the "striated" (Deleuze and Guattari 1986) space of delimited territories. Beginning just before 1500 B.C., the political landscape of the South Caucasus underwent a rapid transformation. After almost a millennium of communities predicated on mobility and pastoralism, new built environments appeared on hilltops across the South Caucasus (fig. 36). One of the earliest regions to witness the shift from the mobile communities of the Middle Bronze Age to the emplaced institutions of the Late was the Tsaghkahovit Plain in central Armenia (see chapter 3).

At the end of the Early Bronze Age, the villages of the region, such as the one at Gegharot, had been rapidly abandoned under the new social pressures of the mobilizing world of the dawning Middle Bronze Age (see chapter 4). The archaeological record of the Tsaghkahovit Plain during the succeeding Middle Bronze Age is, at present, completely silent, suggesting a long hiatus in permanent regional occupation from around 2600 to 1500 B.C. The end of this hiatus is most conspicuously visible in the assemblages from a field of kurgan burials found just below the fortress of Gegharot.[3] Kurgan 1 (fig. 37), one of the best preserved of the excavated tombs, consisted of two main chambers (Badalyan et al. 2008: 59–60). The west chamber contained a diverse collection of animal bones and a ceramic repertoire that constitutes a perfect transitional Middle to Late Bronze Age assemblage, including wares continuous with earlier Sevan-Uzerlik traditions and initial iterations of Late Bronze Age styles. The central chamber contained

[3] Gegharot Kurgans Burial Cluster 1 (Smith et al. 2009: 123).

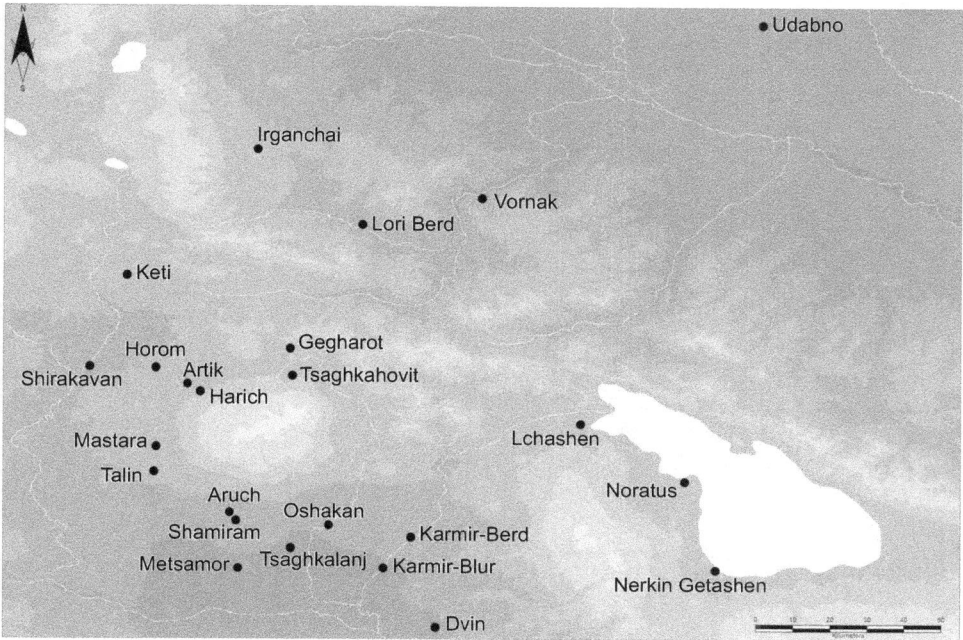

Fig. 36. Major Late Bronze Age archaeological sites in the South Caucasus. (Map Credit: Adam T. Smith.)

the skeleton of an adult male, thirty-five to forty years of age, laid to rest atop fragments from the body of a young infant. The human skeletons were bracketed by the heads and forelimbs of two horses. Ceramic vessels in the chamber all belong to the emergent traditions of the Late Bronze Age, as do the obsidian and bronze arrowheads and the single bronze knife. But what harkens back to the earlier era of the Middle Bronze Age is a mortuary assemblage still focused on instruments of mobility, violence, and, quite possibly, human sacrifice.

Within a few years of the kurgan's construction, the new object world of the Late Bronze Age was emphatically emplaced within a series of fortified hilltop sites constructed along the margins of the Tsaghkahovit Plain. Radiocarbon dates and material assemblages suggest that the fortresses at Gegharot (fig. 14) and Tsaghkahovit (fig. 38) were built sometime just before 1500 B.C. Two other major fortified sites followed no later than the early fourteenth century B.C. Eight other small fortresses and outposts appear to have been in place by the mid-fourteenth century B.C. Evidence to

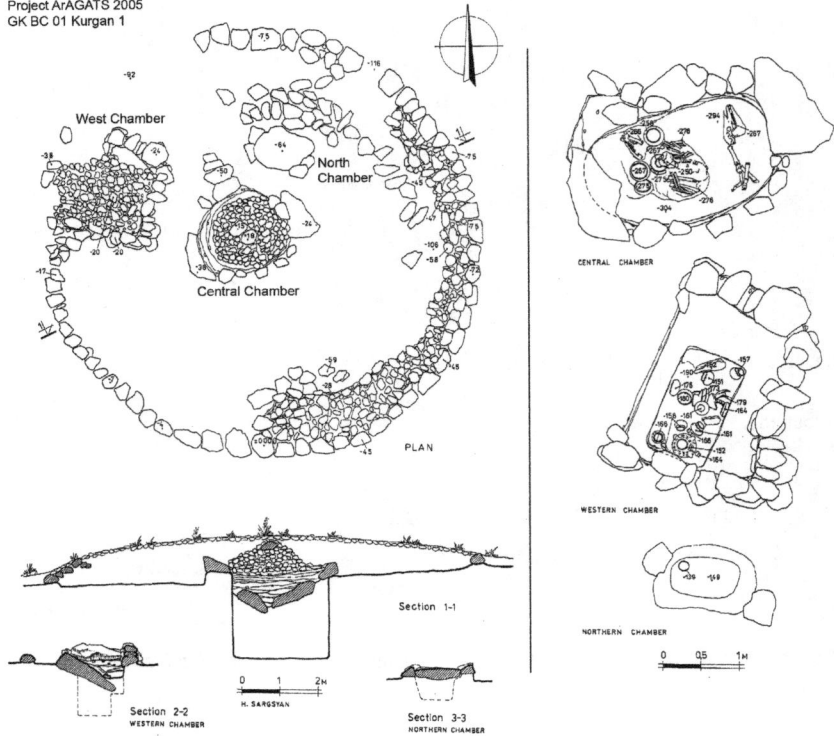

Fig. 37. Plan of Gegharot kurgan 1. (Drawing by Hasmik Sarkisyan, courtesy of Project ArAGATS.)

date suggests that this coordinated process of fortress construction was part of the emergence of a single polity that built and occupied multiple sites in the region (Badalyan et al. 2003; Smith et al. 2004).

It is not clear at present whether sovereign power in the region was formally seated in a single authoritative site or was more diffusely spread across many or all of the major fortified citadels. However, it is clear that the complex cut into the conical outcrop at Tsaghkahovit commanded the most labor and resources in its construction. The site's massive cyclopean terrace and fortification walls set on a rigorously sculpted outcrop attest to a mobilization of people and things that exceeds the region's other fortified sites. The site extends across 39.6 hectares in total, an area that includes the fortified citadel, terraces, and surrounding terrain.[4] The fortress outcrop it-

---

[4] How much of the surrounding terrain was occupied during the Late Bronze Age is a matter of uncertainty because of the later construction of an Iron 3 period settlement at the

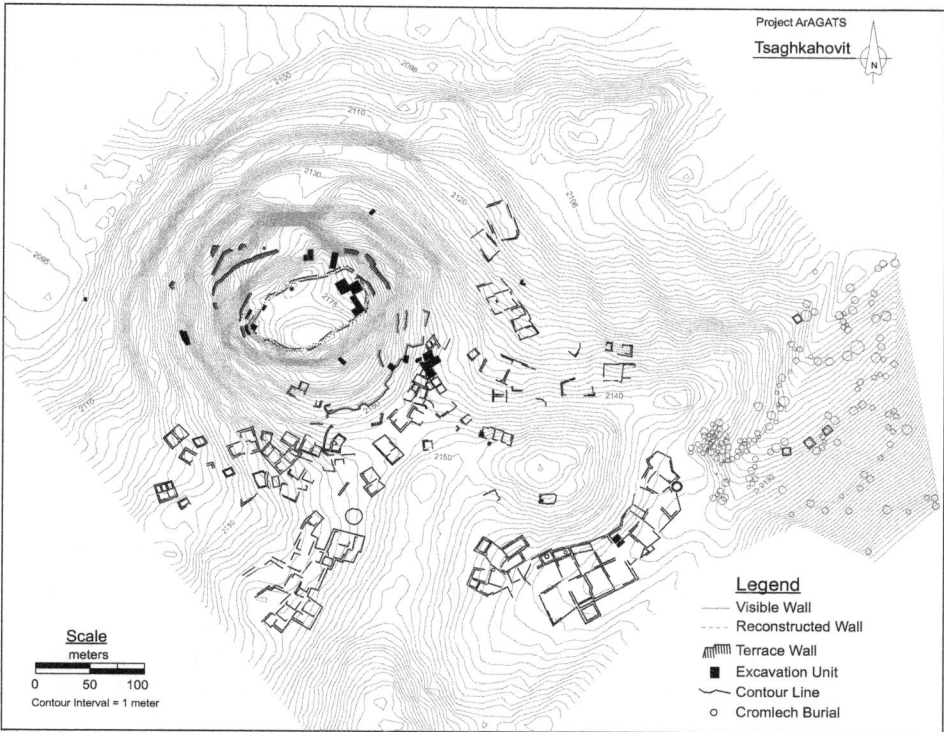

Fig. 38. Plan of the Late Bronze Age fortress at Tsaghkahovit. (Map Credit: Adam T. Smith.)

self (7.59 ha) rises 80 meters above the plain to surveil the road that links the Shirak Plain in the west to the north–south routes between the Ararat Plain and the Kura River basin. The later Achaemenid-era occupation of the citadel disturbed most of the earlier levels, but we have uncovered the remains of a large Late Bronze Age ashlar masonry structure that may well have been a key center of regional authority.

The contemporary occupation at the site of Gegharot, on the north side of the Tsaghkahovit Plain, was comparatively small. The Late Bronze Age constructions and the surface materials at the site cover an area of just 3.43 hectares, with the primary focus of occupation inside the 0.36-hectare citadel and western terrace. The earliest Late Bronze Age constructions appear to have been built on the western terrace at the end of the sixteenth century

---

site. Ian Lindsay's (2006) research in the extramural areas of the site clearly demonstrate a Late Bronze Age occupation beyond the fortress hill. But we are not able to assess the scale of the extramural precincts.

B.C., but the site was razed by an encompassing destruction episode some-time in the late fifteenth or early fourteenth centuries, leaving only scattered traces of the initial Late Bronze (LB I) occupation (Smith et al. 2004). When the site was rebuilt at the beginning of the fourteenth century B.C. (LB II), the formal built environment included workrooms, middens, small storage areas, and paved courtyards. However, the most highly elaborated spaces at the site housed a series of three spatially distinct shrines—one on the west terrace, one on the east side of the citadel, and one on the west side of the citadel (Smith and Leon 2014). The shrines, about which I shall say much more below, were small in scale, with little apparent accommodation for public spectacle, and yet they appear to have been religiously charged places hosting esoteric rituals that utilized a diverse assemblage of conse-crated objects.

The Late Bronze Age resettlement of the Tsaghkahovit Plain (fig. 39) also included substantial fortified complexes at Hnaberd (Smith et al. 2009: 302) and Aragatsiberd (Greene 2013), with smaller fortified complexes around the perimeter of the plain (e.g., Gekhadzor, Lernapar) and atop the initial high peaks of the Pambakh range (e.g., Berdidosh, Poloz Sar). Con-struction techniques employed at the Late Bronze Age Tsaghkahovit Plain sites were highly varied, with irregular "cyclopean" stone masonry fortifica-tion and terracing walls yielding to small informal partitions in many parts of the interior. Aside from these fortified precincts, the ArAGATS survey recorded no settlements that could be definitively dated to the Late Bronze Age. Ian Lindsay's (2005, 2006; Badalyan et al. in press) excavations outside the walls of Tsaghkahovit have documented the presence of an extramural community. However, it does not appear to have hosted the kind of dense residential district that the extended network of fortified sites presupposes. Thus my colleagues and I have elsewhere suggested (Smith et al. 2009: 398) that significant segments of Late Bronze Age communities retained prac-tices of movement derived from the highly mobile lifeways of the Middle Bronze Age. But by the second half of the second millennium, mobile prac-tices were set within an increasingly restricted spatial field of competing territorial polities.

The fortified settlements of the Late Bronze Age Tsaghkahovit Plain were set within a vast mortuary landscape that dotted the surrounding mountain slopes with a dense array of tombs set in discrete clusters (Smith et al. 2009). The Project ArAGATS regional survey identified a total of 199 burial clus-ters with mortuary features broadly describable as typical of the Late Bronze Age, an overall density of 2.05 cemeteries per square kilometer (Smith et al.

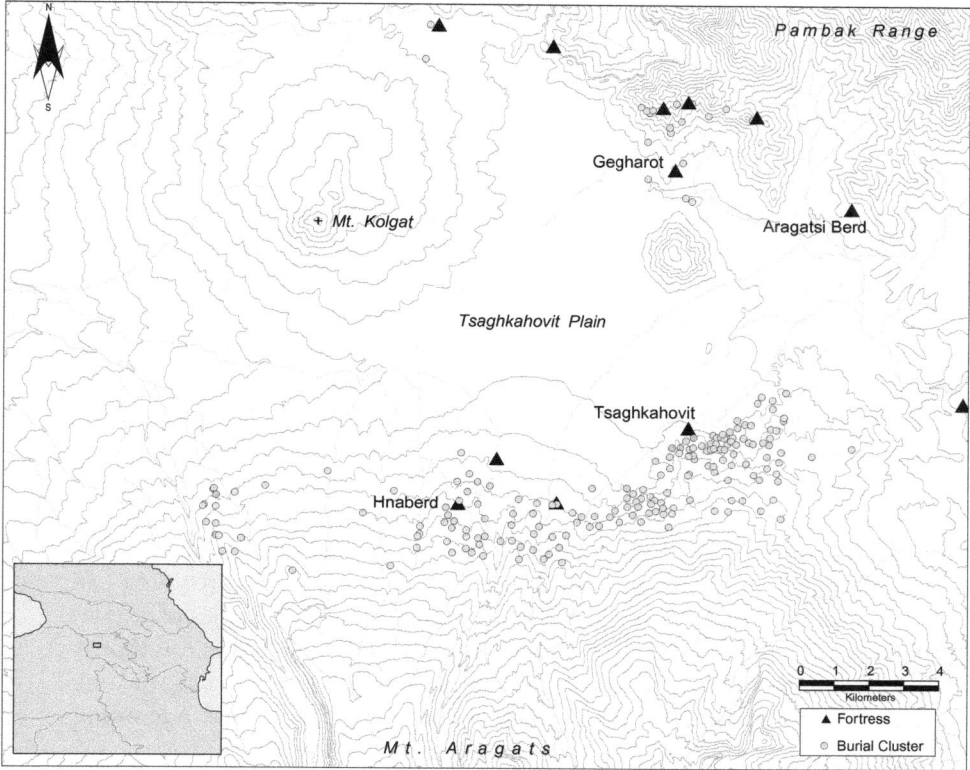

Fig. 39. The Tsaghkahovit Plain in the Late Bronze Age. (Map Credit: Adam T. Smith.)

2009: 396). Although kurgan burials did continue into the Late Bronze Age (as documented in the Tsaghkahovit Plain at the kurgan cemetery below Gegharot [Badalyan et al. 2008: 59–60]), the predominant form of mortuary architecture was the cromlech, a single circle of stones surrounding a sub-terranean earth or stone chamber, covered by large capstones (Smith et al. 2009: 106–7). A conservative estimate based on our survey suggests an average of thirty to fifty burials per cemetery, yielding an estimated total of 5,970 Late Bronze burials surrounding the Tsaghkahovit Plain. Based on excavations across the plain at mortuary sites ranging from Mantash Burial Cluster 8 (Smith et. al 2009: 148) and Hnaberd Burial Cluster 4 (Badalyan et. al 2003: 162–63; Smith et al. 2009: 126) in the west to Tsaghkahovit Burial Cluster 12 (Marshall 2014; Smith et al. 2009: 191) and the Gegharot cemeteries (Badalyan and Avetisyan 2007: 98ff; Martirosyan 1964: 92ff) in the east, it appears that Late Bronze Age tombs in the region generally included the remains of one to three individuals, resulting in an estimated interred population of roughly 10,000 to 12,000.

Perhaps the most compelling feature of the Late Bronze Age burial clusters is their spatial distribution, which appears to provide a unique window into the practices of territorialization that accompanied the emergence of a new order of formal sovereignty. The cemeteries are tightly packed within the central 30 square kilometers of the north Aragats slope, extending in an east–west line from approximately 0.5 kilometers west of Hnaberd fortress to 3 kilometers east of Tsaghkahovit fortress, but they virtually disappear beyond these limits. West of Hnaberd fortress, this hiatus in mortuary architecture persists up to the eastern bank of Mantash gorge; east of Tsaghkahovit fortress, the hiatus extends southwest into the Kasakh River valley. The crisp boundaries in the Late Bronze Age mortuary landscape suggest an emerging territorialization of the region conditioned by claims to regional sovereignty radiating from the new fortified settlements. We currently lack data on the social logics that sustained the clustering of tombs, but one possibility is that obligations to a descent group or social class required patterns of mobility that entangled mobile communities in cycles of regular return to traditional burial grounds. Given the close link between authority and entombment during the Middle Bronze Age, it is not at all surprising that the frontiers of formal sovereignty during the Late Bronze Age would be etched most conspicuously in the mortuary landscape

In addition to a radically transformed settlement pattern and innovations in mortuary architecture, new ceramic styles and metal repertoires also mark the transition between the Middle and Late Bronze Age in the South Caucasus. As the painted pottery of the Karmir-Berd, Karmir-Vank, and Trialeti horizons waned, the punctate designs of the Sevan-Uzerlik tradition were folded into an enduring new ceramic assemblage known as the Lchashen-Metsamor horizon (Smith et al. 2009: 68ff). These black, gray, and buff vessels with incised and pressed circumferential decorations spread rapidly across the South Caucasus and, by the Iron 1 period, areas of the adjacent Armenian Highland (Areshian et al. 1990). In addition, the scale, intensity, and diversity of bronze production increased dramatically during the Late Bronze Age as manufacturing shifted to employing both openwork and lost wax casting, and the repertoire of artifacts expanded to include new forms, such as battle-axes, mace-heads, shaft-hole daggers, bits, flanged-hilt weapons, personal adornments, and statuettes.[5]

---

[5] Key metal assemblages related to the Middle to Late Bronze transition have been re-

How did this new object world of the Late Bronze Age participate in the formalization of sovereignty across the region? What role did these new things play in establishing a new sense of authority, new sentiments of aesthetic attachment to the polity, and a new sensibility of the physical articulation of subjects and objects? Let us turn first to sensibility, to the flows of things and the transubstantiations that they made as they moved.

SENSIBILITY

Flows

Although Project ArAGATS's initial work in the region focused on the fortress of Tsaghkahovit, our attention was drawn to the much smaller site of Gegharot, on the northern flank of the Tsaghkahovit Plain, by the results of compositional analyses of ceramic materials collected during the systematic regional survey. In the course of these investigations, we gathered samples from fifteen clay beds in the plain and surrounding regions known to local potters (fig. 40). Thanks to the underlying geological diversity of the region, clay sources even short distances apart possess relatively distinct chemical compositions. Instrumental Neutron Activation (INA) analysis of the clay sources along with 458 sherds from across the plain indicated that during the Late Bronze Age, three primary clay source groups were in use: one adjacent to Gegharot, another near Tsaghkahovit, and one that remains unidentified but is geologically related to clay beds near Jrashen, just across the northern pass into the Pambakh valley (Minc, in Smith et al. 2009: 381ff; Lindsay et al. 2007).

The INA data indicate two key dynamics in regional material flows during the Late Bronze Age as they pertained to ceramic containers. First, as Lindsay and colleagues (2007: 1680) have noted, out of the total sample of 458 sherds from the plain, only 21 were classified as products of clay sources located outside the Tsaghkahovit Plain, suggesting that an economic insularity accompanied Late Bronze Age political territorialization. Interestingly, the largest proportion of these nonlocal wares came from the citadel and terrace of Gegharot.[6]

---

corded at Nerkin Getashen (burial 21), Oshakan, Aruch III, Harich, and other sites (Smith et al. 2009: 77).

[6] If we compare the roughly similar samples drawn from Gegharot (n=182) and from the extramural settlement at Tsaghkahovit (n=150), it appears that a higher percentage of ceramics made from nonlocal clays were found at Gegharot (7.69%) than outside Tsaghkahovit (1.33%).

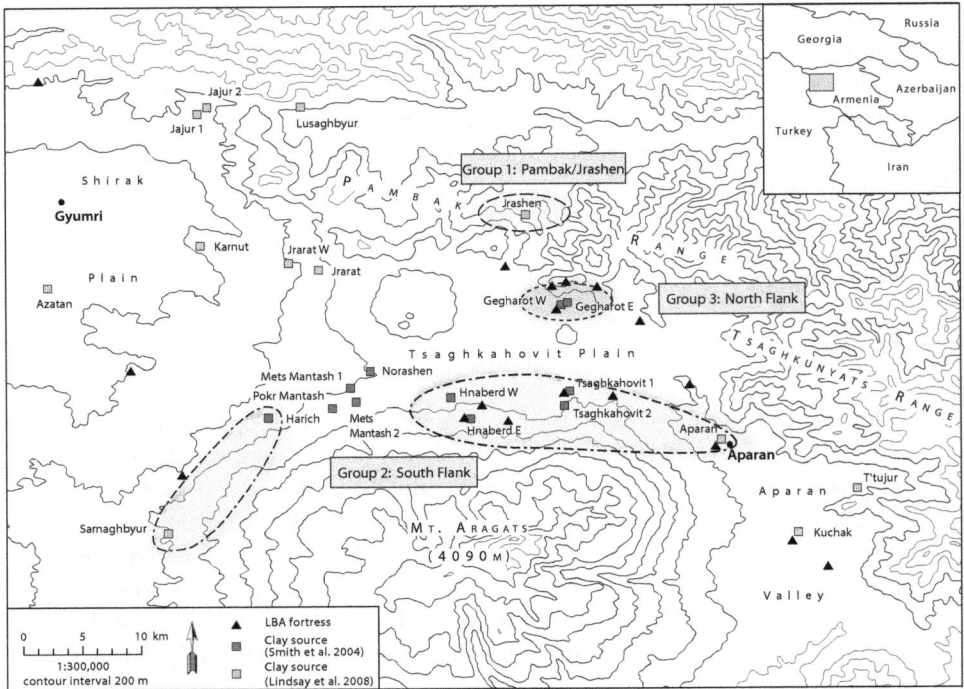

Fig. 40. Map of the Tsaghkahovit Plain showing clay sources and elemental source groups based on instrumental neutron activation analysis. (Map Credit: Ian Lindsay, used with permission.)

This hint at Gegharot's possible privileged position within the flows of things is underscored by the apparent movements of ceramics made from local clays (Smith et al. 2004: 35–39). All three of the main local source groups were well represented in the ceramic assemblages from Gegharot, and ceramics from other, sometimes larger, sites on the plain were more restricted to their local sources (table 1). Whereas greater than 75 percent of the sample sherds from Tsaghkahovit Fortress came from its local source group (2) on the southern flank of the plain, Gegharot received only 19 percent of its ceramic wares from the source in the immediate vicinity (3) and more than 65 percent from the clay sources to the south (2) and to the north (1). In other words, it appears that goods were moving into Gegharot far more than they were moving out to other fortresses, again suggesting an asymmetry in local material flows.

Unfortunately, sample sizes from the other locations on the plain are not robust enough to provide meaningful comparisons.

Table 1. Results of INAA Analysis of Ceramics from Four Sites in the Tsaghkahovit Plain

	Group 1 (likely Pambak)	Group 2 (Mt. Aragats north slope)	Group 3 (Gegharot vicinity)	Local indeterminate	Nonlocal outlier	Total
Gegharot Fortress	65 (35.71%)	56 (30.77%)	35 (19.23%)	12 (6.59%)	14 (7.69%)	182
Tsaghkahovit Fortress	8 (17.02%)	36 (76.60%)	2 (4.26%)	0 (0%)	1 (2.13%)	47
Tsaghkahovit residential complex	7 (4.67%)	132 (88.0%)	5 (3.33%)	4 (2.67%)	2 (1.33%)	150
Hnaberd Fortress	1 (3.03%)	25 (75.76%)	3 (3.03%)	2 (6.06%)	2 (6.06%)	33

Source: After Lindsay et al. 2007.

Belinda Monahan's (2012; Badalyan et al. in press) analysis of caprine survivorship and body-part representation for the faunal remains recovered from Late Bronze Age Gegharot extended our understanding of asymmetries in local material flows into a very different medium. Sheep and goat remains together comprise more than 60 percent of the identified specimens. Intriguingly, only 30 percent of the sheep/goat herd survived to the age of three, the point at which females become reproductively viable. Indeed, caprine kill-off was so great that it is unclear whether the herd would have been able to sustain itself. Monahan's conclusion is that the caprine profile does not resemble that of a pastoral group anxious to maintain a sustainable herd, but that it more likely represents a community supplied with animals from multiple herds. Monahan's examination of the caprine body parts from Gegharot has added further support to this suggestion, indicating that the meat brought to the site was traveling in discrete packages composed primarily of the fore- and hindlimbs. These data indicate that the denizens of Gegharot were supplied with specific cuts of meat, reinforcing the suggestion that there was a significant flow of goods into the site.

This differential flow suggests, at the very least, a politicization of the regional economy, requiring not only institutions of rule but also a more or less well-constituted community of subjects, a public responsive to the demands of authority. What is distinctive, therefore, about the patterns in the ceramic and faunal data is not simply the evidence for a privileged command upon resources—those were already visible in the conspicuous consumption of Middle Bronze Age kurgans. Rather what is new is the circulation of this flow through the mediating institutions of the fortresses. The flow of things thus calls our attention to the sensible transubstantiations that occurred as materials moved through the emplaced institutions of fortified sites like Tsaghkahovit and Gegharot.

Transubstantiation

The Late Bronze Age occupation at Gegharot has produced evidence of a number of spaces that appear to have served as workshops for processing raw materials into finished products. The best preserved of these is room 15–01, located on the southwestern edge of the citadel (Badalyan et al. 2008: 62). The room appears to have been first constructed during the initial occupation of the site when the bedrock substrate was cleared and cut. After the site's first destruction episode, sometime during the late fifteenth or early fourteenth century B.C., debris from the original occupation was piled against the remains of the old eastern wall and bedrock scarp, and a new curvilinear wall was constructed against this midden of blackened soil, burned beam fragments, and material culture. The artifacts found within the midden included a shattered Late Bronze Age pithos, a square carved tuff object (perhaps an idol or threshing stone), and an intriguing ceramic statuette (fig. 41b) that appears to depict a horned human figure with a cloak (or skin) covering its head and shoulders.

The occupation floor of the rebuilt room contained an assemblage that appears to have been primarily dedicated to manufacturing (fig. 41a, c–n). Most notably, the presence of hammerstones, anvils, pits, crucibles, and a stone mold (fig. 41a) suggest that the room was a site of metalworking. More specifically, the stone mold indicates that one of the primary products of the room was jewelry. The mold from T15, likely half of a two-faced closed mold, was carved from a quartz diorite native to the area around Gegharot. On one surface, it was engraved with eight distinct motifs, including weapons (daggers, swords) and spoked wheels, and more enigmatic designs, such as a two-headed spear enveloped by two circles. A similar mold was also found in the destruction debris from the West Terrace shrine at Gegharot (fig. 42a). The terrace mold had designs carved into both sides, suggesting it served as the middle piece of a tripartite mold that was held together by a pin or dowel set through the holes drilled on two opposing corners. Like the T15 mold, the West Terrace Shrine mold was also used to produce jewelry. Engraved on each face of the stone were distinct motifs (on

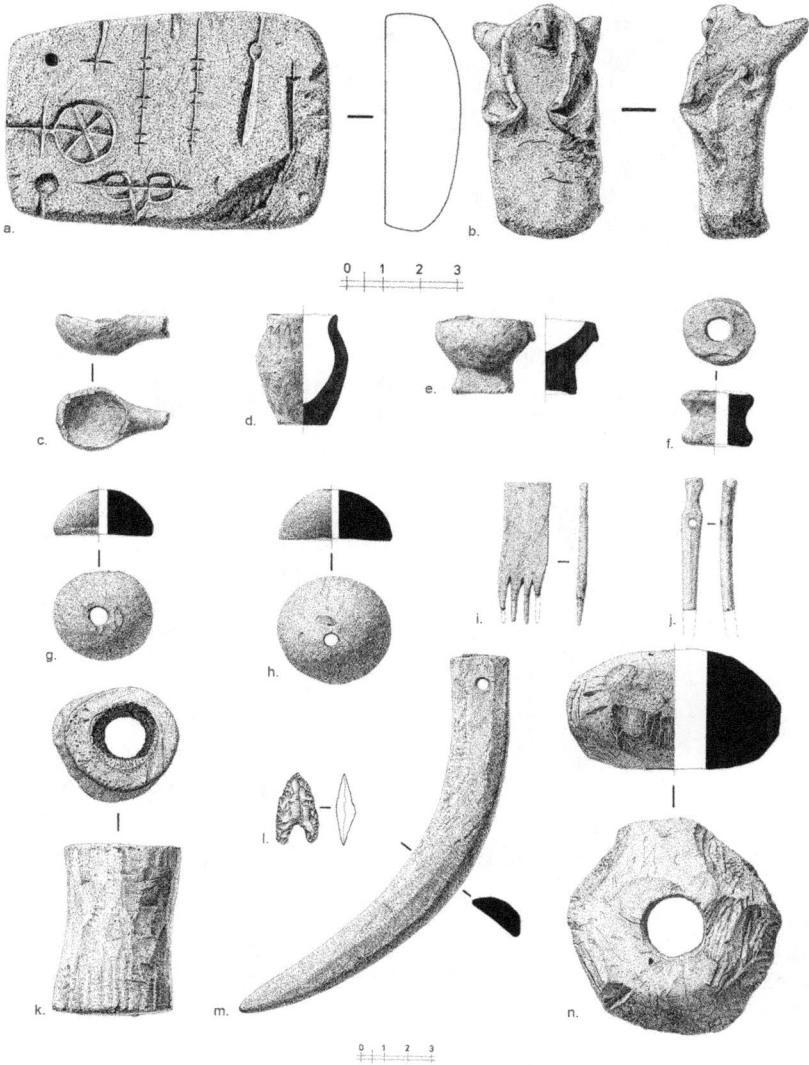

Fig. 41. Materials from room 15–01 at Gegharot. (Drawings by Hasmik Sargisyan, courtesy of Project ArAGATS.)

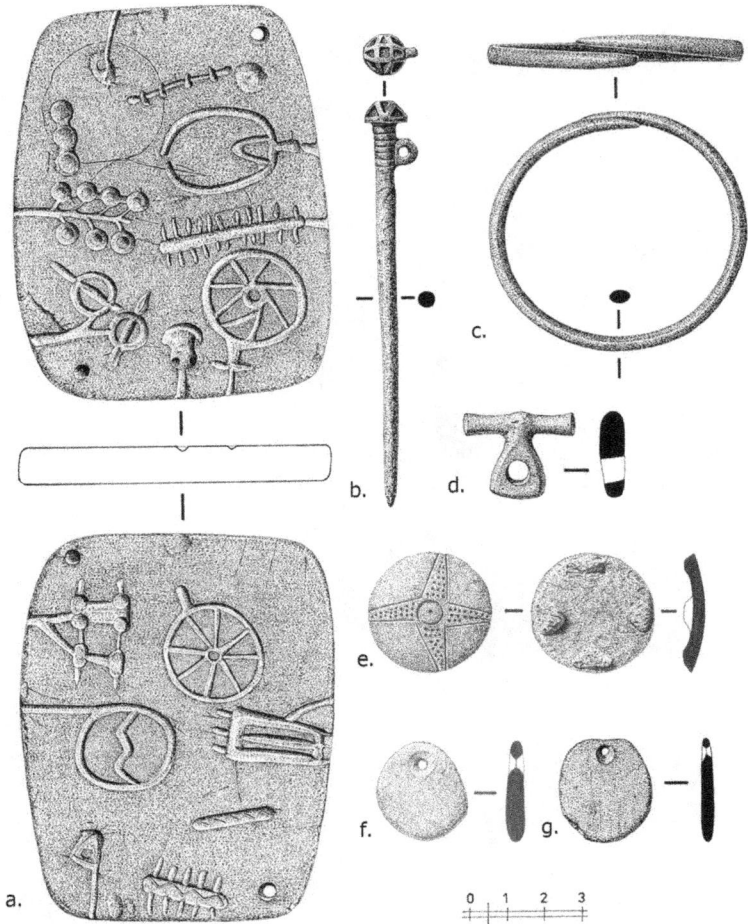

Fig. 42.The jewelry industry at Gegharot: (a–d, f) from West Terrace shrine, (e) from West Citadel shrine. (Drawings by Hasmik Sargisyan, courtesy of Project ArAGATS)

the obverse 7 designs, on the reverse 10) including spoked wheels, arboreal forms, a frog,[7] a four-wheeled wagon, and, again, spears piercing circles.

Given the evidence for jewelry manufacturing at the site, it is perhaps not surprising that the majority of finished metalwork from Gegharot are bronze ornaments, including buttons, fibulae, and bracelets (fig. 42b–c).

[7] The frog motif is highly reminiscent of a gold plated frog (1.75 cm long) from kurgan 2 at Lchashen (Mnatsakahnyan 1961: 70, fig. 24.1).

Interestingly, we find a similar repertoire of personal adornments in bone and stone (fig. 42d–g), suggesting that the production of jewelry at Gegharot was an industry that operated across different material media yet generated an assemblage of closely related products. The focus of Gegharot's manufacturing on items of personal display indicates an industry primarily dedicated to the production of social difference. As Michelle Marcus (1993) points out in her study of lion pins from Iron Age Hasanlu, items of personal adornment work to simultaneously define group cohesion and reinforce hierarchical divisions by enveloping elite bodies within a "social skin" of distinction (after Turner 1980).

Thus, it appears that the wider flows in material so suggestive of a well-constituted political community fueled transubstantiations dedicated to its fragmentation through display. Jewelry molds similar to those found at Gegharot are known from Late Bronze Age sites across the South Caucasus, including the nearby site of Aragatsiberd, indicating that Gegharot did not hold a local monopoly on metalworking. However, as at Gegharot, almost all of the comparanda recovered from settlement contexts were found in close association with locations of ritual practice (Badalyan et al. 2008: 72). It is thus important to note that the sensible transubstantiations accomplished at Gegharot, supported by a dense network of material flows from the region, were set within a built environment devoted to ritual practices. To move to these aspects of the political machine in the Late Bronze Age is to move away from the strictly sensible elements of circulation and manufacturing and towards the domain of sense.

SENSE

Metamorphosis

The sensual domain of the Late Bronze Age political machine is most strikingly apparent in the devotional assemblages that have been uncovered from three shrines at Gegharot (fig. 43).[8] The extensive assemblages from the shrines certainly include objects tied to the flow of goods and practices of manufacturing. However, they are socially intelligible only in terms of their ability to mediate human ties to the sacred. Each of the shrines consisted of a single room. Where the surrounding walls have survived, they

[8] Portions of this discussion appeared previously in Smith and Leon (2014). Special thanks to Jeffrey Leon for his contribution to the analysis of Gegharot's shrines.

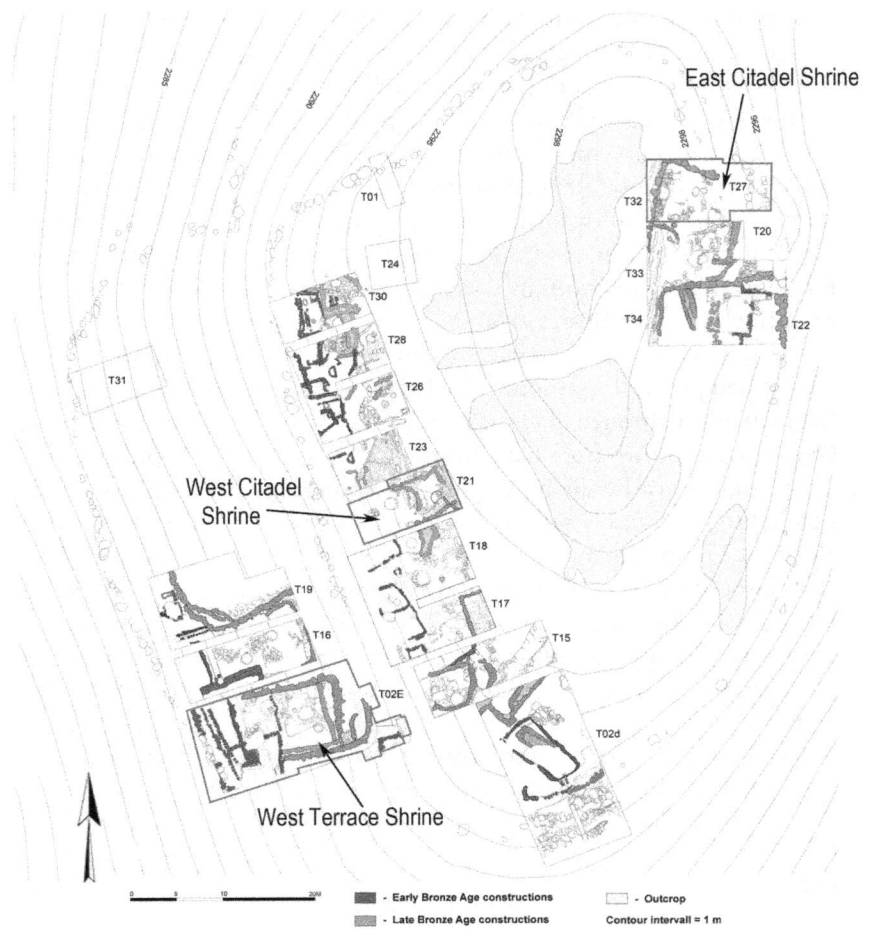

Fig. 43. Map of Gegharot citadel showing outlines and locations of the site's three Late Bronze Age shrines. (Courtesy of Project ArAGATS; architectural drawings by Hasmik Sargisyan and Lilit Ter-Minasyan; topographic map by Adam T. Smith.)

were rectilinear, constructed of worked granite blocks or shaped bedrock. In the center of the upslope wall was a circular packed clay basin filled with ash and ceramic vessels. The floors of the shrines were littered with artifacts of devotion, including censers and idols, an assemblage that was augmented by a daunting array of large and small ceramic vessels related to storage and consumption. The spaces are thus immediately recognizable as hosting broadly similar social practices, even as each presents distinctive features.

The West Terrace shrine was the largest and most architecturally complex of the three shrines at Gegharot, yet it shares the same basic layout and features as the other two (Badalyan et al. 2008: 65ff). The interior space of the room was organized around a large semicircular packed clay basin situated towards the back of the room and set atop a clay platform. A stone stele at the back of the basin likely served as focal point for ritual attention. A pit dug into bedrock lay to the south of the clay basin. The ceramic assemblage recovered from the West Terrace shrine was remarkably large and diverse, including numerous in situ storage vessels, pots, bowls, cups, and a series of variously elaborated censers.

The West Citadel shrine was the smallest and most incomplete of the three shrines (Badalyan et al. in press). Like the one just below on the west terrace, the West Citadel shrine was focused on a clay basin oriented to the west and contained a number of ceramics and layers of ash. A deep pit containing a complete storage vessel and sherds from other large jars was again found just adjacent to the basin. The ceramic assemblage from the floor of the shrine contained a diverse collection of vessels from small cups and bowls to storage vessels. Of particular note was an unusual ceramic form found inside the basin. Known in Armenian as a *manghal*, the object is oval with flat straight sides and openings at both ends (for an example, see fig. 45q).

The East Citadel shrine has yielded the most diverse assemblage of artifacts linked to practices of divination (Badalyan et al. in press). Like the other two, the East Citadel shrine was also focused on a clay basin (fig. 44 midground), but this one was set atop a raised clay platform. The basin was flanked on the north side by a stone bench, atop which we uncovered a large storage vessel slumped onto its side, and on the south side by a small clay platform, where a ceramic manghal (fig. 45q) was perched (similar to the one found in the West Citadel shrine). Near the southern limit of the room (the foreground in fig. 44) was a grinding installation with a groundstone platform, a small grain bin made of clay, and at least two complete, handheld grinding stones. Adjacent to the platform were two largely complete mid-size storage jars.

The eastern portion of the East Citadel shrine contained an encompassing array of in situ ceramic vessels (fig. 45a–r), including everything from large pithoi to small jars, cups, and bowls (more than 45 complete vessels in all). Interestingly, this storage area included several vessels identical to those found in and around the clay basin, including a number of storage jars, cups and bowls, and an additional manghal. Macrobotanical, phytolith, and pollen analyses from the ceramic assemblage indicate wheat processing

Fig 44. The altar (midground) and grinding area (foreground) in the East Citadel shrine at Gegharot. (Photo credit: Adam T. Smith.)

and storage and the likely presence of wine (Cummings and Yost 2011). The clay basin in the East Citadel shrine, centered on the interior wall running north–south, contained ceramic assemblages dominated by relatively small, closed vessels that may have been used in the consumption of substances stored in the larger vessels that sat off the clay platform.

This shrine assemblage as a whole appears to have been focused upon the transformation of value, the manufacture of sacred things out of profane materials. But there appear to be different registers within which such transformations took place. Metamorphosis is visible in the transformation of everyday things into objects of deep affective significance. Indeed, the hieratic nature of these spaces is most demonstrably indicated by the clay idols, three of which were found in the West Terrace shrine, and two more from the basin in the East Citadel shrine. Although, in sensible terms, the idols (fig. 45s) are rather simple figures of unlevigated baked clay, they must have borne a formidable sensual power of signification that was the product not of their manufacture but of their metamorphosis from clay into deity. The idols were found in close proximity to ceramic forms that are

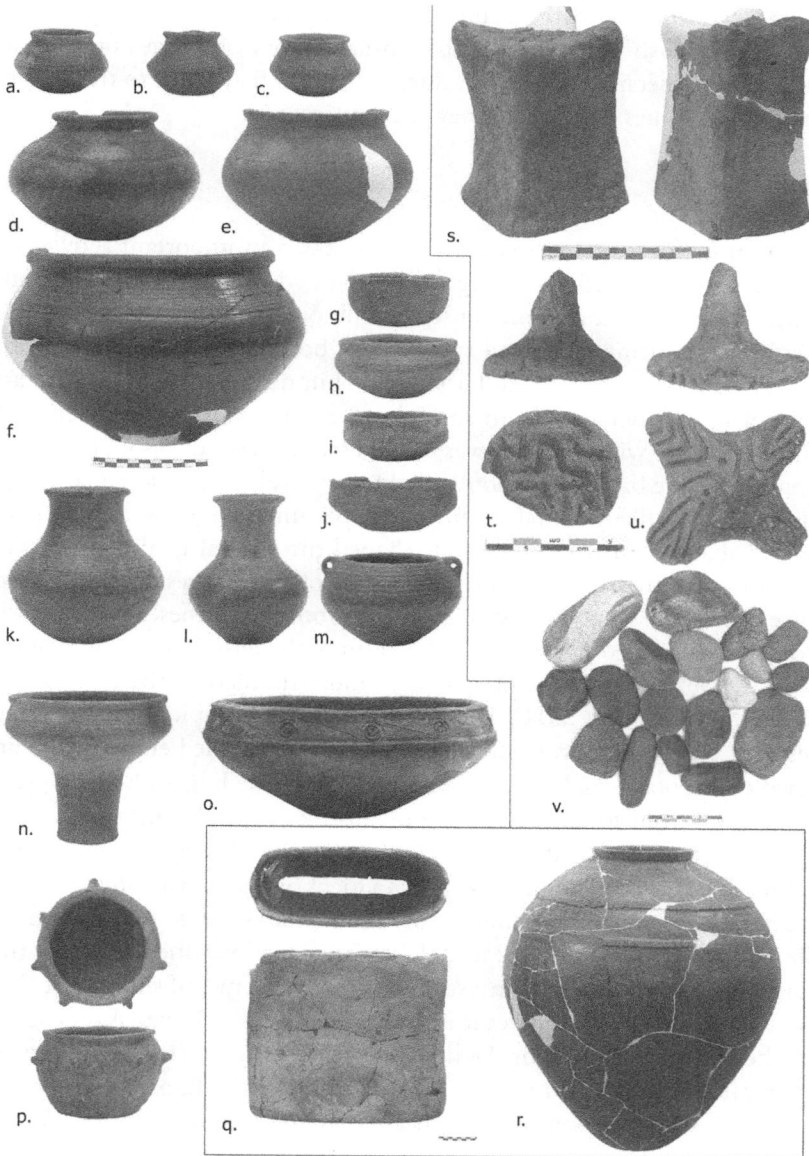

Fig. 45. Gegharot's East Citadel shrine assemblage: (a–m, o–p) jars, cups, and bowls, (n) censer, (q) manghal, (r) storage jar, (s) clay idol, (t–u) clay stamps, (v) collection of small stones from the shrine basin. (Courtesy of Project ArAGATS.)

most clearly linked to the combustion of aromatic or other substances. Hence, they push us to consider the sensual efficacy of things not solely as they achieve metamorphoses in value, but also as they work to transfigure the human bodies with which they came into contact.

Transfiguration

The burning of substances appears to have been an important activity associated with the shrines at Gegharot, indicated by the presence of both simple and elaborate ceramic censers within or adjacent to the basins. The West Terrace shrine contained two censers, both ornately decorated with incised wave-like patterns, and a simple "chimney"; the basin of the East Citadel shrine included an in situ "chimney" (fig. 45n) with evidence of burning on the wide end that was found embedded in the ash. The vessels from inside the basins were dominated by relatively small, closed jars (e.g., fig. 45k, l) that likely contained unguents, perfumes, incense, or other substances that would have powerfully shaped the sensual qualities of devotional ritual—the smells, tastes, and sounds of sacred rites. In addition to the evidence of wine in the storage vessels from the shrines, a pollen wash from a two-handled pot found in the basin of the East Terrace shrine indicated the possible presence of ephedra, a mild stimulant native to Armenia (Cummings and Yost 2011). The presence of psychotropic substances suggest that transfiguration in the Late Bronze Age included embodied pharmacological practices. However, the alteration of the human body appears to have also been accomplished in more distinctly social registers.

As noted earlier in this chapter, the centrality of jewelry within Gegharot's metalworking industry suggests a focus on manufacturing emblems of aesthetic distinction reminiscent of Adam Smith's (1976: 185) account of the political power of the beautiful (see introduction). Indeed, across the South Caucasus there was an explosion in jewelry manufacturing during the Late Bronze Age. And yet it is during the Middle Bronze Age that we see the clearest evidence for the kinds of charismatic rule that would seem to emphasize pomp and regalia. What then drove the fluorescence of the complex material assemblage dedicated to the manufacture of bodily adornments during the Late Bronze Age just as institutions of rule appear to have become more formalized?

One possibility is that as new manufacturing capacities transformed objects of adornment during the second millennium from rare preciosities to widely distributed emblems of status, a key transfiguration was also at work. An increase in the scale of production would have meant that authority could no longer be manufactured from simple scarcity, from the value generated by a personal command over the object world. And so the sensual relationship between object and value began to move in reverse as the ornament itself became the repository of value capable of authorizing the body of the aspiring ruler. Jewelry in the Late Bronze Age was not only a result of authority's ability to command resources, but it was also more significantly part of an assemblage that made authority possible. As Deleuze and Guattari note in their examination of the subordination of the war machine to the apparatus of the state: "Jewelry are the affects that correspond to weapons" (Deleuze and Guattari 1986: 86). The figure of the Late Bronze Age bejeweled body had, in this sense, become critical to the reproduction of formal sovereign authority: rulers came and went, but the continuity of the polity now rested squarely in the durable authority of things. Here we see a critical element in the operation of a political machine—instead of our actions imbuing things with significance, we find things gaining efficacy in lending their significance to us. Human bodies may temporarily occupy roles, but the things *reproduce* the roles across generations. The products of Gegharot's jewelry industry thus worked to transfigure a human body into an authoritative one, inseparable from the authorizing machinery.

A similar transfiguration may be at work in two cylinder seals found at Gegharot (fig. 46). Both are of the Mitannian Common Style that gained popularity across southwest Asia and the eastern Mediterranean during the fifteenth and fourteenth centuries b.c. (Collon 1987). In the Near East, these objects are most often interpreted as tools of administration (Rothman 1994); however, they also appear to have worked as amulets. Cylinder seals in the South Caucasus have traditionally been understood as simply imported prestige goods—baubles whose value rested solely in the distance they traveled from their source. But their salience in the South Caucasus should not be entirely divorced from their role in the Near East as devices of authorization. But what was being authorized if not shipments of goods? Cylinder seals found in mortuary contexts in the South Caucasus indicate that the objects were worn around the necks of individuals as pendants, suggesting that perhaps what was being authorized was an individual—a singular body again transfigured into an authoritative one through the efficacious workings of a material assemblage.

Transfiguration relies not simply on the immediacy of things—their presence on, or in, the body—but also on their location within a shared imagination of the efficacy of assemblages, a collection of sentiments that shaped human understandings of the capacities of objects. So let us now

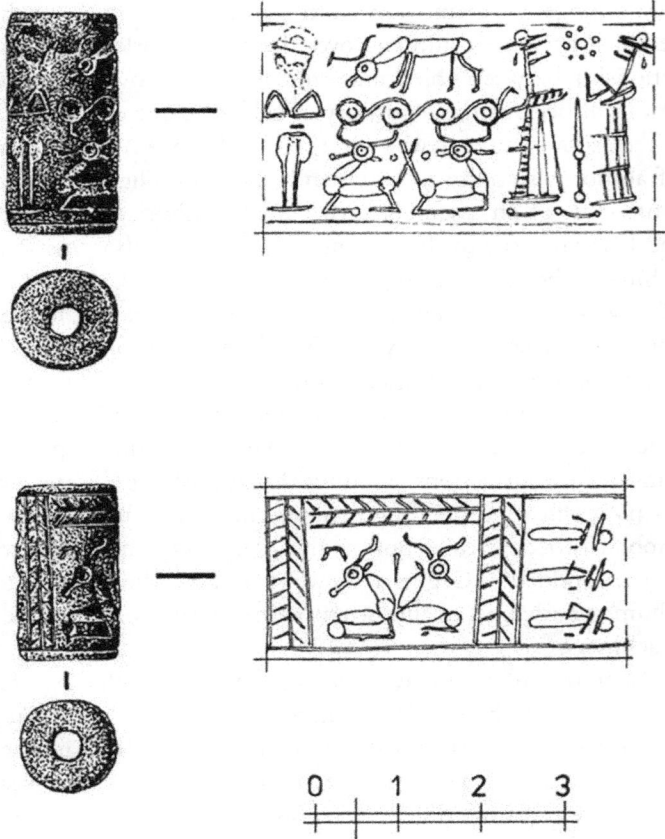

Fig. 46. Two cylinder seals from Gegharot. (Drawings by Hasmik Sargisyan, courtesy of Project ArAGATS.)

turn to this last aspect of the Late Bronze Age political machine in the Tsa-ghkahovit Plain.

SENTIMENT

Sense is linked to the human encounter with form; sentiment describes the imagined capacities of things. The shrines at Gegharot contained an array of things whose operation testifies to the emergence of a new form of capti-vation during the Late Bronze Age—a fascination with the power of things to peer into the workings of the world. Across the three shrines we have recovered what appears to be evidence for three distinct forms of divinatory practice: osteomancy (specifically astragalomancy using knucklebones of quadrupeds), lithomancy (divination by stones), and aleuromancy (divination with flour).

Evidence for osteomancy was found in all three shrines, where caches of cattle and ovicaprid astragali included "dice" that were polished, burned, and often incised with regular patterns of linear striations on one side. *Bos* (cattle) astragali are more numerous than *ovicaprid* (sheep/goat) astragali in all three shrine contexts, with ninety-seven total cattle astragali representing at least sixty-one individual animals.[9] Though there does not appear to be a preference for curating left or right ovicaprid, there does appear to be a strong bias towards left cattle astragali within each of the shrines.[10] In the West Terrace Shrine, forty-eight cattle astragali were recovered, thirty (62.5%) of which were from the left side of the animal, and the remaining eighteen (37.5%) were from the right side. The East Citadel shrine contained thirty-six cattle astragali, with twenty-three (63.9%) left and thirteen right (36.1%). A similar propensity for left astragali is found in the West Citadel shrine, where eight out of thirteen (61.5%) were left astragali. In all three cases, a ratio of approximately two left astragali to every one right astragalus indicates a predilection towards curating astragali from the left side of the animal. This emphasis on left astragali from these contexts is all the more striking when taken alongside the more balanced cattle astragali recovered from nonshrine contexts, which include eighty-four left astragali (49% of the assemblage) and eighty-eight right astragali (51% of the assemblage). The large number of cattle astragali, and especially an asymmetrical ratio of left and right astragali, appears to have played a significant role in the activities associated with the shrines.

Astragali are often associated with cultic activities in the ancient Caucasus, Near East, and Aegean. At the site of Horom in the southern Shirak Plain, just 28.3 kilometers west of Gegharot, excavators uncovered a cultic complex that included a cache of forty-five astragali, which they suggest

[9] Minimum number of individuals calculated based on left astragali.

[10] Sixty-two total ovicaprid astragali represent at least 31 animals (the minimum number of individuals calculated based on left and right astragali). Ovicaprid astragali occur in perfect symmetry across the whole site, with 31 left and 31 right present, and this 1:1 left-to-right ratio is roughly preserved in both the West Terrace and East Citadel shrines. The West Citadel shrine contained more left than right ovicaprid astragali, but the small sample size in this shrine (only 7 total) may account for this offset. Overall, there does not appear to be a preference for curating left or right ovicaprid astragali. My thanks to Belinda Monahan for her analysis of the shrine fauna and to Jeff Leon for his work with the statistical data.

may have been used for divination (Badaljan *et al*. 1994, 17–18). Garth Gilmour (1997) and others (e.g., Binsbergen 2013) have argued that the rolling of the knucklebones functioned as a divinatory activity; indeed the term astragalomancy today describes any form of divination by the casting of lots or dice. Yasur-Landau and colleagues (2012) note that in Mesopotamian and Canaanite texts there is evidence for reserving sacrifices from the right side of the animal for the gods and their attendants. Perhaps the predominance of left cattle astragali from all three shrines indicates a similar allocation of right-sided astragali to the divinity at Gegharot. The striated markings on the astragali likely served to differentiate the dice, which, along with their distribution once thrown, would have been read to indicate a response to a question posed of the diviner.

Evidence for lithomancy at Gegharot has been found only in the East Citadel shrine, where a cache of eighteen small pebbles was found inside the basin (fig. 45v). These stones appear to have been selected for their smooth, rounded shape and their color palette, with hues ranging from black and dark gray to white, green, and red. All of the pebbles were smoothed, but none displayed any conspicuous markings. The use of so-called divining stones is not well attested in textual sources from the ancient Mediterranean, Caucasus, and Near East, but it has been ethnographically documented in Eurasian shamanic traditions (e.g., Pedersen 2001: 422). Powerful stones have been previously recovered archaeologically, most notably those associated with caches of "spirit materials" that include other, better-known media of divination (e.g., Leone 2005: 203). In the case of the Gegharot shrines, when the stones are taken as part of the larger corpus of "spirit materials" found within the East Citadel shrine, it is quite difficult to provide an explanation for their presence that does not implicate them in lithomantic practices.

Evidence for aleuromancy at Gegharot is almost entirely circumstantial and is likewise generally limited to the East Citadel shrine, where the presence of the grinding installation is conspicuous. Aleuromancy is not well attested in the omen literature from the ancient Near East, perhaps because it appears to have been a vernacular tradition of the poor as opposed to a technique favored by professional diviners (George and al-Rawi 1996). The use of flour in ancient divinatory practice appears to have been highly variable. One form involved reading piles of ground flour (Brown 2006), another required mixing flour with water to form a slurry that could be read directly (cf. lecanomancy) or poured out and the residue interpreted (Annus 2010). Another form required that the flour be made into a paste and formed into a cosmogram or effigies (Faraone 1991; Lambert 1957; Reiner

1960). Still another form worked flour into balls of dough that were marked and baked to reveal portents through the behavior of the dough in the fire (Forbes 1959: 540).

The grinding installation in the East Citadel shrine (fig. 44) is particularly conspicuous given the lack of a formal oven for baking. The basin was clearly used for burning materials and certainly could have been used to bake small balls of dough, but it is unlikely that it would have been used to cook loaves of bread. If small lumps of dough were being prepared in the basin, how might they have been marked to help distinguish the portents? This question may help us to understand another set of instruments prominent within the shrine assemblages: clay stamps. The presence of ceramic stamps (fig. 45t, u) in the West Terrace and East Citadel shrines presents a curious archaeological problem. Clay stamps are known from Late Bronze Age sites across the South Caucasus, but to date no clay sealings—the traditional medium of seal impressions in the Near East—have been recorded. We therefore have little evidence for what these stamps were used to mark in the Caucasus, but it does seem likely that it was a perishable material that has not survived in the archaeological record. One possibility (admittedly among many others) is that the stamps marked the divinatory dough that was then used for aleuromancy.

The sequestering of varied divinatory practices behind the fortress walls of Gegharot implies a significant link between sovereignty and prognostication. The shrines at Gegharot suggest that the mystery of sovereign power is not limited to the forms of mediation attendant to the aesthetic potency of "pomp" and the technologies of publicity. As a site of divinatory practice, formalized within the distributed spaces of the shrines, Late Bronze Age Gegharot was, in effect, also a novel apparatus of captivation, placed at the heart of the Tsaghkahovit Plain's political machine. This is not to argue for the generalizability of a kind of oracular sovereign, but rather to suggest that there is a principle critical to the formalization of sovereignty that was shaped at Gegharot into an apparatus of esoteric practice. In one sense, the operation of the divinatory assemblage would have provided a critical bulwark to sovereignty by bolstering claims to specialized knowledge and a privileged relation to the divine (Smith and Leon 2014). But what is especially fascinating about the oracular focus of Gegharot's material world is its institutionalization within the highly restricted space of the fortress.

In this respect, the captivation of the divinatory assemblage lies in the capacity of the sovereign to discipline the world of powerful things, to bring them into the polity and thus appropriate them to the work of governance. Divination, as a means of peering into the inner workings of the

Fig. 47. Anthropomorphic figure on a Late Bronze Age ceramic sherd from Gegharot. (Photo credit: Adam T. Smith.)

cosmos through portents of possible futures, is a theosophical discipline quite similar to those that Foucault (1979: 5) called "the arts of government." Divinatory practices thus anticipate approaches to "simplification" that James Scott (1998) has observed in early modern states. After all, divination makes complex presents and inscrutable futures appear to be more legible and hence more susceptible to calculation. The form of sovereignty at work during the Late Bronze Age at Gegharot was a significant shift in the imagination of rule from the Middle Bronze Age. Let me illustrate what I mean in relation to a single unique find from the site.

In 2008, amidst a dense midden adjacent to the terrace shrine, we came upon a striking fragment of a large storage jar (fig. 47). Set on the shoulder of the jar, in high relief, was a crude human figure. The head is sadly missing, but what is most extraordinary about the piece is the small fragment of an obsidian blade stabbed into the figure's midsection. The violence of the image is of course inescapable, recalling the brutality of the scenes on the Karashamb goblet from several centuries prior. But the Gegharot figure is not a technically skilled adornment for a silver drinking vessel of elite ceremony buried with its owner. It is instead a decidedly unembellished representation of the human figure applied to a nondescript storage jar that was unceremoniously disposed of in a midden.

What is of interest here, I suggest, is not solely the possibility that the Gegharot figure worked as a kind of poppet, even as that is certainly notable. Instead, what is curious is the reductive abstraction of the image—a stick figure rendered in clay—and the apparently unceremonious deposition of the object in a midden. The figure, object, and midden, taken together, are, I suggest, indicative of a form of captivation similar to what Alfred Gell (1992) described as "enchantment." Whereas earlier Middle Bronze Age political aesthetics were staked firmly on the martial heroics of charismatic rulers—sentiments captured in the scenes on the Karashamb goblet—Late Bronze Age political communities were grounded instead in an increasingly depersonalized, routinizing material apparatus that captivated through its own operation. Sovereignty itself, in other words, became an object in the Late Bronze Age, entrancing subjects through the regular operation of governance. Affective commitments to charismatic rulers were transformed into affective commitments to a material apparatus of rule— from an organic body onto a political machine—whose smooth operation, to recall Adam Smith (1976: 185; see introduction), generated aesthetic pleasure and a durable commitment far in excess of the limited powers of coercion and consent.

THE ENDURING POLITICAL MACHINE

Let me bring this examination of the South Caucasus during the epochal Bronze Age to a historical, perhaps even cinematic, conclusion. The operation of the Tsaghkahovit Plain's Late Bronze Age political machine was brought to an end sometime in the late thirteenth or early twelfth century B.C. in a paroxysm of violence that swept through the region. The fortresses at Tsaghkahovit and Gegharot were destroyed ushering in another phase of regional depopulation that endured for the next 500 years. But although the sovereigns of the Tsaghkahovit Plain were undone, the basic engineering of the political machine had metastasized across the South Caucasus and neighboring regions. By the end of the Late Bronze Age, around 1150 B.C., hilltops and rock outcrops from eastern Anatolia to the Great Caucasus had been sculpted into fortified emplacements of the political machine. This political machine worked to transform the polity itself into a kind of object, possessed of a remarkable power to order, authorize, discipline, and captivate.

Karin Knorr-Cetina and Urs Bruegger (2000) have observed a similar kind of machinic object in their study of how currency traders relate to the abstraction of "the market." They describe how the market exists for traders as objects of attachment. As one trader described the market: "It's a life form that has being in its own right. [...] It has form and meaning" (151). The market appears to traders through a series of representations carried on digital displays that present price information, deal requests, deal histories, news feeds, and internal analyses. The market thus appears as a vast totality ("everything" in the words of one trader) impossible to completely comprehend and constantly changing under the pressure of new events. Knorr-Cetina and Bruegger (2000: 150) conclude that "markets are objects of observation because they are not neatly defined within trading environments, they do not have clear borders, and do not reduce to known groups of players engaging in transparent deals." Markets are therefore, to use the terminology used here, kinds of machines independent of any particular subject yet clearly encompassing of their actions. The market expresses its "wants" or "lacks" through the signals on digital-display messages that bind traders to it through structures of perpetual desire.

The political machine assembled in the Late Bronze Age Caucasus, I suggest, worked in a similar fashion. It is clear from the sustained flow of goods into the citadel at Gegharot that a well-ordered public was made aware of the sovereign's lacks and were caught up in a structure of desire that created a kind of reciprocity. Resources flowed into the political machine, and what flowed out was an account of the world, one that made "everything" legible through its own workings. Like the twenty-first-century market, the new polity of the Late Bronze Age was visible most consequentially through its shimmering surfaces—transfigured bodies bedecked in jewelry rather than flickering LCDs. However, these emblems were not just the regalia of political pomp, they were themselves made and made possible by the new configuration of sovereignty. Hence the transubstantiations and transfigurations, metamorphoses and captivations, accomplished within Late Bronze Age citadels like Gegharot provided not simply the material of power but manufactured the affective regimes at the heart of the political.

I should underline that the political machine of the Late Bronze Age did not by any means replace the earlier war machine or civilization machine. Indeed, the political machine would have been unthinkable without the continued operation of those apparatuses. Absent a coherent public bound by a civilization machine there would have been no well-ordered public to respond to the claim to supremacy at the heart of sovereignty. Absent a war machine, there would have been no apparatus of constituted power to divide the social body and define territorial distinction. Thus the political machine was heavily conditioned by the continued operation of older elements in the sovereign assemblage. The efficacy of the political machine lay in its ability to reproduce the desire to be subject to a regularized order of sovereign rule, to attempt to fulfill the machine's endless lacks through the performance of the obligations of subjection. The consequential innovation of the political machine was thus to displace the affective commitments of subjects to sovereigns from the elevated body itself and onto the machinery of reproduction. Hence the death of one sovereign no longer entailed the reordering of the political but merely the substitution of another bejeweled body into the particular relations maintained by the machine.

This is not to suggest that the human capacity for action was ever after confined within an iron cage of constant reproduction. The political machine does not operate simply by entangling or entrapping us. Rather, we are deeply attached to its continued operation; our desire for its continued working is the political machine's most consequential product. Hence, the observation of an apparatus of reproduction in no way guarantees its continual operation or its immunity from tinkering and reengineering. David Hume (1826: 147), for example, marveled at how Henry VIII "was able to set the political machine in that furious movement, and yet regulate and even stop its career: He could say to it, Thus far shalt thou go and no farther: And he made every vote of his parliament and convocation subservient, not only to his interests and passions, but even to his greatest caprices." The vernacular idea of "political will"—overused and undertheorized (cf. Raile et al. 2014)—concedes the consequential operation of the political machine to reproduce existing conditions and the formidable application of agency required to dislodge or redirect its workings. An archaeology of the political machine thus ultimately leads to both a reassessment of our theoretical understanding of the efficacy of objects and a critical reappraisal of the very premises of our constitution as political subjects in our engagement with a host of things.

Conclusion ||||||||||||||||||||||||||||||||||||||||||||||||||||||||||||||||||||||||||||||||||||||||||||||||||||||||

You are the big dream of our small land,
The object of our centuries of longing, our beloved of stone.

(Sevak, in Isabekyan 1968)

On December 17, 2010, a policewoman in the Tunisian city of Sidi Bouzid, 300 kilometers south of Tunis, confiscated an unlicensed produce cart from twenty-six-year- old Mohamed Bouazizi, the sole income earner for a large extended family. When Bouazizi went to the governor's office to complain, officials refused to even see him. Humiliated by the brutality of the police and the imperious disregard of local officials, Bouazizi acquired a can of gasoline and set himself on fire in front of the headquarters of the provincial government. Video of the incident, along with subsequent images of Bouazizi in a hospital bed covered head to foot in white gauze, sparked riots across Tunisia that ultimately led to the downfall of then president Zine El Abidine Ben Ali and cascaded into popular uprisings across northeast Africa and the Middle East.[1] By 2012, governments had also fallen in Libya and in Egypt; mass demonstrations had elicited crackdowns in Iran, Yemen, and Bahrain; and Syria had collapsed into a violent civil war. In the aftermath of Tunisia's Jasmine Revolution, Bouazizi and his cart were immortalized on a postage stamp, and an anonymous Kuwaiti businessman offered to pay $10,000 for the produce cart itself in the hope of erecting a monument in central Tunis. This patron of revolution noted: "This cart changed the course of history."[2]

My focus in this book has been to examine the efficacy of things in political reproduction. But this theoretical and empirical project also necessarily entails rethinking the conditions of historical transformation: how do things fall apart when such a dense apparatus appears to be dedicated to

---

[1] *New York Times*, 1/21/2011. http://www.nytimes.com/2011/01/22/world/africa/22sidi.html ?pagewanted=all&module=Search&mabReward=relbias%3As&_r=0.
[2] *Al Arabiya News*, 1/20/2011. http://www.alarabiya.net/articles/2011/01/20/134314.html.

reproducing the conditions of sovereignty? We might be tempted to pose this query as two distinct lines of investigation: one, an inquiry into the role of things in undermining reproduction and another that returns to the human subject, the *locus classicus* of political thought, to retheorize agency after the material turn. But the collaboration of Bouazizi and his cart suggest that these are in fact the same question, that agency can only be understood in reference to the things mustered to effectively alter the machinery of reproduction.

The things of Sidi Bouzid's revolution were not entirely distinct from the traditional machinery of sovereign reproduction that had long stabilized authoritarian rule. The all-too-quotidian shakedown of an unlicensed fruit seller by an agent of the police could have served as just another moment of political reproduction—a reaffirmation of sovereign authority to discipline subjects by restricting their relations to some things (e.g., the fruit cart) through the mediation of other things (e.g., a license). Bouazizi, however, redrew the points of articulation between the elements of the assemblage. License and cart were spliced into an alternative assemblage of gasoline, bandages, and burned flesh. This newly configured set of material relations that orbited around Bouazizi worked against the machinery of reproduction, metamorphosing an apparatus of indisputable authoritarian intimidation into a fragile infrastructure of domination. In the process, an unlicensed produce cart was transformed into a $10,000 memorial to the Jasmine Revolution.

What spliced the things of authoritarian rule into a new assemblage of resistance was what traditional social thought would call "political action," or, in a wider sociological field, human agency. The machine analytic that I have outlined in the theoretical interventions and empirical studies of this book suggests that political action should not be understood in the narrow sense advanced by Collingwood (1928: 165) as "regulation, control, the imposition of order and regularity upon things"; nor should political action be restricted to an emancipatory sense of *praxis* that demands a dramatic reordering of things (e.g., Habermas 1973). Rather, a theorization of political action that embraces things into the polity describes any activity that manipulates the points of articulation between the object assemblages and human assemblies constitutive of the body politic. Political action, in other words, strives to transform sense, sensibility, and sentiment in order to reconfigure the logics of association.

It was the sensible workings of things on Bouazizi's body that loomed largest in press accounts, the working of gasoline and spark on outraged flesh. But it is impossible to overlook the sensual workings of things on

Bouazizi, that is, their transfiguration of a merchant into an iconic figure of the Arab Spring. Moreover, if prerevolutionary Tunisia was captivated by the working of a seemingly unchallengeable political machine, Bouazizi's actions reconfigured the field of sentiment, exposing the frailty of order and undoing the magical spell of state solidity that Bourdieu (1992: 208) described as political fetishism. Bouazizi's defiant protest was, of course, it self located within an assemblage—gas can, gasoline, ignition—and his act was disseminated to the wider public through a wide variety of mediating technologies, including YouTube and Twitter.

Human capacities for political action are always embedded in a world of things. What Bouazizi accomplished was to challenge the coherence of Tunisia's political machine, to undermine the linkages between objects and subjects, and thus reframe machinic operations. Hence, what had been an unchallengeable apparatus of domination was recast as a fragile web of illegitimate relations. Political action, Bouazizi's example suggests, lies not in simply resisting the machine, but in rewiring it to other ends. Social transformation must then lie in the overlapping power of human agency and efficacy to forestall reproduction, in the collaboration of assemblies and assemblages.

The assemblages of the Jasmine Revolution lie rather far removed from the region at the center of this book's primary empirical concerns. So let me draw these examinations to a close by considering the collaboration of assemblages and assemblies in the Caucasus. Fittingly, returning to the Caucasus also brings us back onto the terrain of archaeology and the efficacy of the things it summons from the earth.

EREBUNI-YEREVAN

On October 25, 1950, an Armenian archaeologist conducting reconnaissance and reconstruction work atop the small hill of Arin-Berd, on the southern outskirts of Yerevan, uncovered a rectangular basalt stone. [3] The face of the stone had been cut and smoothed, and a brief cuneiform inscription was etched into the surface. The inscription read:

> For the greatness of god Khaldi, Argishti, son of Menua, built this majestic fortress and gave it the name Irpuni (Erebuni). It was built for the great land of Biainili and for the pacification of the enemy lands. Argishti speaks: The earth was wilderness; I accomplished great deeds there. For the greatness of

[3] An earlier version of this discussion appeared in Smith (2012b).

god Khaldi, Argishti, son of Menua, powerful king, King of the lands of Biainili, ruler of Tushpa. (Arutyunian 2001: #197–198)

Built in 782 b.c., the fortress of Erebuni had once guarded the northern
reaches of Biainili, better known today as the kingdom of Urartu. Urartu,
was an Iron Age descendant of the South Caucasus's Late Bronze Age political machine (Smith 2012c), an expansionary polity that emerged on the
shores of Lake Van during the early first millennium b.c. A formidable apparatus of military power, bureaucratic regulation, and religious piety, the
Urartian polity spread rapidly during the ninth and eighth centuries b.c. to
unite a large swath of the Armenian Highland under a single imperial regime. However, pressures from surrounding rivals and internal instability
led to the collapse of Urartu sometime during the late seventh century b.c.,
after which it slowly receded from historical memory (Khatchadourian
2008b, 2013).

So it is quite extraordinary that in 1968 the Soviet Union held a year-
long series of all-union events commemorating the founding of the Urartian fortress at Erebuni, on the outskirts of Yerevan, to mark what was billed
as the 2,750th anniversary of the city's founding. Yerevan, capital of the Armenian Soviet Republic, was saluted as the oldest city in the Soviet Union,
and the anniversary celebrations made it into most of the major papers, including *Literaturnaya Gazetta*, *Pravda*, and *Moscow News*. The celebration
culminated with a mass gathering on October 19 held amidst Erebuni's re-
constructed ruins that was attended, according to *Moscow News*, by an estimated 300,000 residents—roughly half the population of the city. The celebration in itself is quite remarkable—a rare Soviet-era episode of an
authorized mass national rally. But still more compelling was how the event
inaugurated a new archaeologically derived assemblage that transformed
the material fabric of Yerevan—its architecture and its everyday commodities—and in so doing opened new possibilities for collaborations between
assemblages and assemblies.

The Museum of the Founding of Yerevan (a.k.a. the Erebuni Museum),
located at the bottom of Arin-Berd hill, was one of the first substantial de-
ployments of the new assemblage to the remaking of Yerevan. The building
was designed as a square box surrounding a central courtyard, mimicking
the square designs of Urartian temple cellas. The façade is decorated with
applied friezes that re-present the iconographic palette of Urartian sources
within the formal repertoire of socialist realism (fig. 48). At the center,
above the entryway, the head of Argishti stares out *en face* toward the center
of Yerevan. He is flanked on the left by eight figures bearing the round

Fig. 48. The façade of the Museum of the Founding of Yerevan. (Photo credit: Adam T. Smith.)

shields and weapons of Urartian soldiers. On the right, also in profile, are eight attendants with hands in traditional positions of supplication, bearing goods to the king.

The Erebuni Museum was by no means the only appearance of the new, archaeologically inspired assemblage on the streets of Yerevan. Commodities from brandy to cigarettes were rebranded with names and emblems derived from archaeological sites (fig. 49a). Decorations and wall murals inspired by archaeological motifs appeared on the city's major arteries. On Lenin Prospect, stone reliefs (fig. 49b) and wire friezes deployed iconography drawn directly from artifacts and decorative art recovered by the excavations at Erebuni. On Tumanyan St., an embossed mural repurposed an array of Urartian-inspired motifs (fig. 49c). The year 782, the founding date for Erebuni, appears on the upper-right-hand corner above an Urartian cauldron. The three warrior figures with round shields and short skirts echo the relief on the Erebuni Museum façade, while to the left is the traditional Urartian figure of a winged genie tending a stylized tree of life. At the center of the composition one figure hands a stylized tower with crenellated battlements to another figure. A small tree rises from the center, with the entire element surrounded by a radiant corona.

Fig. 49. Yerevan's archaeological assemblage: (a) Arin-Berd cigarette pack with the tower and tree logo and 1968 anniversary date, (b) Bull and Lion stone relief on Lenin (now Mashtots) Prospect derived from Erebuni wall paintings, (c) Urartian-inspired wall mural on Tumanyan Street. (Photo credit: Adam T. Smith.)

The tree and tower motif is known from an array of Urartian materials, including a clutch of bronze bowls discovered at the site of Karmir-Blur, which, like Erebuni, is located within the territory of modern Yerevan. The tower and tree appears on the Karmir-Blur bowls as a hieroglyph incised on the interior, often alongside an inscription that claims the objects as property of the king (fig. 50 inset). We see this same tower and tree motif repeated in what is perhaps the most peculiar of the Soviet National redeployments of a recuperated archaeological repertoire: a monument erected in 1970 to commemorate the fiftieth anniversary of Soviet Armenia (fig. 50). Set into a steep rock outcrop at the northern apex of the city's circular central precinct, a cascading stairway ascends to an elevated platform on which stands a 50-meter-high stone obelisk. Surmounting the obelisk is a sculpture depicting the same fortified tower with a stylized tree rising from its crenellated battlements.

In working toward an understanding of the archaeologically derived assemblage that flourished on Yerevan's streets and in its stores after 1968, Yerevan's obelisk poses a unique interpretive challenge. What can this hieroglyph of kingly privilege have possibly meant as an emblem of the Bol-

Fig. 50. Monument commemorating the fiftieth anniversary of Soviet Armenia (photo credit: Adam T. Smith). Inset: bronze bowl from Karmir-Blur with detail of tower and tree hieroglyph and Urartian inscription (after Piotrovskii 1969).

shevik Revolution in Armenia? In the most straightforward sense, the reuse of the tower and tree insignia atop the Yerevan obelisk would seem to stamp the city itself as an object of sovereign possession. Just as the emblem on the bowls from Karmir-Blur claimed them as property of the king, so too their reuse on Yerevan's obelisk would seem to claim Armenia as property of the Soviet Union. However, this reading of the obelisk makes little sense given the role of local officials of the Armenian Soviet Republic in the production of Yerevan's monuments.

A subtler understanding of the reuse of a recuperated Urartian symbol atop a memorial to the Bolshevik Revolution situates the monument within a wider effort, diffused across the built landscape and commodity sphere, to appropriate the array of things erupting from archaeological sites across Armenia to the work of Soviet nationalities policy. As Rogers Brubaker (1996: 29) and other scholars have noted (Slezkine 1994: 450; Suny 1993: 155), Soviet efforts to assimilate non-Russian nationalities to the project of the "new Soviet man" (seen most keenly in linguistic Russification; Gorenberg 2006) were paralleled by policies that actively promoted ethnic identification, particularly among communities of the Soviet Union's ethno-federal republics, such as the Armenian Soviet Republic. As Ronald Suny (1993: 155) has noted, the Kremlin "foster[ed] the development in many republics of native cultures, encouraging education in the local languages, and promoting, through a peculiar form of affirmative action, cadres from the dominant nationality" (see also Martin 2001).

Lenin argued vociferously at the founding of the Soviet Union that only through the cultivation of nationality could the country propel "less developed" cultures into a communist future: "We are going to help you develop your Buriat, Votiak, etc. language and culture, because in this way you will join the universal culture, revolution and communism sooner" (Lenin, quoted in Slezkine 1994: 420). National cultivation was thus securely framed by the historical mission of the Soviet Union as a Marxist-Leninist "dictatorship of the proletariat." However, by the 1970s, "Identification with nationality was for most non-Russians a far more palpable touchstone than the eroded loyalty to social class" (Suny 1993: 171). What accounts for such a dramatic refashioning of non-Russian Soviet subjects from the slogan "national in form, socialist in content" to national in form and content? In Armenia, part of the answer lies in the material assemblage derived from archaeological materials that, during the late 1960s and 1970s, were woven into the fabric of everyday life.

The 1968 celebration at Erebuni was, in most respects, a theatrical enactment of Leninist nationality doctrine. At the opening ceremony, Anton Kochinyan, first secretary of the Central Committee of the Armenian Communist Party, declared, "Yerevan today symbolizes the freedom loving aspirations of our people, the historic victory which it achieved in the arduous and protracted struggle for independence and freedom" (*Moscow News*, October 20,1968). News reports of the occasion reinforced the official account of the ceremony, focusing on Yerevan as a capital reborn under the protection of the Soviet Union. The event was thus presented as an object lesson in Soviet historiography, a reminder of Yerevan's turbulent past as victim of conquerors, from the Urartians to the Ottomans, and its salvation under socialism.

But when the celebration reached its climax at Erebuni, the anthem written to mark the occasion by the poet Payrur Sevak shifted the celebration away from a triumphal celebration of the oldest city in the Soviet

Union to a direct veneration of an Armenian national imaginary. The hymn opens with an apostrophe addressed to the capitals of Armenia past:

Yerevan, born of my Erebuni.
You are our new Dvin, our new Ani.
You are the big dream of our small land,
The object of our centuries of longing, our beloved of stone.

(Sevak, in Isabekyan 1968)[4]

Sevak's poem utilized the object matter of Yerevan—its sensible stone, its sensual histories, its sentimental conjuring of past places and things—to define a public—the first- person plural ("our") of the poetic voice. As such, it stimulated a new collaboration between political action and material efficacy much like that seen in Bouazizi's transformational act of self-immolation, one that transformed "our" Yerevan from a Soviet Armenian first-person plural into an exclusively Armenian one.

Although Sevak's poem did not catalyze an immediate revolutionary uprising, it did effectively resituate the archaeological things that linked Armenia's present to its past and contribute to the ascendency of a national form of identification over the allegiances to class that had been the bedrock of the Soviet project. Erebuni and the archaeologically inspired forms and symbols of Yerevan's built environment and commodity sector did not captivate as memorials to Soviet protection. Rather, they captivated as durable reminders of a distinctly Armenian antiquity.

As a result, these things were effectively detached from the Soviet political machine's apparatus of national cultivation and spliced into an assemblage that proved to be highly efficacious in manufacturing exclusively national Armenian subjects. With the collapse of the Soviet Union, political authorities in the newly independent Armenia did not need to manufacture a new sense of the nation. The redeployed archaeological assemblages that remade Yerevan after the 1968 celebration at Erebuni had already made sensible a distinctly national understanding of the Armenian public, weaving it into the experience of everyday life.

BROTHER AXE

The redeployment of the places and things of Armenia's archaeological past to a distinctly national politics suggests that the material world can

4 Thanks to Lori Khatchadourian for providing this translation.

plays as potent a role in undermining, weakening, and undoing political order as it does in reproducing sovereignty. The machines that reproduce the conditions of sovereignty do not only suffer epochal breakdowns, as was the case in Tunisia's revolution. They also can be retooled, as was the case with the archaeological assemblages that came to promote a sectional account of the Armenian public that would eventually undermine the aspirations of the Soviet political machine. But neither the Tunisian revolution nor the collapse of the Soviet Union dismantled the machinery of sovereign reproduction. Instead, they reconfigured it. If sovereignty lies in the capacity to secure sociopolitical reproduction through the matter that shapes our sense, sensibility, and sentiment, then the hope of a new politics lies not simply in a novel policy idea or a newly anointed charismatic, but in our collective ability to retool our machines. But to do so we must first understand the assemblages that are at work in our lives, attending to their unique ways of working in the world. To misrecognize things as either entirely "other"—solid and unchanging in contrast to human dynamism and flux—or entirely "us"—working in ways fundamentally similar to the way our own bodies move in the world—is to overlook their unique capacities and to ignore their articulation with our human capacities for political action.

Arguably the most amusing caution against misrecognizing our forms of action for the capacities of things also comes from the Caucasus. The Armenian poet Hovannes Toumanyan is best known as a writer whose tales captured the harsh realities of village life in the South Caucasus at the turn of the twentieth century. But Toumanyan also wrote a series of fairy tales that remain staples of children's literature in Armenia today, including the tale of Brother Axe:

Once a man went to a far-off land in search of work. He came to a village where he saw people breaking up firewood with their bare hands.

"Brothers" he said, "why do it with your hands? Have you no axe?"

"What's an axe?" asked the villagers.

The man took an axe from his belt, chopped up the wood and stacked it into a neat pile. [...]

Seeing this, the peasants ran through the village calling: "Hey everybody! Come see what Brother Axe has done!" [...]

They decided to take turns to use the axe. The first day the landlord took his turn. As he swung the first blow the axe landed on his foot and cut it. He rushed through the village roaring with pain.

"Come here, everybody! Brother Axe has run amok. He has bitten my foot."

The peasants ... began to beat the axe. When they saw the axe was none the worse for the heavy beating, they piled wood on it and set fire to it. When the fire had died ... [they] discovered that the axe had turned red.

"Alas!" they cried, "Brother Axe is angry. Look how red he has turned! He will bring some calamity upon us. What shall we do?"

They ... decided to throw the axe in prison. So they took it and flung it into the landlord's barn.... As soon as the red-hot axe touched the hay a fire burst out.

Terrified, the villagers ran after the axe's owner ... and pleaded, "Come, for God's sake, and bring Brother Axe to his senses!" (Toumanyan 1969)

The fable of Brother Axe is a comedy of misrecognition. The stolidity of the axe and its unflinching material properties is set in comical contradistinction to the abjectness of the villagers who seek to reason with it. Theirs is a Promethean misrecognition, a desire to understand the operation of things as isomorphic with the traditional sociology of human action. If an archaeology of the political machine provides a clear analytical imperative, it is to resist anthropomorphic theorizations of things and to accord our vast assemblages a presumption of difference. In doing so, we will undoubtedly uncover a raft of machines working away at reproducing our religious practices, social interactions, economic relations, theologies, cultural entanglements, and worldviews. It is only by closely examining their unique operations that we can ever hope to intervene in their work, not to overcome them but to collaborate with them in reengineering the machinery of political reproduction.

References Cited

Abay, E.
2005 The Expansion of Early Transcaucasian Culture: Cultural Interaction or Migration? *Altorientalische Forschung* 32(1):115–31.
Abibullaev, O. A.
1982 *Eneolit i Bronza na Teritorii Nakhichevanskoy ASSR*. Elm, Baku.
Abramishvili, M.
2010 In Search of the Origins of Metallurgy—An Overview of South Caucasian Evidence. In *Von Majkop bis Trialeti: Gewinnung und Verbreitung von Metallen und Obsidian in Kaukasien im 4.–2. Jt. v. Chr.*, edited by S. Hansen, A. Hauptmann, I. Motzenbäcker and E. Pernicka, 167–78. Dr. Rudolf Habelt GmbH, Bonn.
Adams, R. M.
1966 *The Evolution of Urban Society*. Aldine, New York.
Agamben, G.
1998 *Homo Sacer: Sovereign Power and Bare Life*. Stanford University Press, Stanford, CA.
2004 *The Open: Man and Animal*. Stanford University Press, Stanford, CA.
2005 *State of Exception*. University of Chicago Press, Chicago.
2009 *What Is an Apparatus? and Other Essays*. Stanford University Press, Stanford, CA.
2011 *The Kingdom and the Glory: For a Theological Genealogy of Economy and Government*. Translated by L. Chiesa and M. Mandarini. Stanford University Press, Stanford, CA.
Agnew, J. A.
2009 *Globalization and Sovereignty*. Rowman & Littlefield, Lanham, MD.
Alcock, S.
1993 *Graecia Capta*. Cambridge University Press, Cambridge.
2002 *Archaeologies of the Greek Past: Landscape, Monuments, and Memories*. Cambridge University Press, Cambridge.
Algaze, G.
2001 The Prehistory of Imperialism: The Case of Uruk Period Mesopotamia. In *Uruk Mesopotamia and Its Neighbors: Cross-Cultural Interactions in the Era of State Formation*, edited by M. S. Rothman, 27–83. School of American Research Press, Santa Fe, NM.
Aliev, V. G.
1991 *Kul'tura Epokhi Srednej Bronzy Azerbajdzhana*. Elm, Baku.

Alizadeh, K., H. Eghbal, and S. Samei
   In press   Approaches to Social Complexity in Kura-Araxes Culture: A View
      from Köhne Shahar (Ravaz) in Chaldran, Iranian Azerbaijan. *Paléorient*.
Amiran, R.
   1965   Yanik Tepe, Shengavit, and the Khirbet Kerak Ware. *Anatolian Studies*
      15:165–67.
Anderson, B.
   1983   *Imagined Communities*. Verso, London.
   1990   *Language and Power: Exploring Political Cultures in Indonesia*. Cornell Uni-
      versity Press, Ithaca, NY.
Ankersmit, F. R.
   1996   *Aesthetic Politics: Political Philosophy beyond Fact and Value*. Stanford Uni-
      versity Press, Stanford, CA.
Annus, A.
   2010   *Divination and Interpretation of Signs in the Ancient World*. Oriental Insti-
      tute of the University of Chicago, Chicago.
Anthony, D. W.
   2007   *The Horse, the Wheel, and Language: How Bronze-Age Riders from the Eur-
      asian Steppes Shaped the Modern World*. Princeton University Press, Princeton,
      NJ.
Appadurai, A. (ed.)
   1986   *The Social Life of Things*. Cambridge University Press, Cambridge.
Aquinas, T.
   1964   *Summa Theologiae*, Vol. 13, *Man Made to God's Image*. Blackfriars, New
      York.
   1965   *Summa Theologiae*, Vol. 50, *The One Mediator*. Blackfriars, New York.
Arendt, H.
   1958   *The Human Condition*. University of Chicago Press, Chicago.
Areshian, G., K. Kafadarian, A. Simonian, G. Tiratsian, and A. Kalantarian
   1977   Arkheologicheskie Issledovaniya v Ashtarakskom i Nairiskom Raionakh
      Armyanskoi SSR. *Vestnik Obshchesvennikh Nauk* 4:77–93.
Areshian, G. E.
   1970   Orudiya Truda Artikskogo Mogil'nika. *Istoriko-Filologichskikh Zhurnal*
      3:251–60.
Areshian, G. E., B. Z. Gasparyan, P. S. Avetisyan, R. Pinhasi, K. Wilkinson, A. Smith,
   R. Hovsepyan, and D. Zardaryan
   2012   The Chalcolithic of the Near East and Southeastern Europe: Discoveries
      and New Perspectives from the Cave Complex Areni-1, Armenia. *Antiquity*
      86:115–30.
Areshian, G. E., V. E. Oganesyan, F. M. Muradyan, P. S. Avetisyan, and L. A. Petrosyan
   1990   Konets Srednego Bronzovogo Veka v Mezhdurech'e Araksa i Kury.
      Istoriko-Filologicheskij Zhurnal 128(1):53–74.
Aristotle
   1966   *Metaphysics*. Indiana University Press, Bloomington.
Arkin, R. C.
   2009   *Governing Lethal Behavior in Autonomous Robots*. CRC, Boca Raton, FL.

Arutyunian, N. V.
2001 *Korpus Urartskikh Klinoobraznykh Nadpisej*. Izdatel'stvo "Gitutyun" NAN RA, Yerevan.

Asaro, P.
2006 What Should We Want from a Robot Ethic? *International Review of Information Ethics* 6: 10–16.

Ausch, R., R. Doane, and L. Perez
2000 Interview with Elizabeth Grosz. *Found Object* 9:1–16.

Austen, J.
1922 *Sense and Sensibility*. J. M. Dent and Sons, London.

Avetisyan, P.
2003 Predvaritelnye Raskopok Pamyatnika Agarak. In *Archaeology, Ethnology, and Folklore of the Caucasus: Papers of the International Conference, Yerevan, November 17–18, 2003*, 52–57. Institute of Archaeology and Ethnography NAN RA, Echmiadzin.

Avetisyan, P., R. Badalyan, and A. T. Smith
2000 Preliminary Report on the 1998 Archaeological Investigations of Project ArAGATS in the Tsakahovit Plain, Armenia. *Studi Micenei ed Egeo-Anatolici* 42(1):19–59.

Avetisyan, P., and A. Bobokhyan
2008 The Pottery Traditions of the Armenian Middle to Late Bronze Age "Transition" in the Context of Bronze and Iron Age Periodization. In *Ceramics in Transitions: Chalcolithic through Iron Age in the Highlands of the Southern Caucasus and Anatolia*, edited by K. Rubinson and A. Sagona, 123–83. Peeters, Leuven.

Bachand, B. R.
2006 Preclassic Excavations at Punta de Chimino, Peten, Guatemala: Investigating Social Emplacement on an Early Maya Landscape. Anthropology, University of Arizona, Tucson.

Badaljan, R. S., C. Edens, R. Gorny, P. L. Kohl, D. Stronach, A. V. Tonikajan, S. Hamayakjan, S. Mandrikjan, and M. Zardarjan
1993 Preliminary Report on the 1992 Excavations at Horom, Armenia. *Iran* 31:1–24.

Badaljan, R. S., P. Kohl, D. Stronach, and A. Tonikian
1994 Preliminary Report on the 1993 Excavations at Horom, Armenia. *Iran* 32:1–29

Badalyan, R.
1984 Rannebronzovoe Poselenie Bliz s Karnut. *Istoriko-Filologichskikh Zhurnal* 1:229–37.
1996 Problema Absolyutnoy Khronologii "Shengavitskogo" Kompleksa v Kontekste Kalibrovannykh Radiouglerodnykh Dannykh. In *Tezisy Dokladov 10-oy Nauchnoy Sessii, Posvyashchennoy Itogam Arkheologicheskikh Issledovaniy v Respublike Armenii (1993–1995 gg.)*. Yerevan.

Badalyan, R., and P. Avetisyan
2007 *Bronze and Early Iron Age Archaeological Sites in Armenia I: Mt Aragats and Its Surrounding Region*. British Archaeological Reports International Series S1697. Archeopress, Oxford.

Badalyan, R., P. Avetisyan, and A. T. Smith
  2004a Proekt ArAGATS—Issledovanie Pamyatnikov Pozdnego Bronzovogo Beka v Tsakhkaovitskoj Ravninie. In *Mezhdunarodnaya Nauchnaya Konferentsiya "Arkheologiya, Etnologiya, Fol'kloristika Kavkaza" Sbornik Kratkikh Soderzhanij Dokladov*, 34–35. Nekeri, Tbilisi.
Badalyan, R., C. Chataigner, and P. L. Kohl
  2004b Trans-Caucasian Obsidian: The Exploitation of the Sources and Their Distribution. In *A View from the Highlands: Archaeological Studies in Honour of Charles Burney*, edited by A. Sagona, 437–65. Peeters, Leuven.
Badalyan, R., A. T. Smith, I. Lindsay, L. Khatchadourian, and P. Avetisyan
  2008 Village, Fortress, and Town in Bronze and Iron Age Southern Caucasia: A Preliminary Report on the 2003–2006 Investigations of Project ArAGATS on the Tsaghkahovit Plain, Republic of Armenia. *Archäologische Mitteilungen aus Iran und Turan* 40:45–105.
Badalyan, R., A. T. Smith, I. Lindsay, L. Khatchadourian, A. Harutyunyan, A. Greene, M. Marshall, B. Monahan, and R. Hovsepyan
  In press A Preliminary Report on the 2008, 2010, and 2011 Investigations of Project ArAGATS on the Tsaghkahovit Plain, Republic of Armenia. *Archäologische Mitteilungen aus Iran und Turan*.
Badalyan, R., A. T. Smith, and P. S. Avetisyan
  2003 The Emergence of Socio-Political Complexity in Southern Caucasia. In *Archaeology in the Borderlands: Investigations in Caucasia and Beyond*, edited by A. T. Smith and K. Rubinson, 144–66. The Cotsen Institute of Archaeology at UCLA, Los Angeles.
Bahrani, Z.
  1995 Assault and Abduction: The Fate of the Royal Image in the Ancient Near East. *Art History* 18(3):363.
  2008 *Rituals of War: The Body and Violence in Mesopotamia*. Zone, New York.
Baiburtyan, E. A.
  1938 Kul'tovyj Ochag iz Raskopok Shengavitskogo Poselenija v 1936–37 gg. *Vestnik Drenej Istorii* 4:255–59.
Baines, J.
  2006 Public Ceremonial Performance in Ancient Egypt: Exclusion and Integration. In *Archaeology of Performance: Theaters of Power, Community, and Politics*, edited by T. Inomata and L. S. Coben, 261–302. AltaMira, Lanham, MD.
Baines, J., and N. Yoffee
  1998 Order, Legitimacy, and Wealth in Ancient Egypt and Mesopotamia. In *Archaic States*, edited by G. Feinman and J. Marcus, 199–260. School of American Research Press, Santa Fe, NM.
Barry, A.
  2001 *Political Machines: Governing a Technological Society*. Athlone, London.
Bartelson, J.
  1995 *A Genealogy of Sovereignty*. Cambridge University Press, Cambridge.
Bataille, G.
  1988 *The Accursed Share*, Vol. 1: *An Essay on General Economy*. Zone, New York.

1993   *The Accursed Share*, Vol. 2–3: *An Essay on General Economy*. Zone, New York.

Batuman, E.

2009   The Bells. *The New Yorker*, April 27, 22–29.

Bauer, A.

2010   Socializing Environment and Ecologizing Politics: Social Differentiation and the Production of "Nature" in Iron Age Northern Karnataka. Ph.D. dissertation, University of Chicago, Chicago.

Beebe, B.

2010   Intellectual Property Law and the Sumptuary Code. *Harvard Law Review* 123: 809–85

Benjamin, W.

1968   The Work of Art in the Age of Mechanical Reproduction. In *Illuminations*, edited by H. Arendt, 217–51. Translated by H. Zohn. Schocken, New York.

1978   Critique of Violence. In *Reflections*, edited by P. Demetz, 277–300. Schocken, New York.

Bennett, J.

2010   *Vibrant Matter: A Political Ecology of Things*. Duke University Press, Durham, NC.

Bennett, T., and P. Joyce (eds.)

2010   *Material Powers: Cultural Studies, History and the Material Turn*. Routledge, London.

Bergson, H.

1911   *Creative Evolution*. Translated by A. Mitchell. Henry Holt, New York.

Bermingham, A.

1986   *Landscape and Ideology: The English Rustic Tradition, 1740–1860*. University of California Press, Berkeley.

Bhabha, H. K.

1994   *The Location of Culture*. Routledge, London.

Binford, L.

1962   Archaeology as Anthropology. *American Antiquity* 28(2):217–25.

1964   A Consideration of Research Design. *American Antiquity* 29(4):425–41.

1965   Archaeological Systematics and the Study of Cultural Process. *American Antiquity* 31:203–10.

Binsbergen, W. van

2013   African Divination across Time and Space: Typology and Intercultural Epistemology. In *Reviewing Reality: Dynamics of African Divination*, edited by W. E. A. van Beek and P. M. Peek, 339–75. Lit, Vienna.

Boelhower, W.

2005   Mnemohistory: The Archaeological Turn in the Humanities from Winckelmann to Calvino. *Symbiosis* 9(2):99–116.

Boivin, N.

2008   *Material Cultures, Material Minds: The Impact of Things on Human Thought, Society, and Evolution*. Cambridge University Press, Cambridge.

Boroffka, N., J. Cierny, J. Lutz, H. Parzinger, E. Pernicka, and G. Weisgerber

2002   Bronze Age Tin from Central Asia: Preliminary Notes. In *Ancient Interac-*

tions: East and West in Eurasia, edited by K. V. Boyle, C. Renfrew and M. Levine, 135–59. McDonald Institute for Archaeological Research, Cambridge.

Bourdieu, P.
1984 *Distinction: A Social Critique of the Judgment of Taste*. Translated by R. Nice. Harvard University Press, Cambridge, MA.
1992 *Language and Symbolic Power*. Polity, Cambridge

Bowden, B.
2009 *The Empire of Civilization: The Evolution of an Imperial Idea*. University of Chicago Press, Chicago.

Boyle, M. J.
2013 The Costs and Consequences of Drone Warfare. *International Affairs* 89(1):1–29.

Bradley, R.
1998 *The Significance of Monuments: On the Shaping of Human Experience in Neolithic and Bronze Age Europe*. Routledge, London.

Braidwood, R. J., L. Braidwood, J. G. Smith, and C. Leslie
1952 Matarrah: A Southern Variant of the Hassunan Assemblage, Excavated in 1948. *Journal of Near Eastern Studies* 11(1):1–75.

Brandt, R.
1982 Das Titelblatt des Leviathan und Goyas El Gigante. In *Furcht und Freiheit: Leviathan, Diskussion 300 Jahre nach Thomas Hobbes*, edited by U. Bermbach and K.-M. Kodalle, 201–31. Westdeutscher, Opladen.
1987 Das Titelblatt des Leviathan. *Leviathan: Zeitschrift für Sozialwissenschaft* 15:163–86.

Braun, B., and S. Whatmore (eds.)
2010a *Political Matter: Technoscience, Democracy, and Public Life*. University of Minnesota Press, Minneapolis.

Braun, B., and S. Whatmore
2010b Political Matter: Technoscience, Democracy, and Public Life. In *Political Matter: Technoscience, Democracy, and Public Life*, edited by B. Braun and S. Whatmore, ix–xl. University of Minnesota Press, Minneapolis.

Bray, T. L. (ed.)
2003 *The Archaeology and Politics of Food and Feasting in Early States and Empires*. Kluwer Academic/Plenum, New York.

Breasted, J. H.
1919 The Origins of Civilization. *Scientific Monthly* X:268–89.

Bredekamp, H.
1995 *The Lure of Antiquity and the Cult of the Machine: The Kunstkammer and the Evolution of Nature, Art, and Technology*. Markus Wiener, Princeton, NJ.
1999 *Thomas Hobbes Visuelle Strategien: Der Leviathan, Urbild des modernen Staates, Werkillustrationen und Portraits*. Akademie, Berlin.
2007 Thomas Hobbes's Visual Strategies. In *The Cambridge Companion to Hobbes's Leviathan*, edited by P. Springborg, 29–60. Cambridge University Press, Cambridge.

Brooks, D.
2008 No Whining about the Media. *New York Times*, April 16, 2008. http://

campaignstops.blogs.nytimes.com/2008/04/16/no-whining-about-the-media/?hp.

Brown, B.
2001 Thing Theory. *Critical Inquiry* 28(1):1–16.

Brown, D.
2006 Astral Divination in the Context of Mesopotamian Divination, Medicine, Religion, Magic, Society, and Scholarship. *East Asian Science, Technology, and Medicine* 25:69–126.

Brubaker, R.
1996 *Nationalism Reframed: Nationhood and the National Question in the New Europe*. Cambridge University Press, Cambridge.

Brumfiel, E.
1998 Huitzilopochtli's Conquest: Aztec Ideology in the Archaeological Record. *Cambridge Archaeological Journal* 8(1):3–13.

Bryson, N.
1990 *Looking at the Overlooked: Four Essays on Still Life Painting*. Harvard University Press, Cambridge, MA.

Burney, C.
1975 Excavations at Haftavan Tepe 1973: Fourth Preliminary Report. *Iran* 8:157–71.

Burney, C., and D. M. Lang
1972 *The People of the Hills: Ancient Ararat and Caucasus*. Praeger, New York.

Butler, J.
1990 *Gender Trouble: Feminism and the Subversion of Identity*. Routledge, New York.
1993 *Bodies That Matter: On the Discursive Limits of "Sex."* Routledge, New York.

Bynum, C. W.
2011 *Christian Materiality: An Essay on Religion in Late Medieval Europe*. Zone, New York.

Callon, M., and B. Latour
1981 Unscrewing the Big Leviathan: How Actors Macro-structure Reality and How Sociologists Help Them To Do So. In *Advances in Social Theory and Methodology*, edited by K. Knorr-Cetina and A. V. Cicourel, 275–303. Routledge & Kegan Paul, Boston.

Campbell, R. B.
2009 Toward a Networks and Boundaries Approach to Early Complex Polities: The Late Shang Case. *Current Anthropology* 50(6):821–48.

Carneiro, R.
1970 A Theory of the Origin of the State. *Science* 169:733–39.

Carter, H., and A. C. Mace
1977 *The Discovery of the Tomb of Tutankhamen*. Dover, New York.

Cassirer, E., and P. Gay
1954 *The Question of Jean-Jacques Rousseau*. Columbia University Press, New York.

Cathcart, L. L.
1983 *American Still Life, 1945–1983*. Contemporary Arts Museum, Houston.

Cattelino, J.
    2006   Florida Seminole Housing and the Social Meanings of Sovereignty. *Comparative Studies in Society and History* 48(3):699–726.

Chapman, R.
    2003   *Archaeologies of Complexity.* Routledge, London.
    2007   Evolution, Complexity, and the State. In *Socialising Complexity: Structure, Interaction and Power in Archaeological Discourse,* edited by S. Kohring and S. Wynne-Jones, 13–28. Oxbow, Oxford.

Chataigner, C., P. Avetisyan, G. Palumbi, and H.-P. Uerpmann
    2010   Godedzor: A Late Ubaid-Related Settlement in the Southern Caucasus. In *Beyond the Ubaid: Transformation and Integration in the Late Prehistoric Societies of the Middle East,* edited by R. A. Carter and G. Philip, 377–94. Oriental Institute Press, Chicago.

Chernykh, E. N.
    1992   *Ancient Metallurgy in the USSR: The Early Metal Age.* Cambridge University Press, Cambridge.

Childe, V. G.
    1925   *The Dawn of European Civilization.* A. A. Knopf, New York.
    1931   *Skara Brae, a Pictish Village in Orkney.* Kegan Paul, London.
    1942   Prehistory of the U.S.S.R. II: The Copper Age in Southern Russia. *Man* 74:130–36.
    1950a *Prehistoric Migrations in Europe.* Aschehoug, Oslo.
    1950b The Urban Revolution. *Town Planning Review* 21:3–17.
    1957   The Bronze Age. *Past & Present* 12:2–15.

Claessen, H.J.M.
    1984   The Internal Dynamics of the Early State. *Current Anthropology* 25(4):365–79.

Clark, G.
    1954   The Economic Approach to Prehistory. *Proceedings of the British Academy* 39:215–38.

Clarke, D.
    1973   Archaeology: The Loss of Innocence. *Antiquity* 47:6–18.
    1968   *Analytical Archaeology.* Methuen, London.

Clastres, P.
    1989   *Society against the State.* Zone, New York.

Clifford, J.
    1988   *The Predicament of Culture.* Harvard University Press, Cambridge, MA.

Coben, L. S.
    2006   Other Cuzcos: Replicated Theaters of Inka Power. In *Archaeology of Performance: Theaters of Power, Community, and Politics,* edited by T. Inomata and L. S. Coben, 223–59. AltaMira, Lanham, MD.

Cole, J. P., and F. C. German
    1961   *A Geography of the USSR.* Butterworths, London.

Collingwood, R. G.
    1928   Political Action. *Proceedings of the Aristotelian Society* 29:155–76.

Collon, D.
1987 *First Impressions: Cylinder Seals in the Ancient Near East*. British Museum Publications, London.

Conner, S., and A. Sagona
2007 Environment and Society in the Late Prehistory of Southern Georgia, Caucasus. In *Les Cultures du Caucase: Leurs Relations avec le Proche-Orient*, edited by B. Lyonnet, 21–36. CNRS Éditions, Paris.

Connolly, W. E.
2013 *The Fragility of Things: Self-Organizing Processes, Neoliberal Fantasies, and Democratic Activism*. Duke University Press, Durham, NC.

Cook, A. G., and M. Glowacki
2003 Pots, Politics, and Power: Huari Ceramic Assemblages and Imperial Administration. In *The Archaeology and Politics of Food and Feasting in Early States and Empires*, edited by T. L. Bray, 173–202. Kluwer Academic/Plenum, New York.

Coole, D. H.
2010 The Inertia of Matter and the Generativity of Flesh. In *New Materialisms: Ontology, Agency, and Politics*, edited by D. H. Coole and S. Frost, 92–115. Duke University Press, Durham, NC.

Coole, D. H., and S. Frost (eds.)
2010 *New Materialisms: Ontology, Agency, and Politics*. Duke University Press, Durham, NC.

Cooper, L.
2010 States of Hegemony: Early Forms of Political Control in Syria during the Third Millennium B.C. In *The Development of Pre-State Communities in the Ancient Near East*, edited by D. Bolger and L. C. Maguire, 87–94. Oxbow, Oxford.

Courcier, A.
2010 Metalliferous Potential, Metallogenous Particularities and Extractive Metallurgy: Interdisciplinary Research on Understanding the Ancient Metallurgy in the Caucasus during the Early Bronze Age. In *Von Majkop bis Trialeti: Gewinnung und Verbreitung von Metallen und Obsidian in Kaukasien im 4.–2. Jt. v. Chr.*, edited by S. Hansen, A. Hauptmann, I. Motzenbäcker, and E. Pernicka, 75–93. Dr. Rudolf Habelt GmbH, Bonn.
2014 Ancient Metallurgy in the Caucasus from the Sixth to the Third Millennium BCE. In *Archaeometallurgy in Global Perspective: Methods and Syntheses*, edited by B. W. Roberts and C. P. Thornton, 579–664. Springer, New York.

Crossland, Z.
2010 Materiality and Embodiment. In *The Oxford Handbook of Material Culture Studies*, edited by D. Hicks and M. C. Beaudry, 386–405. Oxford University Press, Oxford.

Cummings, L. S., and C. Yost
2011 Pollen and Phytolith Analysis of Samples from a Shrine at the Site of Gegharot, Armenia. *PaleoResearch Institute Technical Report* 11–060.

Cuvier, G.
1818 *Essay on the Theory of the Earth*. Kirk & Mercein, New York.

Daston, L.
    2004 *Things That Talk: Object Lessons from Art and Science*. Zone, New York.
Daston, L., and P. Galison
    2007 *Objectivity*. Zone, New York.
de Beauvoir, S.
    1953 *The Second Sex*. Knopf, New York.
de Montmollin, O.
    1989 *The Archaeology of Political Structure*. Cambridge University Press, Cambridge.
de Vries, J.
    1999 Luxury and Calvinism/Luxury and Capitalism: Supply and Demand for Luxury Goods in the Seventeenth-Century Dutch Republic. *Journal of the Walters Art Gallery* 57:73–85.
Dedabrishvili, S. S.
    1979 *Kurgany Alazanskoy Doliny*. Metsniereba, Tbilisi.
DeLanda, M.
    2006 *A New Philosophy of Society*. Continuum, London.
Deleuze, G., and F. Guattari
    1986 *Nomadology: The War Machine*. Semiotext(e), New York.
    1987 *A Thousand Plateaus: Capitalism and Schizophrenia*. University of Minnesota Press, Minneapolis.
Deleuze, G., and C. Parnet
    2002 *Dialogues II*. Columbia University Press, New York.
Demarest, A. A., and G. W. Conrad
    1992 *Ideology and Pre-Columbian Civilizations*. School of American Research Press, Santa Fe, NM.
Derrida, J.
    2009 *The Beast and the Sovereign*. University of Chicago Press, Chicago.
Descartes, R.
    2006 *Meditations, Objections, and Replies*. Translated by R. Ariew and D. A. Cress. Hackett, Indianapolis, IN.
Devedjian, S. G.
    1981 *Lori-Berd I*. Izdatel'stvo AN Armyanskoj SSR, Erevan.
    2006 *Lori Berd II*. Nairi, Yerevan.
Dewdney, J. C.
    1979 *A Geography of the Soviet Union*. Pergamon, Oxford.
Dieter, M.
    2013 New Materialism and Non-Humanisation, an Interview with Jussi Parikka. In *Blowup: Speculative Realities*, edited by M. Kasprzak, 23–36. V2, Rotterdam.
Dietler, M.
    2001 Theorizing the Feast: Rituals of Consumption, Commensal Politics, and Power in African Contexts. In *Feasts: Archaeological and Ethnographic Perspectives on Food, Politics, and Power*, edited by M. Dietler and B. Hayden, 65–114. Smithsonian Institution Press, Washington, D.C.
Dietler, M., and B. Hayden (eds.)
    2001 *Feasts: Archaeological and Ethnographic Perspectives on Food, Politics, and Power*. Smithsonian Institution Press, Washington, D.C.

Donnan, C. B.
1976 *Moche Art and Iconography*. UCLA Latin American Center, Los Angeles.
Donnan, C. B., and D. McClelland
1999 *Moche Fineline Painting: Its Evolution and Its Artists*. UCLA Fowler Museum of Cultural History, Los Angeles.
Dzhaparidze, N. O.
1988 *Yuverlirnoye Iskusstvo Epokhi Bronzy v Gruzii*. Metsniereba, Tbilisi.
Dzhaparidze, O.
1969 *Arkeologicheskiye Raskopki v Trialeti v 1957–1958 gg*. Sabchota Sakartvelo, Tbilisi.
1993 Über die Ethnokulturelle Situation in Georgien gegen Ende des 3. Jahrtausends v Chr. In *Between the Rivers and over the Mountains: Archaeologica Anatolica et Mesopotamica Alba Palmieri Dedicata*, edited by M. Frangipane, H. Hauptmann, M. Liverani, P. Matthiae, and M. Mellink, 475–91. Dipartimento di Scienze Storiche Archeologiche e Antropologiche dell'Antichità, Università di Roma "La Sapienza", Rome.
1994 Trialetskaya Kul'tura. In *Epokha Bronzy Kavkaza i Srednei Azii: Rannyaya i Srednyaya Bronza Kavkaza*, edited by K. K. Kushnareva and V. I. Markovin, 75–92. Nauka, Moscow.
1998 *K Etnokul'turnoj Istorii Gruzinskikh Plemen v III Tysyacheletii do n. e*. Izdatel'stvo Tbilisskogo Universiteta, Tbilisi.
Eagleton, T.
1990 *The Ideology of the Aesthetic*. Blackwell, Oxford.
Earle, T.
1997 *How Chiefs Come to Power*. Stanford University Press, Stanford, CA.
Ebert-Schifferer, S.
1999 *Still Life: A History*. Abrams, New York.
Elias, N.
1994 *The Civilizing Process*. Blackwell, Oxford.
Engels, F.
1990 The Origin of Family, Private Property, and the State. In *Karl Marx-Frederick Engels: Collected Works*, Vol. 26, 129–276. International, New York.
Erdal, Y. S., and Ö. D. Erdal
2012 Organized Violence in Anatolia: A Retrospective Research on the Injuries from the Neolithic to Early Bronze Age. *International Journal of Paleopathology* 2(2–3):78–92.
Esaian, S. A.
1966 *Oruzhie i Voennoe Delo Drevnei Armenii*. Izdatel'stvo AN Armyanskoi SSR, Yerevan.
Evans, G., and M. Sahnoun
2002 The Responsibility to Protect. *Foreign Affairs* 81(6):99–110.
Faraone, C. A.
1991 Binding and Burying the Forces of Evil: The Defensive Use of "Voodoo Dolls" in Ancient Greece. *Classical Antiquity* 10(2):165–220.
Faris, D. M.
2012 *Dissent and Revolution in a Digital Age: Social Media, Blogging and Activism in Egypt*. I. B. Tauris, London.

Félibien, A.
  1668 Conférence de l'Académie Royale de Peinture et de Sculpture. Leonard, Paris.
Feuerbach, L. A.
  1966 Principles of the Philosophy of the Future. Translated by M. H. Vogel. Bobbs-Merrill, Indianapolis, IN.
Findlen, P. (ed.)
  2013 Early Modern Things: Objects and Their Histories, 1500–1800. Routledge, New York.
Fine, G.
  1993 On Ideas: Aristotle's Criticism of Plato's Theory of Forms. Clarendon, Oxford.
Fiskesjö, M.
  2003 The Thanksgiving Turkey Pardon, the Death of Teddy's Bear, and the Sovereign Exception of Guantánamo. Prickly Paradigm, Chicago.
Flannery, K. V.
  1968 Archaeological Systems Theory and Early Mesoamerica. In Anthropological Archaeology in the Americas, edited by B. Meggers, 67–87. Anthropological Society of Washington, Washington, D.C.
  1972 The Cultural Evolution of Civilizations. Annual Review of Ecology and Systematics 3:399–426.
Forbes, T. R.
  1959 The Prediction of Sex: Folklore and Science. Proceedings of the American Philosophical Society 103(4):537–44.
Foucault, M.
  1979 On Governmentality. Ideology and Consciousness 6:5–21.
  1989 The Order of Things: An Archaeology of the Human Sciences. Tavistock/Routledge, London.
  2003 "Society Must Be Defended": Lectures at the Collège de France, 1975–76. Translated by D. Macey. Picador, New York.
  2007 Security, Territory, Population: Lectures at the Collège de France, 1977–1978. Translated by D. Macey. Picador, New York.
Frangipane, M.
  2007–2008. The Arslantepe "Royal" Tomb: New Funerary Customs and Political Changes in the Upper Euphrates Valley at the Beginning of the Third Millennium BC. Scienze Dell'Antichità 14(1):169–94.
Frangipane, M., G. M. di Nocera, A. Hauptmann, P. Morbidelli, A. Palmieri, L. Sadori, M. Schultz, and T. Schmidt-Schultz
  2001 New Symbols of a New Power in a "Royal" Tomb from 3000 BC Arslantepe, Malatya (Turkey). Paleorient 27(2):105–36.
Frangipane, M., and G. Palumbi
  2007 Red-Black Ware, Pastoralism, Trade, and Anatolian-Transcaucasian Interactions in the 4th–3rd Millennium B.C. In Les Cultures du Caucase: Leurs Relations avec le Proche-Orient, edited by B. Lyonnet, 233–56. CNRS Éditions, Paris.
Frankfort, H.
  1956 The Birth of Civilization in the Near East. Doubleday Anchor, Garden City, NY.

Frow, J.
2010   Matter and Materialism: A Brief Prehistory of the Present. In *Material Powers: Cultural Studies, History and the Material Turn*, edited by T. Bennett and P. Joyce, 25–37. Routledge, London.

Gamboni, D.
2005   Composing the Body Politic: Composite Images and Political Representation, 1651–2004. In *Making Things Public: Atmospheres of Democracy*, edited by B. Latour and P. Weibel, 162–95. MIT Press, Cambridge, MA.

Garber, J. F.
1983   Patterns of Jade Consumption and Disposal at Cerros, Northern Belize. *American Antiquity* 48(4):800–807.

Geertz, C.
1977   Centers, Kings, and Charisma: Reflections on the Symbolics of Power. In *Culture and Its Creators*, edited by J. Ben-David and T. N. Clark, 150–71. University of Chicago Press, Chicago.
1980   *Negara: The Theater-State in Nineteenth Century Bali*. Princeton University Press, Princeton, NJ.
2004   What Is a State If Not a Sovereign? *Current Anthropology* 45(5):577–93.

Gell, A.
1992   The Technology of Enchantment and the Enchantment of Technology. In *Anthropology, Art, and Aesthetics*, edited by J. Coote and A. Shelton, 40–63. Clarendon, Oxford.

George, A. R., and F.N.H. Al-Rawi
1996   Tablets from the Sippar Library VI. Atra-ḫasīs. *Iraq* 58:147–90.

Gerbaudo, P.
2012   *Tweets and the Streets: Social Media and Contemporary Activism*. Pluto, London.

Gero, J.
2003   Feasting and the Practice of Stately Manners. In *The Archaeology and Politics of Food and Feasting in Early States and Empires*, edited by T. L. Bray, 285–88. Kluwer Academic/Plenum, New York.

Giddens, A.
1984   *The Constitution of Society: Outline of the Theory of Structuration*. Polity, Cambridge.

Gilmour, G. H.
1997   The Nature and Function of Astragalus Bones from Archaeological Contexts in the Levant and Eastern Mediterranean. *Oxford Journal of Archaeology* 16(2):167–75.

Glanville, L.
2013   The Myth of Traditional Sovereignty. *International Studies Quarterly* 57(1):79–90.

Glatz, C.
2009   Empire as Network: Spheres of Material Interaction in Late Bronze Age Anatolia. *Journal of Anthropological Archaeology* 28(2):127–41.

Gledhill, J., B. Bender, and M. T. Larsen
1988   *State and Society: The Emergence and Development of Social Hierarchy and Political Centralization*. Unwin Hyman, London.

Glenn, J., and C. Hayes
    2007 *Taking Things Seriously: 78 Objects with Unexpected Significance*. Princeton Architectural Press, New York.

Gogadze, E. M.
    1972 *Periodizatsiya i Genezis Kurgannoy Kultury Trialeti*. Metsniyereba, Tbilisi.

Gopnik, H., and M. S. Rothman
    2011 *On the High Road: The History of Godin Tepe, Iran*. Mazda, Costa Mesa, CA.

Gorenberg, D.
    2006 Soviet Nationalities Policy and Assimilation. In *Rebounding Identities: The Politics of Identity in Russia and Ukraine*, edited by D. Arel and B. A. Ruble, 273–303. Woodrow Wilson Center Press, Washington, D.C.

Gosden, C., and Y. Marshall
    1999 The Cultural Biography of Objects. *World Archaeology* 31(2):169–78.

Gosselain, O. P.
    1999 In Pots We Trust: The Processing of Clay and Symbols in Sub-Saharan Africa. *Journal of Material Culture* 4(2):205–30.

Gould, R. J., and P. J. Watson
    1982 A Dialogue on the Meaning and Use of Analogy in Ethnoarchaeological Reasoning. *Journal of Anthropological Archaeology* 1:355–81.

Graves, J.
    1853 The Pagan Cemetery at Ballon Hill, County of Carlow. *Transactions of the Kilkenny Archaeological Society* 2(2):295–303.

Greenberg, R.
    2007 Transcaucasian Colors: Khirbet Kerak Ware at Khirbet Kerak (Tel Bet Yerah). In *Les Cultures du Caucase: Leurs Relations avec le Proche-Orient*, edited by B. Lyonnet, 257–68. CNRS Éditions, Paris.

Greene, A.
    2013 The Social Lives of Pottery on the Plain of Flowers: An Archaeology of Pottery Production, Distribution, and Consumption in the Late Bronze Age South Caucasus. Ph.D. dissertation, University of Chicago, Chicago.

Grosz, E.
    2008 Darwin and Feminism: Preliminary Investigations for a Possible Alliance. In *Material Feminisms*, edited by S. Alaimo and S. J. Hekman, 23–51. Indiana University Press, Bloomington.

Gummel, Y. I.
    1939 Raskopki v Nagorno-Karabakhskoj Avtonomnoj Oblasti v 1938 Godu. *Izvestiya Azerbaydzhanskogo Filiala Akademii Nauk SSSR* 4:77–85.
    1948 Nekotorye Pamyatniki Rannebronzovoy Epokhi Azerbaydzhana. *Kratkiye Soobshcheniya o Dokladakh i Polevykh Issledovaniyakh Instituta Istorii Material-noy Kultury* 20:15–28.

Habermas, J.
    1973 *Theory and Practice*. Beacon, Boston.
    1984 *The Theory of Communicative Action*, Vol. 1. Translated by T. McCarthy. Heinemann Educational Books, London.

Halperin, C. T., and A. E. Foias
    2010 Pottery Politics: Late Classic Maya Palace Production at Motul de San José Petén, Guatemala. *Journal of Anthropological Archaeology* 29(3):392–411.

Hansen, D. P.
1998 Art of the Royal Tombs of Ur: A Brief Interpretation. In *Treasures from the Royal Tombs of Ur*, edited by R. L. Zettler and L. Horne, 43–72. University of Pennsylvania Museum, Philadelphia.

Hansen, T. B., and F. Stepputat
2006 Sovereignty Revisited. *Annual Review of Anthropology* 35:295–315.

Haraway, D.
1985 A Manifesto for Cyborgs: Science, Technology, and Socialist Feminism in the 1980s. *Socialist Review* 80:65–107.
1991 *Simians, Cyborgs, and Women: The Reinvention of Nature*. Routledge, New York.

Harman, G.
2010 Object-Oriented Philosophy. In *Towards Speculative Realism: Essays and Lectures*, 93–104. Zero, Ropley, UK.

Harmanşah, Ö.
2007 "Source of the Tigris": Event, Place and Performance in the Assyrian Landscapes of the Early Iron Age. *Archaeological Dialogues* 14(2):179–204.

Harshaw, T.
2008 It's the Lapel Pins, Stupid. *New York Times*, April 17, 2008. http://opinionator.blogs.nytimes.com/2008/04/17/its-the-lapel-pins-stupid/.

Harvey, D.
1989 *The Condition of Postmodernity*. Blackwell, Oxford.

Haury, E. W.
1950 *The Stratigraphy and Archaeology of Ventana Cave, Arizona*. University of Arizona Press, Tucson.

Hegel, G.W.F.
1988 *Aesthetics*. Translated by T. M. Knox. Oxford University Press, Oxford.
2011 *Lectures on the Philosophy of History: Complete and Unabridged*. Translated by R. Alvarado. Wordbridge, Aalten.

Heidegger, M.
2001 *Poetry, Language, Thought*. Translated by A. Hofstadter. Perennial Classics, New York.

Henare, A.J.M., M. Holbraad, and S. Wastell
2007 *Thinking through Things: Theorising Artefacts Ethnographically*. Routledge, London.

Herder, J. G. v.
1986 *On the Origin of Language*. Translated by J. H. Moran. University of Chicago Press, Chicago.

Hewsen, R. H.
1997 The Geography of Armenia. In *The Armenian People from Ancient to Modern Times*, edited by R. G. Hovannisian, 1–17. St. Martin's, New York.
2001 *Armenia: A Historical Atlas*. University of Chicago Press, Chicago.

Hicks, D.
2010 The Material-Cultural Turn: Event and Effect. In *The Oxford Handbook of Material Culture Studies*, edited by D. Hicks and M. C. Beaudry, 25–98. Oxford University Press, Oxford.

Hill, G.
   2013   Living with Less. A Lot Less. In *The New York Times*, March 9, SR1.
Hobbes, T.
   1991   *Leviathan*. Cambridge University Press, Cambridge.
Hodder, I.
   1986   *Reading the Past*. Cambridge University Press, Cambridge.
   1999   *The Archaeological Process: An Introduction*. Blackwell, Oxford.
   2006   *The Leopard's Tale: Revealing the Mysteries of Çatal Höyük*. Thames & Hudson, New York.
   2012   *Entangled: An Archaeology of the Relationships between Humans and Things*. Wiley-Blackwell, Malden, MA.
Honig, E. A.
   1998   *Painting and the Market in Early Modern Antwerp*. Yale University Press, New Haven, CT.
Hopkins, R.
   2008   *The Transition Handbook: From Oil Dependency to Local Resilience*. Green, Totnes.
Houston, S., and K. Taube
   2000   An Archaeology of the Senses: Perception and Cultural Expression in Ancient Mesoamerica. *Cambridge Archaeological Journal* 10(2):261–94.
Houston, S. D.
   2006   Impersonation, Dance, and the Problem of Spectacle. In *Archaeology of Performance: Theaters of Power, Community, and Politics*, edited by T. Inomata and L. S. Coben, 135–55. Altamira, Lanham, MD.
Howland, D., and L. White (eds.)
   2009   *The State of Sovereignty: Territories, Laws, Populations*. Indiana University Press, Bloomington.
Hume, D.
   1826   *The History of England*. Talboys and Wheeler, Oxford.
Humphrey, C.
   2004   Sovereignty. In *A Companion to the Anthropology of Politics*, edited by D. Nugent and J. Vincent, 418–36. Blackwell, Oxford.
Hunt, A.
   2004   Getting Marx and Foucault into Bed Together! *Journal of Law and Society* 31(4):592–609.
Hutson, S. R.
   2002   Built Space and Bad Subjects: Domination and Resistance at Monte Alban, Oaxaca, Mexico. *Journal of Social Archaeology* 2(1):53–80.
Ingold, T.
   2007   Materials against Materiality. *Archaeological Dialogues* 14(1):1–16.
   2012   No More Ancient; No More Human: The Future Past of Archaeology and Anthropology. In *Archaeology and Anthropology: Past, Present, and Future*, edited by D. Shankland, 77–89. Bloomsbury, London.
Inomata, T.
   2006   Politics and Theatricality in Mayan Society. In *Archaeology of Performance: Theaters of Power, Community, and Politics*, edited by T. Inomata and L. S. Coben, 187–221. AltaMira, Lanham, MD.

Inomata, T., and L. S. Coben (eds.)
  2006 *Archaeology of Performance: Theaters of Power, Community, and Politics.*
        AltaMira, Lanham, MD.
Inomata, T., and D. Triadan
  2009 Culture and Practice of War in Maya Society. In *Warfare in Cultural Con-
        text: Practice, Agency, and the Archaeology of Violence*, edited by A. E. Nielsen
        and W. H. Walker, 56–83. University of Arizona Press, Tucson.
Irigaray, L.
  1985 *This Sex Which Is Not One.* Cornell University Press, Ithaca, NY.
Isabekyan, H.
  1968 *Erebuni-Erevan: Erevani 2750-amyaki Art`iv.* Obshchestvo Znanie Armian-
        skoj SSR, Yerevan.
Jackson, M. A.
  2008 *Moche Art and Visual Culture in Ancient Peru.* University of New Mexico
        Press, Albuquerque.
Johansen, P. G., and A. Bauer (eds.)
  2011 *The Archaeology of Politics: The Materiality of Political Practice and Action in
        the Past.* Cambridge Scholars Press, Newcastle.
Johnson, M.
  2007 *Ideas of Landscape.* Blackwell, Malden, MA.
Jones, M. P.
  1996 Posthuman Agency: Between Theoretical Traditions. *Sociological Theory*
        14(3):290–309.
Joyce, A. A., and M. Winter
  1996 Ideology, Power, and Urban Society in Pre-Hispanic Oaxaca. *Current
        Anthropology* 37(1):33–47.
Joyce, R., and J. Pollard
  2010 Archaeological Assemblages and Practices of Deposition. In *The Oxford
        Handbook of Material Culture Studies*, edited by D. Hicks and M. C. Beaudry,
        291–311. Oxford University Press, Oxford.
Joyce, R. A.
  2005 Archaeology of the Body. *Annual Review of Anthropology* 34:139–58.
Kant, I.
  1872 *Critique of Pure Reason.* Translated by J.M.D. Meiklejohn. Bell and Daldy,
        London.
Kantorowicz, E. H.
  1957 *The King's Two Bodies: A Study in Mediaeval Political Theology.* Princeton
        University Press, Princeton, NJ.
Kaufman-Osborn, T. V.
  1997 *Creatures of Prometheus: Gender and the Politics of Technology.* Rowman &
        Littlefield, Lanham, MD.
Kavtaradze, G. L.
  1999 The Importance of Metallurgical Data for the Formation of a Central
        Transcaucasian Chronology. In *The Beginnings of Metallurgy*, edited by
        A. Hauptmann, E. Pernicka, T. Rehren, and Ü. Yalçin, 67–101. Deutsches
        Bergbau-Museum, Bochum.
  2004 The Chronology of the Caucasus during the Early Metal Age: Observa-

tions from Central Trans-Caucasus. In *A View from the Highlands: Archaeological Studies in Honour of Charles Burney*, edited by A. Sagona, 539–56. Peeters, Leuven.

Keane, W.
2005 Signs Are Not the Garb of Meaning: On the Social Analysis of Material Things. In *Materiality*, edited by D. Miller, 182–205. Duke University Press, Durham, NC.

Kehoe, A. B.
1998 *The Land of Prehistory*. Routledge, New York.

Kelly-Buccellati, M.
1974 The Early Trans-Caucasian Culture: Geographical and Chronological Interaction. Ph.D. dissertation, University of Chicago, Chicago.
1980 The Outer Fertile Crescent Culture: North Eastern Connections of Syria and Palestine in the Third Millennium B.C. *Ugarit-Forschungen* 11:413–30.
1990 Trade in Metals in the Third Millennium: Northeast Syria and Eastern Anatolia. In *Resurrecting the Past*, edited by E. van Donzel, M. Mellinck, C. Nijland, J. J. Roodenberg, and K. R. Veenhof, 117–31. Nederlands Instituut, Istanbul.
2004 Andirons at Urkesh: New Evidence for the Hurrian Identity of the Early Trans-Caucasian Culture. In *A View from the Highlands: Archaeological Studies in Honour of Charles Burney*, edited by A. Sagona, 67–89. Peeters, Leuven.

Kerouac, J.
1957 *On the Road*. Viking, New York.

Khatchadourian, L.
2008a Social Logics under Empire: The Armenian "Highland Satrapy" and Achaemenid Rule, ca. 600–300 BC. Ph.D. dissertation, University of Michigan, Ann Arbor.
2008b Unforgettable Landscapes: Attachments to the Past in Hellenistic Armenia. In *Negotiating the Past in the Past: Identity, Memory, and Landscape in Archaeological Theory*, edited by N. Yoffee, 43–75. University of Arizona Press, Tucson.
2013 An Archaeology of Hegemony: The Achaemenid Empire and the Remaking of the Fortress in the Armenian Highlands. In *Empires and Diversity: On the Crossroads of Archaeology, Anthropology, and History*, edited by G. Areshian, 108–45. Cotsen Institute Press, Los Angeles.
2014 Empire in the Everyday: A Preliminary Report on the 2008–2011 Excavations at Tsaghkahovit, Armenia. *American Journal of Archaeology* 118(1):137–69.
n.d. The Satrapal Condition: Archaeology and the Matter of Empire. Unpublished manuscript.

Kidder, A. V.
1924 *An Introduction to the Study of Southwestern Archaeology with a Preliminary Account of the Excavations at Pecos*. Yale University Press, New Haven, CT.

Kiguradze, T., and A. Sagona
2003 Origins of the Kura-Araxes Cultural Complex. In *Archaeology in the Borderlands: Investigation in Caucasia and Beyond*, edited by A. T. Smith and

K. S. Rubinson, 38–94. The Cotsen Institute of Archaeology at UCLA, Los Angeles.

Kirch, P. V.

2010   *How Chiefs Became Kings: Divine Kingship and the Rise of Archaic States in Ancient Hawai'i.* University of California Press, Berkeley.

Klass, P.

2013   A Firm Grasp on Comfort. *New York Times*, March 11, D4.

Knappett, C.

2005   *Thinking through Material Culture: An Interdisciplinary Perspective.* University of Pennsylvania Press, Philadelphia.

Knorr-Cetina, K., and U. Bruegger

2000   The Market as an Object of Attachment: Exploring Postsocial Relations in Financial Markets. *Canadian Journal of Sociology* 25(2):141–68.

Kohl, P. L.

1992a The Kura-Araxes "Chiefdom/State": The Problems of Evolutionary Labels and Imperfect Analogies. In *South Asian Archaeology Studies*, edited by G. L. Possehl, 223–32. Oxford & IBH, New Delhi.

1992b The Transcaucasian Periphery in the Bronze Age. In *Resource Power and Regional Interaction*, edited by P. A. Urban and E. M. Schortman, 117–37. Plenum, London.

2003   Integrated Interaction at the Beginning of the Bronze Age: New Evidence from the Northeastern Caucasus and the Advent of Tin-Bronzes in the Third Millennium BC. In *Archaeology in the Borderlands: Investigations in Caucasia and Beyond*, edited by A. T. Smith and K. Rubinson, 9–21. The Cotsen Institute of Archaeology at UCLA, Los Angeles.

2007   *The Making of Bronze Age Eurasia.* Cambridge University Press, Cambridge.

Kolata, A. L.

2006   Before and After Collapse: Reflections on the Regeneration of Social Complexity. In *After Collapse: The Regeneration of Complex Societies*, edited by G. M. Schwartz and J. J. Nichols, 208–21. University of Arizona Press, Tucson.

Kopytoff, I.

1986   The Cultural Biography of Things: Commoditization as Process. In *The Social Life of Things*, edited by A. Appadurai, 64–91. Cambridge University Press, Cambridge.

Koşay, H. Z.

1976   *Keban Project Pulur Excavations, 1968–1970.* Middle East Technical University Keban Project Publications, Ankara.

Kostoff, S.

1991   *The City Shaped.* Thames and Hudson, London.

Krasner, S. D.

2005   The Day After. *Foreign Policy* (146):68–70.

Krickeberg, W.

1928   Mexikanisch-Peruanische Parallelen, Ein Uberblick und Eine Erganzung. In *Festschrift: Publication D'Hommage Offerte au P. W. Schmidt*, edited by W. Koppers, 378–93. Congregations-Buchduckerei, Vienna.

Kroeber, A. L.
   1951   Great Art Styles of Ancient South America. In *The Civilizations of Ancient America*, edited by S. Tax, 207–15. University of Chicago Press, Chicago.
Kuftin, B. A.
   1940   K Voprosu O Rannykh Stadiyakh Bronzovoy Kultury na Territorii Kavkaza. *Kratkiye Soobshcheniya O Dokladakh i Polevykh Issledovaniyakh Instituta Istorii* 8:5–35.
   1941   *Arkheologicheskiye Raskopki v Trialeti*. Izdatel'stvo Akademii nauk Gruzinsko SSR, Tbilisi.
Kunstler, J. H.
   1993   *The Geography of Nowhere*. Touchstone, New York.
Kus, S., and V. Raharijaona
   2006   Visible and Vocal: Sovereigns of the Early Merina (Madagascar) State. In *Archaeology of Performance: Theaters of Power, Community, and Politics*, edited by T. Inomata and L. S. Coben, 303–29. AltaMira, Lanham, MD.
Kushnareva, K. K.
   1994a Pamyatniki Trialetskoj Kul'tury Na Territorii Yuzhnogo Zakavkaz'ya. In *Epokha Bronzy Kavkaza i Srednei Azii: Rannyaya i Srednyaya Bronza Kavkaza*, edited by K. K. Kushnareva and V. I. Markovin, 93–105. Nauka, Moscow.
   1994b Karmirberdskaya (Tazakendskaya) Kul'tura. In *Epokha Bronzy Kavkaza i Srednei Azii: Rannyaya i Srednyaya Bronza Kavkaza*, edited by K. K. Kushnareva and V. I. Markovin, 106–17. Nauka, Moscow.
   1997   *The Southern Caucasus in Prehistory*. University of Pennsylvania Museum, Philadelphia.
Kushnareva, K. K., and V. I. Markovin (eds.)
   1994   *Epokha Bronzy Kavkaza i Srednei Azii: Rannyaya i Srednyaya Bronza Kavkaza*. Nauka, Moscow.
Lamb, W.
   1954   The Culture of North-East Anatolia and Its Neighbours. *Anatolian Studies* 4:21–32.
Lambert, W. G.
   1957   An Incantation of the Maqlû Type. *Archiv für Orientforschung* 18:288–99.
Latour, B.
   1993   *We Have Never Been Modern*. Harvard University Press, Cambridge, MA.
   1999   *Pandora's Hope: Essays on the Reality of Science Studies*. Harvard University Press, Cambridge, MA.
   2004a *Politics of Nature: How to Bring the Sciences into Democracy*. Harvard University Press, Cambridge, MA.
   2004b How to Talk About the Body? The Normative Dimension of Science Studies. *Body & Society* 10(2–3):205–29.
   2005   *Reassembling the Social: An Introduction to Actor-Network-Theory*. Oxford University Press, Oxford.
   2007   Can We Get Our Materialism Back, Please? *Isis* 98(1):138–42.
Layard, A. H.
   1853   *The Monuments of Nineveh*. J. Murray, London.

Lefebvre, H.

1991 *The Production of Space*. Blackwell, Oxford.

Lefort, C.

1988 *Democracy and Political Theory*. Translated by D. Macey. University of Minnesota Press, Minneapolis.

Leibniz, G. W.

1989 *Philosophical Papers and Letters*. Kluwer, Dordrecht.

Leone, M. P.

2005 *The Archaeology of Liberty in an American Capital: Excavations in Annapolis*. University of California Press, Berkeley.

Levi-Strauss, C.

1969 *The Raw and the Cooked*. Harper and Row, New York.

Limbaugh, R.

2008 Obama's Clueless Debate Answers. *The Rush Limbaugh Show*, April 17, 2008. http://www.rushlimbaugh.com/daily/2008/04/17/obama_s_clueless _debate_answers.

Lin, P., K. Abney, and G. A. Bekey

2012 *Robot Ethics: The Ethical and Social Implications of Robotics*. MIT Press, Cambridge, MA.

Lindsay, I.

2005 Yuzhnaya Chast' Nizhnego Kvartala Tsakhkaovitskogo Poseleniya v Pozdnem Bronzovom Beke (Predvaritel'nie rezul'taty raskopok 2003 g.). In *Hin Hayastani Mshakooyte XIII*, edited by A. A. Kalantaryan, R. Badalyan and P. Avetisyan, 116–24. Mughni, Yerevan.

2006 *Late Bronze Age Power Dynamics in Southern Caucasia: A Community Perspective on Political Landscapes*. Ph.D. dissertation, University of California, Santa Barbara.

Lindsay, I., J. Leon, A. Smith, and C. Wiktorowicz

2014 Geophysical Survey at Late Bronze Age Fortresses: Comparing Methods in Diverse Geological Contexts of Northwestern Armenia. *Antiquity* 88:578–95.

Lindsay, I., L. Minc, C. Descantes, R. J. Speakman, and M. D. Glascock

2007 Exchange Patterns, Boundary Formation, and Sociopolitical Change in Late Bronze Age Southern Caucasia: Preliminary Results from a Pottery Provenance Study in Northwestern Armenia. *Journal of Archaeological Science* 35:1673–82.

Lindsay, I., A. T. Smith, and R. Badalyan

2010 Magnetic Survey in the Investigation of Sociopolitical Change at a Late Bronze Age Fortress Settlement in Northwestern Armenia. *Archaeological Prospection* 17(1):15–27.

Locke, J.

1959 *An Essay Concerning Human Understanding*. Dover, New York.

1988 *Two Treatises of Government*, student ed. Cambridge University Press, Cambridge.

Lubbock, J.

1865 *Pre-historic Times, as Illustrated by Ancient Remains, and the Manners and Customs of Modern Savages*. Williams and Norgate, London.

Lucretius, T.
    1997   *On the Nature of the Universe.* Translated by R. Melville. Clarendon, Oxford.
Lupton, A.
    1996   *Stability and Change: Socio-Political Development in North Mesopotamia and South-East Anatolia, 4000–2700 B.C.* Tempus Reparatum, Oxford.
Lurie, A.
    2007   When Is a Building Beautiful? *New York Review of Books* 54(4):19–21.
Lyman, R. L., and M. J. O'Brien
    2003   *W. C. McKern and the Midwestern Taxonomic Method.* University of Alabama Press, Tuscaloosa.
Lyon, P.
    1989   Archaeology and Mythology, II: A Reconsideration of the Animated Objects Theme in Moche Art. *Cultures in Conflict: Current Archaeological Perspectives* 20:62–68.
MacKenzie, D.
    1984   Marx and the Machine. *Technology and Culture* 25(3):473–502.
Makalatiya, S. I.
    1943   Arkheologicheskiye Raskopki Kurganykh Pogrebeniy v sel. Tkviavi. *Trudy Goriyskogo Istoriko-Etnograficheskogo Muzeya* 1.
Malcolm, N.
    2003   The Title Page of Leviathan, Seen in a Curious Perspective. In *Aspects of Hobbes*, edited by N. Malcolm, 200–233. Oxford University Press, New York.
Mapes, M.
    2008   Okay, Now *I'm* Bitter. *Huffington Post*, April 17, 2008. http://www.huffing tonpost.com/mary-mapes/okay-now-iimi-bitter_b_97252.html.
Marcus, A. A., A. Aiyer, and K. Dombrowski
    2012   Droning On: The Rise of the Machines. *Dialectical Anthropology* 36(1/2):1–5.
Marcus, M.
    1993   Incorporating the Body: Adornment, Gender, and Social Identity in Ancient Iran. *Cambridge Archaeological Journal* 3(2):157–78.
Marcuse, H.
    1964   *One Dimensional Man: Studies in the Ideology of Advanced Industrial Society.* Beacon, Boston.
Márquez, B., J. F. Gibaja, J. E. González Urquijo, J. J. Ibáñez, and A. Palomo
    2009   Projectile Points as Signs of Violence in Collective Burials During the 4th and the 3rd millennium Cal. BC in the N.E. of the Iberian Peninsula. Digital. CSIC http://digital.csic.es/handle/10261/10203.
Marshall, M.
    2014   Subject(ed) Bodies: A Bioarchaeological Investigation of Late Bronze—Iron 1 (1500–800 BC) Armenia. Ph.D. dissertation, University of Chicago, Chicago.
Martel, J.
    2006   The Spectacle of the Leviathan: Thomas Hobbes, Guy Debord and Walter Benjamin on Representation and Its Misuses. *Law, Culture and the Humanities* 2(1):67–90.

Martin, E.

1989 The Cultural Construction of Gendered Bodies. *Ethnos* 54:143–60.

Martin, T.

2001 *The Affirmative Action Empire: Nations and Nationalism in the Soviet Union, 1923–1939*. Cornell University Press, Ithaca, NY.

Martirosyan, A. A.

1964 *Armenia v Epokhu Bronzi i Rannego Zheleza*. Akademiya Nauk Armyanskoi SSR, Yerevan.

Marx, K.

1906 *Capital: A Critique of Political Economy*. Charles H. Kerr, Chicago.

1978 Economic and Philosophical Manuscripts of 1844. In *The Marx-Engels Reader*, 2nd ed., edited by R. C. Tucker, 67–125. Norton, New York.

1998 Theses on Feuerbach. In *The German Ideology*. Prometheus, Amherst, NY.

Marx, K., and F. Engels

1998 *The German Ideology*. Prometheus, Amherst, NY.

Marx, L.

1964 *The Machine in the Garden: Technology and the Pastoral Ideal in America*. Oxford University Press, New York.

Maurer, B.

2005 Does Money Matter? Abstraction and Substitution in Alternative Financial Forms. In *Materiality*, edited by D. Miller, 140–64. Duke University Press, Durham, NC.

McEwan, I.

1987 *The Child in Time*. Houghton Mifflin, Boston.

McGuire, R.

1991 Building Power in the Cultural Landscape of Broome County, New York 1880 to 1940. In *The Archaeology of Inequality*, edited by R. H. McGuire and R. Paynter, 102–24. Blackwell, Oxford.

1983 Breaking Down Cultural Complexity: Inequality and Heterogeneity. *Advances in Archaeological Method and Theory* 6:91–142.

Meillassoux, Q.

2008 *After Finitude: An Essay on the Necessity of Contingency*. Continuum, London.

Melikishvili, G. A.

1965 Voznikoveniye Khettskogo Tsartsva i Problema Drevneyshego Naseleniya Zakavkazya i Maloy Azii. *Vestnik Drevnej Istorii* 1:3–30.

Meskell, L.

2004 *Object Worlds in Ancient Egypt: Material Biographies Past and Present*. Berg, Oxford.

2005a Objects in the Mirror are Closer Than They Appear. In *Materiality*, edited by D. Miller, 51–71. Duke University Press, Durham, N.C.

Meskell, L. (ed.)

2005b *Archaeologies of Materiality*. Blackwell, Malden, MA.

Millar, J.

1796 Letters of Sidney, on inequality of property. To which is added, a treatise of the effects of war on commercial prosperity. *Scots Chronicle*. Debrett, London.

Miller, D.
1987 *Material Culture and Mass Consumption*. Blackwell, Oxford.
2005a Materiality: An Introduction. In *Materiality*, edited by D. Miller, 1–50. Duke University Press, Durham, NC.

Miller, D. (ed.)
2005b *Materiality*. Duke University Press, Durham, NC.

Mills, B. J.
2007 Performing the Feast: Visual Display and Suprahousehold Commensalism in the Puebloan Southwest. *American Antiquity* 72(2):210–39.

Mills, B. J. (ed.)
2004 *Identity, Feasting, and the Archaeology of the Greater Southwest*. University Press of Colorado, Boulder.

Minnis, P. E., M. E. Whalen, and R. E. Howell
2006 Fields of Power: Upland Farming in the Prehispanic Casas Grandes Polity, Chihuahua, Mexico. *American Antiquity* 71(4):707–22.

Mirtskhulava, G. I.
1975 *Samshvilde*. Metsniereba, Tbilisi.

Mitchell, W.J.T. (ed.)
1994 *Landscape and Power*. University of Chicago Press, Chicago.

Mnatsakahnyan, A. O.
1961 Lchashenskie Kurgany. *Kratkie Sobshchestva o Dokladakh i Polevykh Issledovaniyakh Instituta Arkheologii AN SSSR* 85:70.

Mohs, F.
1825 *Treatise on Mineralogy; or, The Natural History of the Mineral Kingdom*. A. Constable, Edinburgh.

Mollison, B. C.
1990 *Permaculture: A Practical Guide for a Sustainable Future*. Island, Washington, D.C.

Monahan, B.
2012 Beastly Goods: Pastoral Production in the Late Bronze Age Tsaghkahovit Plain. In *Regimes and Revolutions: Power, Violence, and Labor in Eurasia Between the Ancient and the Modern*, edited by C. Hartley, G. B. Yazıcıoğlu, and A. T. Smith, 337–47. Cambridge University Press, Cambridge.

Montaigne, M. de
1965 *The Complete Essays of Montaigne*. Translated by C. Cotton. Stanford University Press, Stanford, CA.

Morgan, L. H.
1877 *Ancient Society*. Henry Holt, New York.

Mueller, G. E.
1944 The One and the Many. *Philosophical Review* 53(1):46–61.

Mumford, L.
1934 *Technics and Civilization*. Harcourt, Brace, New York.

Munn, N. D.
1986 *The Fame of Gawa: A Symbolic Study of Value Transformation in a Massim (Papua New Guinea) Society*. Cambridge University Press, Cambridge.

Myers, F. R.
2001 *The Empire of Things: Regimes of Value and Material Culture*. School of American Research Press, Santa Fe, NM.

Narimanishvili, G.
    2003   Ritual Roads at Trialeti Barrows. *Dziebani* 11:9–22.
Nelson, S. M.
    2003   Feasting the Ancestors in Early China. In *The Archaeology and Politics of Food and Feasting in Early States and Empires*, edited by T. L. Bray, 65–89. Kluwer Academic/Plenum, New York.
Nojima, H.
    2005   From Everyday Things to Everyday Memories: Two Kinds of Interactions with Objects in a House. In *Ubiquitous Computing Systems*, edited by H. Murakami, H. Nakashima, H. Tokuda, and M. Yasumura, 10–19. Springer, Berlin.
Norton, M. I., D. Mochon, and D. Ariely
    2012   The IKEA effect: When Labor Leads to Love. *Journal of Consumer Psychology* 22(3):453–60.
O'Connor, D.
    2011   The Narmer Palette: A New Interpretation. In *Before the Pyramids: The Origins of Egyptian Civilization*, edited by E. Teeter, 151–59. Oriental Institute of the University of Chicago, Chicago.
O'Connor, R.
    2012   *Friends, Followers, and the Future: How Social Media Are Changing Politics, Threatening Big Brands, and Killing Traditional Media*. City Lights, San Francisco.
Oberman, H. A.
    1987   Via Antiqua and Via Moderna: Late Medieval Prolegomena to Early Reformation Thought. *Journal of the History of Ideas* 48(1):23–40.
Ockham, W.
    1974   *Opera Theologica*, Vol. 2. Editiones Instituti Franciscani Universitatis S. Bonaventurae, St. Bonaventure, NY.
    1992   *A Short Discourse on Tyrannical Government*. Translated by J. Kilcullen. Cambridge University Press, Cambridge.
Oganesian, V. E.
    1988   Serebrianyi Kubok iz Karashamba. *Ostoriko-Filologicheskii Zhurnal* 4:145–61.
    1992a   Raskopki Karashambskogo Mogil'nika v 1987g. In *Arkheologicheskie Raboty na Novostroikakh Armenii*, 26–36. Izdatel'stvo AN Armenii, Yerevan.
    1992b   A Silver Goblet from Karashamb. *Soviet Anthropology and Archeology* 30(4):84–102.
Olsen, B.
    2003   Material Culture after Text: Re-membering Things. *Norwegian Archaeological Review* 36(2):87–104.
    2010   *In Defense of Things: Archaeology and the Ontology of Objects*. AltaMira, Lanham, MD.
Özfirat, A.
    2008   The Highland Plateau of Eastern Anatolia in the Second Millennium BCE: Middle/Late Bronze Ages. In *Ceramics in Transitions: Chalcolithic through Iron Age in the Highlands of the Southern Caucasus and Anatolia*, edited by K. Rubinson and A. Sagona, 101–22. Peeters, Leuven.

Palumbi, G.
2008 *The Red and Black: Social and Cultural Interaction between the Upper Euphrates and Southern Caucasus Communities in the Fourth and Third Millennium* B.C. Sapienza Università di Roma, Roma.

Pauketat, T. R.
2000 Politicization and Community in the Pre-Columbian Mississippi Valley. In *The Archaeology of Communities: A New World Perspective*, edited by M. A. Canuto and J. Yaeger, 16–43. Routledge, London.
2007 *Chiefdoms and Other Archaeological Delusions*. AltaMira, Lanham, MD.

Pedersen, M. A.
2001 Totemism, Animism and North Asian Indigenous Ontologies. *The Journal of the Royal Anthropological Institute* 7(3):411–27.

Pervukhin, A.
2005 Deodands: A Study in the Creation of Common Law Rules. *American Journal of Legal History* 47(3):237–56.

Peterson, D.
2003 Ancient Metallurgy in the Mountain Kingdom: The Technology and Value of Early Bronze Age Metalwork from Velikent, Dagestan. In *Archaeology in the Borderlands: Investigations in Caucasia and Beyond*, edited by A. T. Smith and K. Rubinson, 22–37. The Cotsen Institute of Archaeology at UCLA, Los Angeles.

Petrosyan, L. A.
1989 *Raskopki Pamyatnikov Keti i Voskeaska*. Akademiya Nauk, Yerevan.
1996 Raskopki v Landzhike. In *Tezisy Dokladov Nauchnoy Sessii, Posvyashchennoy Itigam Polevykh Arkheologicheskikh Issledovaniy v Respublike Armeniya (1993–1995 gg.)*. Yerevan.

Picchelauri, K.
1997 *Waffen der Bronzezeit aus Ost-Georgien*. Marie Leidorf, Espelkamp.

Pietz, W.
1993 Fetishism and Materialism: The Limits of Theory in Marx. In *Fetishism as Cultural Discourse*, edited by E. S. Apter and W. Pietz, 119–51. Cornell University Press, Ithaca, NY.

Piotrovskii, B. B.
1969 *Karmir-Blur*. Aurora, Leningrad.
1973 Early Cultures of the Lands of the Scythians. *Metropolitan Museum of Art Bulletin* 32(5):12–25.

Pitt-Rivers, A. H. L.-F.
1887 *Excavations in Cranborne Chase, near Rushmore, on the borders of Dorset and Wilts*. Harrison and Sons, London.

Pkhakadze, G. G.
1963 *Eneolit Kvemo Kartli*. Izdatel'stvo Akademii Nauk Gruzinskoj SSR, Tbilisi.
1976 Arkheologicheskie Issledovaniya v c. Koda na Terrirorii Stroitel'stva Ptitsefermi. In *Arkheologicheskie Issledovaniya na Novostrojkakh Gruzinskoj SSR*, edited by O. D. Lordkipanidze and T. K. Mikeladze, 45–48. Metsniereba, Tbilisi.

Plashchev, A., and V. Chekmarev
  1978   *Gidrografiya SSSR*. Gidrometeoizdat, Leningrad.
Plog, F.
  1975   Systems Theory. *Annual Review of Anthropology* 4:207–24.
Plog, F., and S. Upham
  1983   The Analysis of Prehistoric Political Organization. In *The Development of Political Organization in Native North America*, edited by E. Tooker and M. H. Fried, 199–213. American Ethnological Society, Philadelphia.
Pollock, S.
  2003   Feasts, Funerals, and Fast Food in Early Mesopotamian States. In *The Archaeology and Politics of Food and Feasting in Early States and Empires*, edited by T. L. Bray, 17–38. Kluwer Academic/Plenum, New York.
Polzer, J.
  2002   Ambrogio Lorenzetti's War and Peace Murals Revisited: Contributions to the Meaning of the Good Government Allegory. *Artibus et Historiae* 45:63–106.
Porter, A.
  2010   From Kin to Class—and Back Again! Changing Paradigms of the Early Polity. In *The Development of Pre-State Communities in the Ancient Near East*, edited by D. Bolger and L. C. Maguire, 72–78. Oxbow, Oxford.
Porter, A., and G. M. Schwartz
  2012   *Sacred Killing: The Archaeology of Sacrifice in the Ancient Near East*. Eisenbrauns, Winona Lake, IN.
Preucel, R. W.
  1995   The Postprocessual Condition. *Journal of Archaeological Research* 3(2):147–75.
Puturidze, M.
  2003   Social and Economic Shifts in the South Caucasian Middle Bronze Age. In *Archaeology in the Borderlands: Investigations in Caucasia and Beyond*, edited by A. T. Smith and K. Rubinson, 111–27. The Cotsen Institute of Archaeology at UCLA, Los Angeles.
Quillet, J.
  1988   Community, Counsel and Representation. In *The Cambridge History of Medieval Political Thought, c. 350–c. 1450*, edited by J. H. Burns, 520–72. Cambridge University Press, Cambridge.
Quilter, J.
  1990   The Moche Revolt of the Objects. *Latin American Antiquity* 1(1):42–65.
  1997   The Narrative Approach to Moche Iconography. *Latin American Antiquity* 8(2):113–33.
Raile, E. D., A. N. W. Raile, C. T. Salmon, and L. A. Post
  2014   Defining Public Will. *Politics & Policy* 42(1):103–30.
Rancière, J.
  2006   *The Politics of Aesthetics: The Distribution of the Sensible*. Continuum, London.
Rathje, W. L., and C. Murphy
  1992   *Rubbish! The Archaeology of Garbage*. HarperCollins, New York.

Rawls, J.
 1971   *A Theory of Justice*. Belknap, Cambridge MA.
Reiner, E.
 1960   Fortune-Telling in Mesopotamia. *Journal of Near Eastern Studies* 19(1):23–
  35.
Reinhold, S.
 2003   Traditions in Transition: Some Thoughts on Late Bronze Age and Early
  Iron Age Burial Costumes from the Northern Caucasus. *European Journal of
  Archaeology* 6(1):25–54.
Renfrew, C.
 1986   Introduction: Peer-Polity Interaction and Socio-Political Change. In
  Peer-Polity Interaction and Socio-Political Change, edited by C. Renfrew and J. F.
  Cherry, 1–18. Cambridge University Press, Cambridge.
Reno, J. O.
 2008   Out of Place: Possibility and Pollution at a Transnational Landfill. Ph.D.
  dissertation, University of Michigan.
Reynolds, J.
 1975   *Discourses on Art*. Yale University Press, New Haven, CT.
Richard, F. G.
 2010   Recharting Atlantic Encounters: Object Trajectories and Histories of Value in the Siin (Senegal) and Senegambia. *Archaeological Dialogues* 17(1):1–27.
Richardson, S.
 2012   Early Mesopotamia: The Presumptive State. *Past & Present* 215(1):3–49.
Rohde, D., and K. Mulvihill
 2010   *A Rope and a Prayer: A Kidnapping from Two Sides*. Viking, New York.
Root, M. C.
 1979   *The King and Kingship in Achaemenid Art*. Brill, Leiden
Rosen, S. A.
 1997   *Lithics after the Stone Age: A Handbook of Stone Tools from the Levant*. AltaMira Press, Walnut Creek, CA.
Rostovtzeff, M. I.
 1922   *Iranians & Greeks in South Russia*. Clarendon, Oxford.
Rothman, M. S.
 1994   Sealings as a Control Mechanism in Prehistory: Tepe Gawra XI, X and
  VIII. In *Chiefdoms and Early States in the Near East: The Organizational Dynamics of Complexity*, edited by G. Stein and M. Rothman, 103–20. Prehistory,
  Madison, WI.
 2003   Ripples in the Stream: Transcaucasia-Anatolian Interaction in the Murat/
  Euphrates Basin at the Beginning of the Third Millennium B.C. In *Archaeol-
  ogy in the Borderlands: Investigation in Caucasia and Beyond*, edited by A. T.
  Smith and K. S. Rubinson, 95–110. The Cotsen Institute of Archaeology at
  UCLA, Los Angeles.
 2005   Transcaucasians: Settlement, Migration, and Trade in the Kura-Araxes
  Periods. *Archäologische Mitteilungen aus Iran und Turan* 37:53–62.
Rousseau, J.-J.
 1979   *Emile, or On Education*. Translated by A. Bloom. Basic, New York.

Routledge, B. E.
2004 *Moab in the Iron Age: Hegemony, Polity, Archaeology*. University of Pennsylvania Press, Philadelphia.
Rowlands, M.
2005 A Materialist Approach to Materiality. In *Materiality*, edited by D. Miller, 72–87. Duke University Press, Durham, N.C.
Rowlands, M., and C. Y. Tilley
2006 Monuments and Memorials. In *Handbook of Material Culture*, edited by C. Y. Tilley, W. Keane, S. Küchler, M. Rowlands, and P. Spyer, 500–515. Sage, London.
Rubinson, K.
1976 *The Trialeti Culture*. Ph.D. dissertation, Columbia University.
1977 The Chronology of the Middle Bronze Age Kurgans at Trialeti. In *Mountains and Lowlands: Essays in the Archaeology of Greater Mesopotamia*, edited by L. D. Levine and T.C.J. Young, 235–50. Undena, Malibu, CA.
2005 Second Millennium Painted Potteries and Problems of Terminologies. *Archäologische Mitteilungen aus Iran und Turan* 37:133–38.
2013 Actual Imports or Just Ideas? Investigations in Anatolia and the Caucasus. In *Cultures in Contact: From Mesopotamia to the Mediterranean*, edited by Joan Aruz, Sarah B. Graff, and Yelena Rakic, 12–25. Metropolitan Museum of Art, New York.
Rubinstein, N.
1958 Political Ideas in Sienese Art: The Frescoes by Ambrogio Lorenzetti and Taddeo di Bartolo in the Palazzo Pubblico. *Journal of the Warburg and Courtauld Institutes* 21(3/4):179–207.
Safdie, M., and W. Kohn
1997 *The City after the Automobile: An Architect's Vision*. Basic, New York.
Sagona, A.
1984 *The Caucasian Region in the Early Bronze Age*. BAR International Series, Oxford.
2000 Sos Höyük and the Erzurum Region in Late Prehistory: A Provisional Chronology for Northeast Anatolia. In *Chronologie des pays du Caucase et de l'Euphrate aux IVe–IIIe Millénaires*, edited by C. Marro and H. Hauptmann, 329–73. Institut Français d'Études Anatoliennes Georges Dumezil, Istanbul.
Sagona, A., and C. Sagona
2000 Excavations at Sos Höyük, 1998 to 2000: Fifth Preliminary Report. *Ancient Near Eastern Studies* 37:56–127.
2009 Encounters with the Divine in Late Prehistoric Eastern Anatolia and Southern Caucasus. In *Studies in Honour of Altan Çilingiroğlu: A Life Dedicated to Urartu on the Shores of the Upper Sea*, edited by H. Sağlamtimur, Z. Derin and E. Abay, 537–63. Arkeoloji ve Sanat Yayinlari, Istanbul.
Sahlins, M.
1972 The Original Affluent Society. In *Stone Age Economics*, 1–39. Aldine de Gruyter, Hawthorne, NY.
2004 *Apologies to Thucydides: Understanding History as Culture and Vice Versa*. University of Chicago Press, Chicago.

Sahni, K.

1997   *Crucifying the Orient: Russian Orientalism and the Colonization of the Caucasus and Central Asia.* White Orchid Press, Bangkok.

Santner, E. L.

2011   *The Royal Remains: The People's Two Bodies and the Endgames of Sovereignty.* University of Chicago Press, Chicago.

Sardaryan, S. A.

1967   *Pervobytnoe Obshchestvo v Armenii.* Akademiya Nauk, Yerevan.

Schaffer, S.

2005   Seeing Double: How to Make Up a Phantom Body Politic. In *Making Things Public: Atmospheres of Democracy*, edited by B. Latour and P. Weibel, 196–202. MIT Press, Cambridge, Mass.

Schele, L., and D. Freidel

1990   *A Forest of Kings.* Quill William Morrow, New York.

Schele, L., and M. E. Miller

1986   *The Blood of Kings: Dynasty and Ritual in Maya Art.* George Braziller, New York.

Schiffer, M. B.

1983   Toward the Identification of Formation Processes. *American Antiquity* 48(4):675–706.

1987   *Formation Processes of the Archaeological Record.* University of New Mexico Press, Albuquerque.

Schiller, F.

1982   *On the Aesthetic Education of Man: In a Series of Letters.* Translated by E. M. Wilkinson and L. A. Willoughby. Clarendon, Oxford.

2005   *Schiller's "On Grace and Dignity" in Its Cultural Context: Essays and a New Translation.* Camden House, Rochester, NY.

Schliemann, H.

1875   *Troy and Its Remains: A Narrative of Researches and Discoveries Made on the Site of Ilium, and in the Trojan Plain.* J. Murray, London.

Schmitt, C.

1985   *Political Theology: Four Chapters on the Concept of Sovereignty.* MIT Press, Cambridge, MA.

Schnapp, A.

1997   *The Discovery of the Past.* Harry N. Abrams, New York.

Schwartz, G.

1986   Mortuary Evidence and Social Stratification in the Ninevite V Period. In *The Origins of Cities in Dry-Farming Syria and Mesopotamia in the Third Millennium* B.C., edited by H. Weiss, 45–60. Four Quarters, Guilford.

Scott, A.

1997   Modernity's Machine Metaphor. *British Journal of Sociology* 48(4):561–75.

Scott, J. C.

1998   *Seeing Like a State: How Certain Schemes to Improve the Human Condition Have Failed.* Yale University Press, New Haven, CT.

Sennett, R.

2008   *The Craftsman.* Allen Lane, London.

Serres, M.
1995 *Genesis*. University of Michigan Press, Ann Arbor.

Service, E. R.
1975 *Origins of the State and Civilization*. Norton, New York.

Shackel, P. A.
2001 Public Memory and the Search for Power in American Historical Archaeology. *American Anthropologist* 103(3):655–70.

Shanks, M.
1995 Art and an Archaeology of Embodiment: Some Aspects of Archaic Greece. *Cambridge Archaeological Journal* 5(2):207–44.
1999 *Art and the Early Greek State: An Interpretive Archaeology*. Cambridge University Press, Cambridge.

Shanks, M., and C. Tilley
1987 *Social Theory and Archaeology*. Polity, Cambridge.

Shanshashvili, N., G. Narimanishvili, and G. Narimanishvili
2010 Trade and Trade Roads between South Caucasus and Near East in 3rd–2nd Millenniums B.C. In *Proceedings of the ICEA 2010 TİRE Second International Congress of Eurasian Archaeology: East Anatolian and Caucasian Bronze Age Cultures*, edited by A. S. Güneri, 363–88. Institute of Anatolia & Eurasia, Izmir, Turkey.

Sherratt, A.
1997 *Economy and Society in Prehistoric Europe*. Edinburgh University Press, Edinburgh.

Shingaki, N., and H. Nojima
2006 How Many Objects Are There around a Baby? Developmental Study of a Child's Interaction with Things. *Proceedings of the Fifth International Conference of Cognitive Science*. Vancouver, B.C. http://csjarchive.cogsci.rpi.edu/proceedings/2006/iccs/p187.pdf.

Shively, D. H.
1955 Bakufu versus Kabuki. *Harvard Journal of Asiatic Studies* 18(3/4):326–56.

Simonyan, A. E.
1982 Karmirberdskaya Kul'tura po Materialam Perioda Sredney Bronzy v Armenii. *Tezesiy Dokladov Vsesoyuznogo Simpoziuma Kul'turnyy Progress v Epokhu Bronzy i Rannego Zheleza* 1978:69–73.
1984 Dva Pogrebeniya Epokhi Sredney Bronzy Mogil'nika Verin Naver. *Sovetskaya Arkheologiya* 3:122–35.
2004 "Tsarskoe" Pogrebenie Epochi Sredney Bronzy Nerkin Naver. In *Mezhdunarodnaya Nauchnaya Konferentsiya "Arkheologiya, Etnologiya, Fol'kloristika Kavkaza" Sbornik Kratkikh Soderzhanij Dokladov*, 126–27. Nekeri, Tbilisi.

Simonyan, A. P.
1963 *Erevan: Ocherk Istorii, Ekonomiki i Kul'tury Goroda*. Izdatel'stvo Erevanskogo Universiteta, Yerevan.

Simonyan, H.
2006 *Verin Naver: 1976–1990 t't' Peghowmneri Ardyownk'nere*. Yerevani Hamalsarani Hratarakch'owt'yown, Yerevan.

Sims, L. S., and S. Rewald
 1996 *Still Life: The Object in American Art, 1915–1995: Selections from the Metro-politan Museum of Art*. Rizzoli, New York.
Singer, P. W.
 2009 *Wired for War: The Robotics Revolution and Conflict in the Twenty-First Century*. Penguin, New York.
Skinner, Q.
 1999 Ambrogio Lorenzetti's Buon Governo Frescoes: Two Old Questions, Two New Answers. *Journal of the Warburg and Courtauld Institutes* 62:1–28.
 2002 *Visions of Politics*, Vol. 2. Cambridge University Press, Cambridge.
Skira, P.
 1989 *Still Life: A History*. Rizzoli, New York.
Slezkine, Y.
 1994 The USSR as a Communal Apartment, or How a Socialist State Promoted Ethnic Particularism. *Slavic Review* 53(2):414–52.
Smith, A.
 1976 *An Inquiry into the Nature and Causes of the Wealth of Nations*. University of Chicago Press, Chicago.
 1982 *The Theory of Moral Sentiments*. Liberty Fund, Indianapolis, IN.
Smith, A. T.
 2001 The Limitations of Doxa: Agency and Subjectivity from an Archaeological Point of View. *Journal of Social Archaeology* 1(2):155–71.
 2003 *The Political Landscape: Constellations of Authority in Early Complex Polities*. University of California Press, Berkeley.
 2004 The End of the Essential Archaeological Subject. *Archaeological Dialogues* 11(1):1–20.
 2005 Prometheus Unbound: Southern Caucasia in Prehistory. *Journal of World Prehistory* 19(4):229–79.
 2006 Urartian Spectacle: Authority, Subjectivity, and Aesthetic Politics. In *Spectacle, Performance, and Power in Premodern Complex Society*, edited by T. Inomata and L. Coben, 103–34. AltaMira, Walnut Creek, CA.
 2011 Archaeologies of Sovereignty. *Annual Review of Anthropology* 40:415–32.
 2012a The Caucasus and the Near East. In *A Companion to the Archaeology of the Ancient Near East*, edited by D. T. Potts, 668–86. Wiley-Blackwell, Oxford.
 2012b "Yerevan, My Ancient Erebuni": Archaeological Repertoires, Public Assemblages, and the Manufacture of a (Post-)Soviet Nation. In *Regimes and Revolutions: Power, Violence, and Labor in Eurasia Between the Ancient and the Modern*, edited by C. Hartley, G. B. Yazıcıoğlu, and A. T. Smith, 57–77. Cambridge University Press, Cambridge.
 2012c The Prehistory of an Urartian Landscape. In *Biainili-Urartu: The Proceedings of the Symposium Held in Munich 12–14 October 2007*, edited by S. Kroll, C. Gruber, U. Hellwag, M. Roaf and P. Zimansky, 39–52. Peeters, Leuven.
Smith, A. T., R. Badalyan, P. Avetisyan, and M. Zardaryan
 2004 Early Complex Societies in Southern Caucasia: A Preliminary Report on the 2002 Investigations by Project ArAGATS on the Tsakahovit Plain, Republic of Armenia. *American Journal of Archaeology* 108:1–41.

Smith, A. T., R. S. Badalyan, and P. S. Avetisyan

2005 Southern Caucasia during the Late Bronze Age: An Interim Report on the Regional Investigations of Project ArAGATS in Western Armenia. In *Anatolian Iron Ages: Proceedings of the Fifth Anatolian Iron Ages Colloquium Held at Van, 6–10 August 2001*, edited by A. Çilingiroglu and G. Darbyshire, 175–85. The British Institute at Ankara, Ankara.

2009 *The Archaeology and Geography of Ancient Transcaucasian Societies I: The Foundations of Research and Regional Survey in the Tsaghkahovit Plain, Armenia.* Oriental Institute Press, Chicago.

Smith, A. T., and J. Leon

2014 Divination and Sovereignty: The Late Bronze Age Shrines at Gegharot, Armenia. *American Journal of Archaeology.* 118: 549–63

Smith, M. L.

2003 *The Social Construction of Ancient Cities.* Smithsonian Books, Washington D.C.

Snodgrass, A. M.

1985 The New Archaeology and the Classical Archaeologist. *American Journal of Archaeology* 89:287–98.

Sofaer, J. R.

2006 *The Body as Material Culture: A Theoretical Osteoarchaeology.* Cambridge University Press, Cambridge.

Spencer, H.

1981 *The Man versus the State.* Liberty Classics, Indianapolis, IN.

Spencer, J.

2007 *Anthropology, Politics and the State: Democracy and Violence in South Asia.* Cambridge University Press, Cambridge.

Spengler, O.

1932 *Man and Technics: A Contribution to a Philosophy of Life.* Translated by C. F. Atkinson. Knopf, New York.

Squier, E. G., and E. H. Davis

1848 *Ancient Monuments of the Mississippi Valley: Comprising the Results of Extensive Original Surveys and Explorations.* Smithsonian Institution, Washington, D.C.

Starn, R.

1994 *Ambrogio Lorenzetti: The Palazzo Pubblico, Siena.* George Braziller, New York.

Stein, Gil

1999 *Rethinking World-Systems: Diasporas, Colonies, and Interaction in Uruk Mesopotamia.* University of Arizona Press, Tucson.

Steward, J.

1955 *Theory of Culture Change.* University of Illinois Press, Urbana.

Stiegler, B.

1998 *Technics and Time.* Stanford University Press, Stanford, CA.

Strathern, M.

1988 *The Gender of the Gift: Problems with Women and Problems with Society in Melanesia.* University of California Press, Berkeley.

Strawser, B. J. (ed.)
  2013   *Killing by Remote Control: The Ethics of an Unmanned Military.* Oxford University Press, Oxford.
Suny, R. G.
  1993   *The Revenge of the Past: Nationalism, Revolution, and the Collapse of the Soviet Union.* Stanford University Press, Stanford, CA.
Sutton, T.
  1997   The Deodand and Responsibility for Death. *Journal of Legal History* 18(3):44–55.
Tallgren, A. M.
  1922   *Zur Archäologie Eestis, I: Vom Anfang der Besiedlung bis etwa 500 n. Chr.* Tartu, Dorpat.
Tardzhumanian, G. V. (ed.)
  1984   *Atlas Selskogo Khoziaistva Armianskoi SSR.* Glavnoe upravlenie geodezii i kartografii pri Sovete ministrov SSSR, Moskva.
Taylor, W. W.
  1948   *A Study of Archaeology.* Southern Illinois University Press, Carbondale.
Thomas, J.
  2012   Archaeology, Anthropology, and Material Things. In *Archaeology and Anthropology: Past, Present, and Future*, edited by D. Shankland, 219–29. Bloomsbury, London.
Thomas, N.
  1991   *Entangled Objects: Exchange, Material Culture, and Colonialism in the Pacific.* Harvard University Press, Cambridge, MA.
Thoreau, H. D.
  1882   *Walden.* Houghton, Mifflin, Boston.
Tilley, C.
  1991   *Material Culture and Text: The Art of Ambiguity.* Routledge, London.
  2004   *The Materiality of Stone.* Berg, Oxford.
Tillich, P.
  1967   *Systematic Theology.* 3 vols. University of Chicago Press, Chicago.
Tolz, V.
  2011   *Russia's Own Orient: The Politics of Identity and Oriental Studies in the Late Imperial and Early Soviet Periods.* Oxford University Press, Oxford.
Tornay, S. C.
  1936   William of Ockham's Nominalism. *Philosophical Review* 45(3):245–67.
Torosyan, R. M., O. S. Khnkikyan, and L. A. Petrosyan
  2002   *Drevnij Shirakavan.* Izdatel'stvo Gitutyun, Yerevan.
Toumanyan, H.
  1969   *Selected Works.* Progress, Moscow.
Trifonov, V. A.
  1994   The Caucasus and the Near East in the Early Bronze Age. *Oxford Journal of Archaeology* 13(3):357–60.
Trigger, B. G.
  2003   *Understanding Early Civilizations: A Comparative Study.* Cambridge University Press, Cambridge.

Turner, T.
1980 The Social Skin. In *Not Work Alone: A Cross-Cultural View of Activities Superfluous to Survival*, edited by J. Cherfas and R. Lewin, 112–40. Sage, Beverly Hills, CA.

Veblen, T.
1994 *The Theory of the Leisure Class*. Dover, New York.

Vincent, J.
1996 Political Anthropology. In *Encyclopedia of Social and Cultural Anthropology*, edited by A. Barnard and J. Spencer, 428–34. Routledge, London.

Walker, W. H.
1995 Ceremonial Trash? In *Expanding Archaeology*, edited by J. M. Skibo, W. H. Walker and A. E. Nielsen, 67–79. University of Utah Press, Salt Lake City.
2002 Stratigraphy and Practical Reason. *American Anthropologist* 104(1):159–77.

Warner, M.
2005 *Publics and Counterpublics*. Zone, New York.

Weber, M.
1968 *Max Weber on Charisma and Institution Building*. University of Chicago Press, Chicago.
1994 *Weber: Political Writings*. Cambridge University Press, Cambridge.

Weibel, P.
2005 Art and Democracy: People Making Art Making People. In *Making Things Public: Atmospheres of Democracy*, edited by B. Latour and P. Weibel, 1008–37. MIT Press, Cambridge, MA.

Wengrow, D.
2010 *What Makes Civilization? The Ancient Near East and the Future of the West*. Oxford University Press, Oxford.

Wesson, C. B.
2008 *Households and Hegemony: Early Creek Prestige Goods, Symbolic Capital, and Social Power*. University of Nebraska Press, Lincoln.

Willey, G., and P. Phillips
1958 *Method and Theory in American Archaeology*. University of Chicago Press, Chicago.

Williams, B. G.
2010 The CIA's Covert Predator Drone War in Pakistan, 2004–2010: The History of an Assassination Campaign. *Studies in Conflict & Terrorism* 33(10):871–92.

Wilson, D.
1862 *Prehistoric Man: Researches in the Origin of Civilization in the Old and the New World*. Macmillan, Cambridge.

Woolley, C. L.
1934 *Ur Excavations*, Vol. 2, *The Royal Cemetery*. Oxford University Press, London.

Worsaae, J. J. A.
1849 *The Primeval Antiquities of Denmark*. Translated by W. Thoms. J. H. Parker, London.

Wright, H.
   1977   Recent Research on the Origin of the State. *Annual Review of Anthropology* 6:379–97.

Yaeger, J.
   2000   The Social Construction of Communities in the Classic Maya Countryside: Strategies of Affiliation in Western Belize. In *The Archaeology of Communities: A New World Perspective*, edited by M. A. Canuto and J. Yaeger, 123–42. Routledge, London.

Yaralov, Y.
   1960   *Yerevan*. Foreign Languages, Moscow.

Yasur-Landau, A., E. H. Cline, N. Goshen, N. Marom, and I. Samet
   2012   An MB II Orthostat Building at Tel Kabri, Israel. *Bulletin of the American Schools of Oriental Research* 367:1–29.

Yoffee, N.
   1993   Too Many Chiefs? or Safe Texts for the 90's. In *Archaeological Theory—Who Sets the Agenda*, edited by A. Sherratt and N. Yoffee, 60–78. Cambridge University Press, Cambridge.

Index

Aeschylus, 27

aesthetics: aesthetic captivation, 29, 89, 124, 156; of awe, 68; of distinction and subjection, 121; political aesthetic and the "pleasure of position," 156–57

Afghanistan, 60

Agamben, Giorgio, 5, 87, 142; on the apparatus of subjectification, 89–90; on "constituting power" and "constituted power," 6; on human sacrifice as the ultimate foundation of sovereignty, 148; on sovereignty, 89

Agarak, 120

Agnew, John, 87

Amsterdam *toebakje* paintings, 41

amulets, 15, 57, 177

Anatolia: eastern Anatolia, 151; expansion of Uruk communities into, 106; Late Chalcolithic period in, 102

ancient Near East, the, 100, 101, 104, 177, 180

Anderson, Benedict, 89, 98

animacy, 35–36, 62

animal sacrifice, 138, 180

animals, 2, 27, 37, 39, 90, 120, 167, 179; domesticated animals, 154; draught animals, 142; game animals, 144; paintings/sculptures of, 40, 42, 74; pastoral animals, 140. *See also* animal sacrifice

Ankersmit, F. R., 156

anthropology, 52; evolutionary anthropology, 84; of the object world, 31–32; political anthropology, 66; Victorian cultural anthropology, 64

antimony ores, 109n7, 139–40

Appadurai, A., 148

Aquinas, Thomas, 34, 36; ontological realism of, 34; on relics, 34

Arab Spring, social networking during, 72

Aragatsiberd, 162, 171

archaeology, 29–30, 43; archeological culture, 45; culture-history and material taxonomy, 44–45; "osteoarchaeology," 53; and the political, 64, 66–67; processual archaeology, 46–47, 66–67

Arendt, Hannah: on *"animal laborans,"* 27; on *Homo faber*, 98

Areshian, Gregory, 131

Arin-Berd, 188

Aristotle, 33, 64, 77; Aristotelian reason, 36; and the concept of the good life, 90; and the great chain of being, 40; response to Plato's theory of the Forms, 33–34

armaments/weaponry: arrows of the Middle Bronze Age, 144; of the Middle Bronze Age, 139–40; projectile points of the Early Bronze Age, 142, 143, 152; projectile points of the Middle Bronze Age, 142–44; and the social reproduction of violence, 144

Armenia: central Armenia, 131; northern Armenia, 144–45; Soviet Armenia, 191, 192. *See also* Armenian Highland, the

Armenian Highland, the, 16, 102, 104, 107, 108, 122, 164, 189

arsenic, 109, 109n7; arsenic-copper alloy, 139; arsenic-tin-copper alloy, 139; copper-arsenic-antimony alloy, 139–40

Arslantepe, "royal" tomb at, 106, 106–7n5, 107

Aruch, 138, 147

assemblages, 32–33, 43, 89, 145; articulation of material assemblages, 54; and assembly, 32–33, 72–73; and civic practices, 4; the coalescence of interdigitated assemblages, 6; as a collection of materials in one location, 44; definition of, 32, 45; "efficacy" of, 21; heterogeneity of, 39; and the inseparable binding of the material and the representational, 3–4; mutable nature of, 48; redefinition of, 46–47; the reproduction of material assemblages, 6;

assemblages (*cont.*)
and the sociological meaningfulness of
objects, 20; use of by naturalists, 44
Aubrey, John, 43
Augustinus Triumphus, 8
Austen, Jane, 57–58
authority, 67; devices of, 177; political authority, 65; production of, 65; and the
responsibility to protect those subject to
authority, 91; sovereign authority, 86–87,
92–93
authorization: devices of (amulets, cylinder
seals), 177; logics of, 64; and subjection,
67–68, 71; techniques of, 5
automatons, 79, 156
Azerbaijan, 152

Baines, John, 68
Balici-Zezvebi, 112
Banquet with Mince Pie (1635), 42
Barry, Andrew, 72
Bataille, Georges, 10–11, 91
Benjamin, Walter, 6
Bennett, Jane, 21, 28, 50
Bet Yerah, 108
biopower, 87
Blashfield, Edwin, 98, 99
Bloomberg, Michael, proposal of to limit
soft-drink size in New York City, 73,
73n9
body, the, 156; conception of as a singular
biological entity, 52; social construction
of, 53
body politic, the, 88
Boelhower, W., on the "archaeological" turn
in the human sciences, 20
Bolshevik Revolution, the, 191–92
Bouazizi, Mohamed, 186, 187–88, 194
Bourdieu, P., 157, 188
Bouzid, Sidi, 187–88
Brae, Skara, 45
Bronze Age. *See* Early Bronze Age; Gegha-
rot, Early Bronze Age of; Kura-Araxes
Early Bronze Age civilization; Middle
Bronze Age; South Caucasus, Early
Bronze Age of
bronze production: increase in during the
Late Bronze Age, 164; workshops for,
140
Brother Axe, tale of, 195–96
Brubaker, Rogers, 192–93
Bruegger, Urs, 183–84

Bryson, Norman, 41
burial clusters, 162–64; Hnaberd Burial
Cluster 4, 163; Mantash Burial Cluster 8,
163; spatial distribution of, 164; Tsaghkahovit Burial Cluster 12, 163
Butler, Judith, 53
Bynum, Caroline, 35, 40

cabinets of curiosity, 43
caprine survivorship, 167
captivation, 15, 39, 88n15, 148, 178, 181,
183; aesthetic captivation, 29, 89, 124,
156; the captivation of objects in the
Kura-Araxes civilization, 124–25; of
divinatory assemblages, 181–82; the
emergence of a new form of captivation
during the Late Bronze Age, 178–79; of
objects, 15, 124; sentiments of captivation, 15, 124; visible forms of, 57
Caravaggio, Michelangelo Merisi da, 41
Cassirer, Ernst, 22
Çatahöyük, 120
Caucasus, the, 16–19, 188; at the beginning
of the Late Bronze Age, 157–65; civilization in, 100, 125–26; the Great Caucasus
range, 16; human migration from, 106;
material flows across the Middle Bronze
Age Caucasus, 138–42. *See also* North
Caucasus; South Caucasus
ceramics, 159, 172; geographic differen-
tiation of ceramic styles, 152; of the
Karmir-Berd horizon, 151–52; of the
Karmir-Vank horizon, 152; of the Late
Chalcolithic, 102, 108; Lchashen-
Metsamor ceramic assemblages, 164;
new ceramic styles during the transition
between the Middle and Late Bronze
Ages in the South Caucasus, 164; of the
Sevan-Uzerlik horizon, 152, 158, 164; of
the Verin Naver horizon, 152
Cezanne, Paul, 41
Chalcolithic period. *See* Late Chalcolithic
Chardin, Jean-Baptiste-Siméon, 41
Chernykh, Evgenii N., 134, 140
Childe, V. Gordon, 45, 100
Chkalovka, 112
Cicero, 7–8
civilization(s), 64, 65, 99; in the ancient
Near East, 100; cosmopolitan model of,
101; as exclusive clubs/communities,
101–2; in southern Russia, 100. *See also*
civilization machine

civilization machine, 22, 98–99, 152, 158, 184; as a machine for manufacturing publics, 102, 130, 136

Clarke, David, 45

Clastres, Pierre, 65, 97; on the "society against the state," 121

clay stamps, 181

Coben, Lawrence, 68

Collingwood, R. G., 187

communities: egalitarian communities, 65; the "imagined community," 98; of the Late Bronze Age, 162; of the Middle Bronze Age, 140, 152; political communities, 2, 21, 85, 86, 183

Connolly, William, 51

conspicuous consumption, 136, 145, 147; in the Arslantepe tomb, 107; in mortuary assemblages, 22, 125, 158

Coole, Diana, 52

Cooper, Lisa, 70

copper-arsenic-antimony alloys, 139–40

Cowgill, George, 67

cremation, in the Middle Bronze Age II, 147

cromlechs, 163

currency traders, and the abstraction of the "market," 183–84

cylinder seals, 177

Daley, Richard J., 7

Daston, L., 43

de Avila, Francisco, 154

de Beauvoir, Simone, 52, 53

DeLanda, Manuel, 47

Deleuze, Gilles, 48, 51, 127, 130, 152, 154; on jewelry and weapons, 177

democracy, 11; participatory democracy, 5; and public rallies, 5

deodands, legal practices governing, 78–79, 79n12

Descartes, René, 54–55

Devedjian, Seda, 145

Dietler, M., 67

divination, as a means of peering into the workings of the cosmos, 181–82

divinatory practices, forms of, 179–80; aleuromancy, 179, 180–81; astragalomancy (*bos* [cattle] and *ovicaprid* [sheep/goat]), 179–80, 179n10; lithomancy, 179, 180; osteomancy, 179; the use of flour in divinatory practices, 180–81

Dolukhanov, Pavel, 131

Donnan, Christopher, 155

drinking vessels, metal, 150

drone warfare, 59–60, 60n6

Eagleton, Terry, 58

Early Bronze Age, 102, 110–11, 122, 140; bronze production in, 131; civilization machine of, 22, 99, 105; collective tombs of, 116, 118, 131; the Early Bronze Age public, 125–26; Early Bronze I, 116; Early Bronze II, 116; material flows in, 138, 140. *See also* armaments/weaponry, projectile points of the Early Bronze Age

Ebla, 70

efficacy, 21, 39, 50, 52, 79; of assemblages, 88, 177; as a capacity to make something new, 50; efficacy of things in political reproduction, 186–87; material efficacy and political action, 194; and the political machine, 185; sensual efficacy, 176; of things/objects, 13, 40, 57, 76, 86, 122, 148, 185, 186, 188. *See also* machines, efficacy of

egalitarianism, 112, 122, 125, 134, 136

El Abidine Ben Ali, Zine, 186

Elar, 103

empiricism, 36, 39, 54; Lockean empiricism, 55

epistemology, 36; classical epistemology, 37; multimodal epistemology, 21

Erebuni, 188–94; fortress of, 189

Euphrates, upper, 102; destruction episodes in, 105, 105n3

Eurasian Steppe, the, 125

feasts/feasting: definition of, 69; key aspects of in relation to sovereignty, 69–70; as a means of bodily training, 70

Félibien, André, 40, 43

festivals, 68

fetishes, 15, 57

Feuerbach, Joseph Anselm, 83

Feuerbach, Ludwig, 83

fortresses/fortifications, 153; "cyclopean" stone masonry fortifications, 162; of Erebuni, 189; fortified complexes at Hnaberd and Aragatsiberd, 162, 164; fortresses at Gegharot and on the Tsaghkahovit Plain, 159–62, 160–61n4, 168; institu-

fortresses/fortifications (*cont.*)
tionalization within the restricted space
of fortresses, 181
Foucault, Michel, 5, 36, 87, 89, 182
Fragile State Index (FSI), 92
Frangipane, Marcella, 106–7n5
funerary rituals, 68

Galison, P., 43
Geertz, Clifford, 89, 91
Gegharot, 107, 124, 165–68; causes of the
abandonment of, 131–32; ceramics of,
165–66, 165–66n6; cylinder seals at, 177;
Early Bronze Age of, 110–12; fire at,
116; flow of material goods into, 184;
"Karnut-Shengavit" ceramics of during
Kura-Araxes occupation, 116; Kurgan 1
of, 158–59; large storage jar of, 182–83;
Late Bronze Age occupation of, 168–71;
period VI A palace complex (building
III) and VI B "royal" tomb of, 116; possible sacred space at, 118, 120; sensual
quality of the Early Bronze Age assemblage at, 118, 120; sovereignty at work in
during the Late Bronze Age, 182. *See also*
Gegharot, shrines of
Gegharot, shrines of, 171–72, 174, 176;
East Citadel shrine, 173–74, 176, 179,
179n10, 180, 181; and the emergence
of a new form of captivation during
the Late Bronze Age, 178–79; forms of
divinatory practice recovered at, 179; importance of substance burning at, 176;
the presence of ceramic censers in, 176;
psychotropic substances found at, 176;
West Citadel shrine, 173; West Terrace
shrine, 168–69, 173, 174, 179, 179n10;
wine found at, 176
Gell, Alfred, 183; on "enchantment of
technology," 14; on "methodological
philistinism," 31; on "technology of enchantment," 14
Georgia, 152
German Ideology, The (Marx and Engels), 84
Gero, J., 70
Gilmour, Garth, 179–80
God, 8n7, 13, 40, 78, 81, 88; intercession of
in the world, 36; mind of, 34; the sovereign as the agent of, 79
Godedzor, 108
Godin Tepe, 106
good life (*eudaimonia*), the, 90

governance, 6, 21, 82, 93, 98, 102, 181, 183;
definition of as an ordering of the world
of things, 82; of human bodies, 78; institutional apparatus of, 70, 158; Lorenzetti's understanding of just governance
depicted in the decoration of Sala dei
Nove, 127, 129–30; machine of, 89; and
sovereignty, 90; technologies of, 87; of
things, 90
Gramsci, Antonio, 70, 71
Graves, James, 43–44
Greenberg, Raffi, 108
Grosz, Elizabeth, 53
Guattari, F., 48, 51, 127, 130, 152, 154; on
jewelry and weapons, 177
Güzelova, 124

Haarlem *banketje* paintings, 41
Habermas, Jürgen, 85
Haftavan Tepe, 152
hallucinogenics, 122
Hansen, T. B., 5–6
Haraway, Donna, 61
Harman, Graham, 38
Harvey, David, 15
Haury, Emil, 45n3
Heda, Claesz, 42
Hegel, Georg Wilhelm Friedrich, 9, 38–39
hegemony: geopolitical hegemony, 70; "he-
gemony without sovereignty" at Ebla, 70
Henry VIII (king of England), 185
Hesiod, 27–28
Hicks, D., on the "material" turn in the
human sciences, 20
Hill, Graham, 30
Hobbes, Thomas, 4, 38, 156; on the duality
of the sovereign, 79–80, 79n13, 80n14
Hodder, Ian, 39, 50, 71, 120; on "entrap-
ment" to themes of contagion, 14
Homo faber (man the creator), 85, 98
Homo loquens (speaking man), 85
Homo sacer (sacred man), as a mirror image
of the sovereign, 89
Horom, 111, 179–80
human agency, 187, 188
human rights, 91, 91n16
human sacrifice, 159; and transfiguration
of the body, 147; as the ultimate foundation of sovereignty, 148
"humanitarian intervention," 91, 91n16
Hume, David, 185
Humphrey, C., 6

Hunt, Alan, 98
Hustwit, Gary, 29

idols, 174, 176
Ikea effect, the, 148
Ingold, Tim, 20, 55, 56
Inomata, Takeshi, 68
Instrumental Neutron Activation (INA)
    analysis, 165
International Commission on Intervention
    and State Sovereignty (ICISS), 91n16
International Criminal Court, 63
Iran, 140, 186; northwestern Iran, 152

Jackson, M. A., 154
Jane Mary of Maillé, 35
Jasmine Revolution, the, 186, 195; assem-
    blages of, 188
jewelry/jewelry manufacturing, 168,
    170–71; and authority, 177; centrality of
    jewelry within Gegharot's metalworking
    industry, 176; and the transfigured body,
    184; transformation of jewelry as objects
    of adornment to emblems of status,
    176–77
John of Sacrobosco, 8
Joint American-Armenian Project for the
    Archaeology and Geography of Ancient
    Transcaucasian Societies. See Project
    ArAGATS
Jrashen, 165
justice: distributive justice, 129; as fairness,
    82–83

Kantorowicz, E. H., 5, 79, 88, 151
Karashamb, Great Kurgan, 145, 148–51;
    architecture of, 149; date of, 148; silver-
    plated goblet found in, 149–51, 157
Karmir-Berd horizon, ceramics of, 151–52
Karmir-Vank horizon, ceramics of, 152
Karnut, 124
Kasakh River valley, 164
Kavtaradze, G. L., 139
Keane, Webb, 4n5
Keti, 112
Khabur drainage, northern Syria, 108
Khatchadourian, Lori, 71, 89, 92
Khirbet Kerak, 108, 109
Kiketi, 112
kingship, institution of, 65
kinship, 65, 66
Kirovakan, 147

Knorr-Cetina, Karin, 183–84
Kochinyan, Anton, 193
Koda, 112
Kohl, Philip L., 108, 132, 132n9, 134
Köhne Shahar, 106, 109n6
Kolata, Alan, 70
Korinth, archaic, 68
Kosovo, NATO air campaign in, 59
Kroeber, A. L., 155
Kuftin, B. A., 147
Kura-Araxes civilization (Early Bronze
    Age), 22, 102–5, 109; alternate names
    for, 102n1; animal forms of, 123; appear-
    ance of tin bronzes in, 139; ceramics
    of, 103, 106, 109n6, 122; the civilization
    machine of, 125–26; collective tombs
    of, 125, 133; Early Bronze II iconogra-
    phy of, 150; "Elar-Aragats" ceramics of,
    110–11; expansion of the decorative tra-
    dition of the ceramics of, 122–23; expan-
    sion of the Kura-Araxes assemblage in,
    103–5, 106, 107–8, 109–10, 116, 122, 138;
    "fortification" walls of, 106n4; hearth as-
    semblages of, 120–21; interactions with
    neighboring communities, 105, 105n2;
    "Karnut-Shengavit" ceramics of, 116; and
    sensibility, 105–10; social boundaries of,
    138, 139; as a "society against the state,"
    121
kurgans, 139, 163; Aruch kurgans, 138, 147;
    Bedeni kurgans, 139, 146; diversity of
    Middle Bronze Age kurgans, 144–45;
    Early Kurgans, 132, 134, 136, 138, 139,
    145; involvement of collective labor in
    kurgan construction, 148; Kirovakan
    kurgans, 147; Lori-Berd kurgans, 147;
    Martkopi kurgans, 139; metal drinking
    vessels found in, 150; of the Middle
    Bronze Age III burial fields at Karmir-
    Berd and Shirakavan, 147; Tsnori
    kurgans, 134–36, 139, 146; Vanadzor
    kurgans, 145, 149, 150. See also Gegharot,
    Kurgan 1 of; Great Karashamb Kurgan;
    Trialeti, kurgan field at; Trialeti-Vanadzor
    complex/horizon, kurgans of

Landjik, 112
landscape, and politics, x–xi, 15; instrumen-
    tality of, 31; painting, 40–41; and things,
    15–16
Late Chalcolithic, 45, 100, 102–3, 106,
    109n6; ceramics of, 102, 108

Latour, B., 47, 48, 51n5; on "idealized materialism," 20; on networks, 53–54
Lefebvre, Henri, 15
Lefort, Claude, 156–57
Leibniz, Gottfried, 8, 8n7
Lenin, Vladimir, 193
Levant, the, 104; southern Levant, 108
Leviathan (Hobbes), frontispiece of, 79–81, 85
Levi-Strauss, C., 154n2
liberalism, 72
Lindsay, Ian, 160–61n4, 162, 165
Locke, John, 55; on the labor theory of property, 81, 82; on the origin of political society, 81–82
Lorenzetti, Ambrogio, 127, 129–30
Lori-Berd, 138, 144–45, 147
Lubbock, John, 44
Lucretius, 37
Luddite movement, 10
Lyon, Patricia, 154

machine politics, 7–11; and the Latin *machina*, 7–8
machines: the "anthropological machine," 90, 91; governmental machines, 86–91; the "leviathan machine," 91; tyrannical machines, 72. *See also* civilization machine; machines, efficacy of; political machine, the; war machine, the
machines, efficacy of, 48, 126; agency and efficacy, 49–50; bodies and machines, 52–54; and reproduction and transformation, 51–52
Maikop, 106, 107, 109, 125; contents of the Great Kurgan burial tumulus/assemblage, 99–100; and the "cultural community" of Maikop, 100; excavation of the Great Kurgan burial tumulus/assemblage of, 99–101, 150; the Maikop assemblage in a wider art historical context, 100–101
Marcus, Michelle, 171
Marcuse, Herbert, 11
Martkopi, 139
Marx, Karl, 10; on commodity "fetishism," 11, 84–85; on human thought itself as a material process, engaged by the physical world, 83–84; materialism of, 84; "production metaphysics" of, 84
Marxism, 72; Western Marxism, 66, 85
material flows: across the Middle Bronze

Age Caucasus, 138–42; during the Early Bronze Age, 138, 140; during the Late Bronze Age, 165–68, 184
"material turn," the, 39
materialism, 83; of Marx, 84; new forms of, 39; speculative materialism, 20
materiality, 30, 55; contemporary materiality, 71; materiality movement, 30; materiality studies, 31; materiality theory, 4
McEwan, Ian, 47
Meillassoux, Q., 38, 50; on "correlationism," 31–32
Melikishvili, Giorgi, 132
memory, 27, 68–69, 189
Mesopotamia, 68, 121, 126
metalworking, 176; metal assemblages, 164, 164–65n5; metal drinking vessels, 150. *See also* armaments/weaponry; jewelry/jewelry manufacturing
metamorphosis, 144–45, 171–74, 176; "miracles of metamorphosis," 35
Middle Ages, the, 35, 40; holy matter in, 35
Middle Bronze Age, 153, 157–58; ceramic assemblages of the terminal Middle Bronze Age, 152; communities of, 140, 152; diversity of Middle Bronze Age tomb assemblages, 144–45; proliferation of the apparatus of violence during the Middle Bronze Age, 144; reproduction of the Middle Bronze Age war machine, 145, 150; variability in the treatment of dead bodies during, 146–48; the violence of elite competition during, 151. *See also* armaments/weaponry
Millar, John, 7
Moche jars, painted, 154–56, 154n1; debates concerning the art of, 155–56; images depicted on, 155
Mokhrablur, 103, 106
Montaigne, Michel de, 8, 97
Morgan, Lewis Henry, 98
mortuary clusters. *See* burial clusters
MQ-1 Predator drones, 59–60; militarization of, 63; as replacing conventional Westphalian geopolitics, 63; threats to the global and political community posed by, 62–63
Mueller, G. E., on the "world-machine," 21
Mumford, Lewis, 11
Museum of the Founding of Yerevan (the Erebuni Museum), 189–91

Nagorno-Karabakh highlands, 152
Narimanishvili, Goderzi, 140
Narmer Palette, 88n15
Near East. *See* ancient Near East, the
Neolithic, the: mining of copper ore in, 82; the Neolithic "revolution," 77–78
Nerkin Naver, 145
noble lie, the, 76–77
nominalism, 35–36, 39, 78
North Caucasus, the, 16, 104; the Chalcolithic North Caucasus, 100; kurgan assemblages of, 132

Obama, Barack, and the flag pin controversy, 1–2, 3–4, 50
objects: abstract category of, 52; anthropomorphizing of, 31; the beautiful object, 39; as a Cartesian division, 38; as conceptual abstractions, 32; defined as any "accident of a body without us," 38; exile of from the *via moderna*, 37, 40; the global number of household objects, 29; and the human body/body parts, 47n4; liberal politics of, 86; Marxist politics of, 86; and modern polity, 72; ontogenetic ties to objects, 30; and political order, 73; quality of, 36; the "revolt of objects," 154, 154n2, 156
Olsen, Bjørnar, 51, 53
ontogeny, 76
Oriental Institute at the University of Chicago, tympanum of, 98, 99

Pakistan, 60; drone war in, 60n4
Palumbi, G., 120
Pambakh Valley, 165
Pauketat, Timothy, 66
Peace of Westphalia (1648), 63
permaculture, 20
Persia, Achaemenid: social logics of empire in, 71; theory of political order in, 89
Persian Gulf, necklaces of, 140
Phillips, Philip, 45
philosophy, 43, 52; classical philosophy, 37; modern philosophy, 39; object-oriented philosophy, 20
Picasso, Pablo, 42
Pindar, 27
Piotrovskii, Boris, 100
Plato, 2–3, 33, 34, 97; allegory of the cave, 2–3; on the ideal *polis*, 76; and the noble

lie, 76–77; on the phylogenic origin myth for polity, 77–78, 85; on the polity as an association, 77
political action, 11, 187–88, 195; and material efficacy, 194
political association, "thingness" of, 85
political economy, 23, 75, 77, 81
political machine, the, 7, 23, 177, 178; efficacy of, 185; as an engine for inculcating civic virtues, 10; innovation of, 185; and the machinery of political reproduction, 156; the sensual domain of the Late Bronze Age political machine, 171–74, 176; the Tsaghkahovit Plain's Late Bronze Age political machine, 183, 184–85
political performance, 70
political theory, contemporary, 71–72
"political will," 185
politics: the economy of commensal politics, 70; politics as politics, 64; predatory politics, 145; and prehistory/archaeology, 64–67
polity: modern polity, 72; origin myths of polity as an association, 77–78; as a product of artifice, 81
Porter, Anne, 65
power, 67; as ceremonial regalia, 89; and human-thing entanglements, 71; as management, 89; "power over," 71; power and pomp, 89; "power to," 71; sovereign power, 87; subjection and sovereign power, 90; things as "powerful," 71. *See also* biopower
Predator drones. *See* MQ-1 Predator drone
prehistory, and the political, 64–67
Project ArAGATS, 18, 110, 162, 165; chronology of for the Bronze Age, 19
Prometheus, 16, 27–28
publicity, 68–69, 98, 99, 124, 181; key aspects of, 68; technologies of, 181
Pulur, 120
purification, 36, 37
psychoanalysis, 52
Puturidze, Marina, 142

Quillet, J., on the "*aporia* of the one and the many," 21, 158
Quilter, J., 155, 156

racial domination, 69
Rancière, Jacques, 58

Rawls, John, 4, 85; on the general principles of justice, 82–83
realism, medieval, 34–35, 34n1
regalia: political work of, 88; the regalia of sovereignty, 88–89
reproduction: apparatus of, 185; of a coherent public, 6, 92, 98, 101–2; efficacy of things in political reproduction, 186–87; the machinery of political reproduction, 156; the machinery of sovereign reproduction, 195; of material assemblages, 6; of the Middle Bronze Age war machine, 145, 150; the role of things in the reproduction of a public, 98; the social reproduction of violence, 144; and transformation, 51–52
resography, 29
Reynolds, Joshua, 40–41
Robinson, Karen, 150
robotic weapons systems, 61–62; and the capacity of for decision making, 62; the moral and legal issues of sending robots to war, 62
Root, M. C., 71
Rostovtzeff, Mikhail, 99
Rousseau, Jean-Jacques, 4; use of the machine analogy by, 8–9
Russia, 22, 100

Sachkhere, 139
sacrifice. See animal sacrifice; human sacrifice
Sagona, Antonio, 107, 118, 120, 122
Sagona, Claudia, 118, 120, 122
Sala dei Nove, decoration of by Lorenzetti, 127, 129–30, 150
Samshvilde, 112
Santner, E. L., on "spectral things," 52
scientific illustration, 42–43
sculptures, 35, 57, 191
sense, 14, 15, 21, 56, 58, 110–12, 116, 188, 120–21; Cartesian privileging of, 55–56; impasse of with sensibility, 55; and metamorphosis, 144–45, 171–74, 176; and the relation of form to value, 122
Sense and Sensibility (Austen), 57–58
sensibility, 14, 15, 21, 54, 56, 58, 105–10; impasse of with sense, 55; and material flows, 138–42, 165–68, 171; and the physicality of things, 57; sovereignty of, 55; understanding as organized by, 55
sentiment, 14, 15, 21, 56, 58, 122–25, 148–

51, 178–83; in Jane Austen's novels, 57–58; and our imagination of the efficacy of things, 122; sentiments of captivation, 15; sentiments of care, 14
Serres, Michel, 51
Sevak, Payrur, 186, 193–94
Sevan-Uzerlik horizon, ceramics of, 152, 158, 164
Shackel, P. A., 68
shamanic traditions, Eurasian, 180
Shane, Scott, 60
Shanks, Michael, 68
Shengavit, 106, 134, 136
Sherratt, Andrew, 100, 106
Shirak Plain, the, 111–12
shrines. See Gegharot, shrines of
Singer, P. W., 61
Smith, Adam, 9–10, 77, 156
Smith, J. Richardson, 44
social evolutionism, 67
social reproduction, machinery of, 52
Socrates, on the ideal polis, 76
Sofaer, Joanna, on "theoretical osteoarchaeology," 53
Somalia, 60, 92
Sos Höyük, 106, 120, 124
South Caucasus, the, 16, 109n7, 150, 151, 153, 171; four geographic provinces of (northern, western, eastern, southern), 16–18; major river systems in (the Kura and the Araks), 16. See also South Caucasus, Early Bronze Age of; South Caucasus, transition of from the Early to the Middle Bronze Age; Tsaghkahovit Plain
sovereign, the: as the agent of God, 79; authority of, 153; as a mirror image of the "sacred man" (Homo sacer), 89; and the right of inheritance, 88; sovereign power, 87, 150–51; territory of, 87. See also sovereign, the dual (the principle of sovereign dualism)
sovereign, the dual (the principle of sovereign dualism), 78–81, 88; duality of the sovereign formalized in political theory by Hobbes, 79–80, 79n13; the sovereign as an agent of God, 79; wayward things and the dual sovereign, 78–81
sovereignty, 4–7, 59–61, 76, 136, 153, 195; in the ancient world, 65n8; apparatus of, 90–91; archaeologies of, 67–72; the body of the sovereign ruler, 5; as a condition of political interaction, 6, 61; dynam-

ics of, 64; formalization of, 181; and governance, 90; as grounded in both *oikonomia* (power as management) and glory (power as ceremonial regalia), 89, 91; and hegemony, 70; the Hobbesian sense of, 5; human sacrifice as the ultimate foundation of, 148; in the Late Bronze Age at Gegharot, 182; mechanics of, 80; nested relations of, 71; and order, 78; as a physical principle of the polity, 87; as practice, 88; proto-sovereignty in the Middle Bronze Age, 151; reduction of to territoriality, 87; and regalia, 88–89; sovereign matter, 86–91; sovereignty disassembled, 61–63; spectacle of, 68–69; and violence, 69, 88n15; Western "myth" of, 87. *See also* authority, sovereign; sovereignty, key conditions of

sovereignty, key conditions of: definition of a sovereign figure, 6, 92; manufacture of an apparatus capable of formalizing governance, 6, 93; reproduction of a coherent public, 6, 92, 98, 101–2

Soviet Union, 189; collapse of, 195; efforts of to assimilate non-Russian nationalities to the project of the "new Soviet man," 193. *See also* Armenia, Soviet Armenia

spectacle/the spectacular, 68–69; and political performance, 69–70

Spencer, Herbert, 9

Spengler, Oswald, 11

Standard of Ur (chamber D of tomb PG 779 [southern Mesopotamia]), 73–76, 73n10, 79, 85, 121, 125; as an account of political community, 75–76; interpretation of as a representation of the twin principles of Sumerian kingship, 76; "peace" mosaic of, 74–75; unknown function of, 74, 74n11; "war" mosaic of, 75

state, the, 97; the aesthetic state, 156; the Balinese "theater state," 89; the ethical state, 156

Stepanakert, 139

Stepputat, F., 5–6

Stiegler, Bernard, 28

still life paintings, 41, 42–43

subjection, 5, 10, 64, 69, 156, 185; aesthetics of, 121; and authorization, 67–68, 71; logics of, 64; of sacrifice, 148; sentiments of, 136; and sovereign power, 90

subjectivization, 70, 92

subservience, 38–39

sumptuary laws, 97–98

Suny, Ronald, 193

Syria, 70, 125; northeastern Syria, 108; northern Syria, 108

Syro-Mesopotamian world, the, 102, 105

Tacitus, 7

talismans, 15, 148

Tallgren, Aarne, 100

Tammany Hall, 7

Taurus Mountains, 105

technology, political preoccupation with the problems posed by, 72–73

territorialization, 87, 157, 164; as a consequence of the war machine, 152; and contradiction, 151–53, 158; Late Bronze Age political territorialization, 165

things, 89; active things, 72; efficacy of, 13, 40, 57, 76, 86, 122, 148, 185, 188; efficacy of in political reproduction, 186–87; exile of from the *via moderna*, 35; governance of, 82, 90; and liberal theory, 81–83; physicality of, 57; possession/ownership of, 72; as "powerful," 71; role of in the reproduction of a public, 98; "spectral things," 52; universals as not things (*res*), 36; "vitality" of, 52; wayward things and the dual sovereign, 78–81. *See also* objects

Thomas, Nicholas, on "entangle," 32

Thoreau, Henry David, 3n4, 59, 72

tin, 139; tin alloys, 139; tin bronzes, 139

Tkviavi, 133

Tokugawa Shogunate, 97, 98

Toumanyan, Hovannes, 195

transubstantiation, 14, 57, 140, 142–45, 168–71

transfiguration, 146–48, 176–78; of the human body into an authoritative body, 177; transfigured bodies and jewelry, 184

Treaty of Westphalia (1648), 63, 87

Trialeti, 139; four major social groups interred in the Trialeti-era kurgans, 142; kurgan field at, 140–42, 150; roads of as egresses from one world to the next, 142

Trialeti-Vanadzor complex/horizon, 157; ceramics of, 136, 151–52; kurgans of, 138–39

Tsaghkahovit, 71, 165

Tsaghkahovit Plain, 18, 107, 110, 178; causes of the abandonment of, 131–32; construction techniques employed at, 162; fortified complexes of at Hnaberd and Aragatsiberd, 162, 164; fortresses of, 159–62, 160–61n4; mortuary clusters of the Late Bronze Age in, 162–64; occupation of near the Gegharot site, 161–62; political machine of in the Late Bronze Age, 183, 184; resettlement of in the Late Bronze Age, 162; shift in from mobile communities to emplaced institutions (fortifications), 158–64; transformation of the local ecology in, 131
Tunisia, 186

Uglich, bell of, 11–13; as an amulet for the protection of children, 13; exile of, 13; peal of as the voice of God, 13; punishment of, 13; sounding of the death knell for Tsarevitch Dmitri, 11–12
unarmed aerial vehicles (UAVs), 59, 70; intrusion of into allied airspace, 63
United States, 92; concern for objects in, 41
universals, 34, 36 36n2
Urartu, kingdom of, 189; collapse of, 189; square designs of the Urartian temple cells, 189; and Urartian images of spectacle, 69
Uruk communities, expansion of into Anatolia, 106
utilitarianism: eco-utilitarianism, 66; liberal utilitarianism, 66

Vanadzor, 139; kurgans of, 145, 149
Veblen, Thorstein, 145
Verin Naver horizon, ceramics of, 152
Veselovskii, Nikolai, 99
via moderna, 36, 37, 40, 41, 43, 54, 87; exile of things from, 35
violence, 152; assemblage of, 150; at the heart of sovereignty, 69; and mobility, 130; political violence, 136; proliferation of the apparatus of violence during the Middle Bronze Age, 144; social reproduction of, 144; and the state, 87. See also war machine, the
Virgil, 7

wagons, and human mobility, 138
war machine, the, 22–23, 127, 130, 136, 138, 152–53, 158, 184; and the flow(s) of things, material, and people, 138–42; and transfiguration, 146–48; and transubstantiation, 142–45; articulation of violence and mobility in the apparatus of, 130; as assembled by "nomads," 130, 153; as outside of the state apparatus, 130; reproduction of the Middle Bronze Age war machine, 145, 150.
Warner, Michael, 98
weaponry. See armaments/weaponry
Weber, Max: account of bureaucratic regimes by, 85–86; on authority, 150; on the state as a "monopoly of physical violence," 87
Weibel, Peter, 157
Willey, Gordon, 45
William of Ockham, 35–36, 36n2, 40; on the exile of objects, 37; as the father of epistemology, 36; nominalism of, 36, 39, 78
workshops, for the processing of raw materials, 168; objects found in and the processing of jewelry, 168, 170–71

Yanik Tepe (level L), 106
Yasur-Landau, A., 180
Yerevan. See also Erebuni-Yerevan; Museum of the Founding of Yerevan (the Erebuni Museum)
Yoffee, Norman, 68

Zagros Mountains, 104, 106

GPSR Authorized Representative: Easy Access System Europe - Mustamäe tee
50, 10621 Tallinn, Estonia, gpsr.requests@easproject.com

www.ingramcontent.com/pod-product-compliance
Lightning Source LLC
Chambersburg PA
CBHW031125270326
41929CB00011B/1497